"I am extremely pleased that Heidi Furey, S
written this impressive text .... In my legal
as an engineering society executive, I have had the opportunity to review a
range of books and publications addressing the issue of engineering ethics.
In my opinion, *Beyond the Code* is singular and exceptional in the manner
in which it addresses the topic of engineering ethics. The text combines
the theoretical and the practical in a way that will delight readers ....
I congratulate the authors on a job well done!"

Arthur E. Schwartz, Deputy Chief Executive Officer,
NSPE (writing in his Foreword to the book)

"*Beyond the Code: A Philosophical Guide to Engineering Ethics* is a unique text
for engineering educators to teach the complex topic of ethics, as well
as for professional engineers seeking to deepen their knowledge on the
subject. It is organized such that each chapter focuses on one of the six
Fundamental Canons of the NSPE Code of Ethics, providing the reader
with underpinnings from a philosophy perspective (ideas and literature that
most engineers may not be exposed to or even seek out on their own)
coupled with relevant case studies for discussion and reflection. A well-
written, interesting, and enjoyable read!"

J. Patrick Abulencia, Chemical Engineering,
Manhattan College, USA

Beyond the Code

For over 80 years, the National Society of Professional Engineers (NSPE) has been a leader in the promotion of ethical practice within the field of engineering. One of the Society's greatest contributions is the formation and adoption of the NSPE Code of Ethics. But the code, with its six "Fundamental Canons," is only truly instructive if engineers can bridge the gap between principles and action. Here there is no substitute for personal reflection on the ethical and philosophical issues that underlie the code. If done well, such reflection provides an indispensable basis for moral problem solving. *Beyond the Code: A Philosophical Guide to Engineering Ethics* is designed to complement the NSPE Code of Ethics by helping readers "go beyond" in their understanding of the philosophical issues bound up in the code. Each chapter addresses one of the Fundamental Canons of the NSPE code, and provides a philosophical analysis of the various parts of each canon by employing contemporary and classical texts. This unique approach to engineering ethics guides students and professionals in their readings of the appended selections to refine their understanding of the code in order to apply it to the practical challenges of today's engineers.

Key Features:

- Is the first introduction to engineering ethics that helps students understand and apply the NSPE Code of Ethics to engineering practice
- Includes a Preface from Arthur E. Schwartz, NSPE Deputy Chief Executive Officer and General Counsel, and NAFE Executive Director
- As a hybrid text, includes primary philosophical texts with extensive introductions from the book's three authors
- Offers case studies from the NSPE Board of Ethical Review, allowing students to see a direct connection between the issues discussed in the text and real-world engineering practice

- Includes the following pedagogical aids:
  - "Key Terms and Concepts" for each chapter
  - "Preparing to Read" sections before each primary source reading
  - "Guided Reading Questions" after each primary source reading
  - "Going Beyond—Our Questions for a Deep Dive" after each case study.

Heidi Furey is Assistant Professor of Philosophy at Manhattan College. She has authored several publications on professional ethics in leading research publications.

Scott Hill is a Lecturer in the Department of Philosophy at the University of Colorado, Boulder. His papers have appeared in *American Philosophical Quarterly*, *Australasian Journal of Philosophy*, *Canadian Journal of Philosophy*, *Ergo*, and *Erkenntnis*.

Sujata K. Bhatia is Professor of Chemical and Biomolecular Engineering at the University of Delaware, where she teaches design courses for chemical engineers and biomedical engineers.

Beyond the Code

A Philosophical Guide to
Engineering Ethics

Heidi Furey, Scott Hill, and
Sujata K. Bhatia

Routledge
Taylor & Francis Group

NEW YORK AND LONDON

First published 2022
by Routledge
605 Third Avenue, New York, NY 10158

and by Routledge
2 Park Square, Milton Park, Abingdon, Oxon OX14 4RN

Routledge is an imprint of the Taylor & Francis Group, an informa business

© 2022 Taylor & Francis

The right of Heidi Furey, Scott Hill, and Sujata K. Bhatia to be identified as authors of this work has been asserted by them in accordance with sections 77 and 78 of the Copyright, Designs and Patents Act 1988.

Library of Congress Cataloging-in-Publication Data
A catalog record for this title has been requested

ISBN: 978-1-138-18385-8 (hbk)
ISBN: 978-1-138-18386-5 (pbk)
ISBN: 978-1-315-64381-6 (ebk)

Typeset in Bembo
by Newgen Publishing UK

Visit the eResources: www.routledge.com/9781138183865

Contents

Foreword by Arthur E. Schwartz, Deputy Chief Executive
  Officer of the NSPE   xi
Fundamental Canons of the NSPE Code of Ethics
  for Engineers   xvii
Note from the Authors   xix
Preface   xxi

Introduction: Background   1
  Normative Ethics 1
  Consequentialism 3
  Deontology 4
  Applied Ethics 6
  Moral Theories as Imperfect Tools 8
  Value Conflicts in Applied Ethics 8
  Morality and Law 11
  Metaethics 11
  Philosophy of Science 16
  Why Metaethics and Philosophy of Science? 20
  Key Terms and Concepts 20
  End of Chapter Reading 21
    Guided Core Reading I.1: '*An ethical framework for evaluating*
      experimental technology' *by Ibo van de Poel (excerpts)* 22
    Guided Core Reading I.2: '*Why ethics matters for autonomous*
      cars' *by Patrick Lin (excerpt)* 27
    Guided Further Reading 33
  Bibliography 39

1 Public Wellbeing   41
  Public Welfare 41
  Paternalism 43

Technological Mediation 45
Distributive Justice 47
Wrapping Up 49
Key Terms and Concepts 50
End of Chapter Reading and NSPE Board of Ethical Review Cases 51
    Guided Core Reading 1.1: *'Integrating ethics in design through the*
        value-sensitive design approach' by Mary L. Cummings (excerpt) 52
    Guided Core Reading 1.2: *'The (mis)framing of social justice: Why*
        ideologies of depoliticization and meritocracy hinder engineers' ability
        to think about social injustices' by Erin A. Cech (excerpts) 56
    NSPE Board of Ethical Review Cases 61
    Guided Further Reading 66
Bibliography 71

2   Competence   73
Complications for Determining Competence 74
Ethical Competence 75
Practical Judgment 76
Moral Exemplars 76
Mentorship 78
Ethical Engagement 79
Technological Rationality 80
Excellence and Expertise 83
Getting it Right 85
Technical and Moral Expertise 86
Key Terms and Concepts 87
End of Chapter Reading and NSPE Board of Ethical Review Cases 88
    Guided Core Reading 2.1: *'Mentoring: Some ethical considerations'*
        by Vivian Weil (excerpts) 89
    Guided Core Reading 2.2: *'Changing the paradigm for engineering*
        ethics' by Jon Alan Schmidt (excerpts) 93
    NSPE Board of Ethical Review Cases 97
    Guided Further Reading 102
Bibliography 107

3   Objectivity   109
Descartes, Objectivity, and Science 109
The Method of Doubt 110
Fallacies and Objectivity 111
Social Engineering 112
Engineering and Scientific Objectivity 113
Scientific Integrity 113
Lack of Integrity in Science and Engineering 114

Academic Pressure 115
The Obligation to Explain Well 116
Conclusion 117
Key Terms and Concepts 117
End of Chapter Reading and NSPE Board of Ethical Review Cases 118
    Guided Core Reading 3.1: *'Fallacies of risk' by Sven Ove Hansson*
        (excerpts) 119
    Guided Core Reading 3.2: *'The integrity of science: What it means,*
        why it matters' by Susan Haack (excerpts) 124
    NSPE Board of Ethical Review Cases 129
    Guided Further Reading 134
Bibliography 139

4   Loyalty   141
Fiduciary Obligations 141
Divided Loyalties in Engineering 141
Predatory Loyalty 143
Narrow Loyalty 144
Attitude Loyalty 145
Whistleblowing 146
Genuine Loyalty 147
Key Terms and Concepts 149
End of Chapter Reading and NSPE Board of Ethical Review Cases 150
    Guided Core Reading 4.1: *The Philosophy of Loyalty by*
        Josiah Royce (excerpt) 151
    Guided Core Reading 4.2: *'Whistleblowing: Professionalism, personal*
        life, and shared responsibility for safety in engineering' by
        Mike W. Martin (excerpts) 155
    NSPE Board of Ethical Review Cases 160
    Guided Further Reading 165
Bibliography 170

5   Honesty and Deception   173
Lying and Deception 173
The Value of Honesty 175
   Honesty and Happiness 175
   Honesty and Power 176
   Honesty and Autonomy 177
The Problem of Full Disclosure 177
Honesty: Some Unanswered Questions 178
Understanding Trust 179
   Trust and Reliance 179
   Trust and Vulnerability 180

Self-Deception 181
   Understanding Self-Deception 182
Questions Regarding Self-Deception 182
Plagiarism and Deception 183
Key Terms and Concepts 186
End of Chapter Reading and NSPE Board of Ethical Review Cases 187
   Guided Core Reading 5.1: *'The ethics of truth-telling and the problem*
      of risk' by Paul B. Thompson (excerpts) 188
   Guided Core Reading 5.2: *'Trust and antitrust' by Annette Baier*
      (excerpts) 191
   NSPE Board of Ethical Review Cases 195
   Guided Further Reading 200
Bibliography 205

6   Professional Honor   207
Problems for Professional Responsibility 208
Rethinking Responsibility 212
Personal Meaning 216
Key Terms and Concepts 218
End of Chapter Reading and NSPE Board of Ethical Review Cases 219
   Guided Core Reading 6.1: *'Ain't no one here but us social forces' by*
      Michael Davis (excerpts) 220
   Guided Core Reading 6.2: *'Moral creativity in science and engineering'*
      by Mike W. Martin (excerpts) 224
   NSPE Board of Ethical Review Cases 227
   Guided Further Reading 232
Bibliography 237

Index   239

Foreword

Arthur E. Schwartz, Deputy Chief Executive Officer of the NSPE

Are there many more significant issues confronting our society today than engineering ethics? I do not think so.

In its essence, engineering ethics constitutes an inquiry and understanding of the role that professional engineers and the technology they employ plays in shaping our everyday world. Because of the profound role that professional engineers possess in conceptualizing, designing, building, manufacturing, operating, maintaining, and disassembling products, structures, buildings, systems, processes, and other we live in, walk in drive in, eat, drink, and breathe, few issues could be more important to us. That is why I am extremely pleased that Heidi Furey, Scott Hill, and Sujata Bhatia have written this impressive text, *Beyond the Code*.

As the book clearly demonstrates, engineering ethics reflects the customs, habits, and values of engineering as a profession, and embodies the time-tested experience, seasoning, and training of practicing engineers. As with law and medicine, professional engineering is a learned profession. Professional engineering involves the exercise of expert judgment and discretion in the performance of services, and professional engineers are expected to use their education, training, and experience in a manner that comports with public health and safety.

Often engineers look for guidance in determining the most appropriate course of action to follow in what is contained in the law. Statutes, regulations, and court decisions certainly provide a basis to make certain decisions about conduct and behavior. The law, however, does not always address the many issues relating to appropriate professional conduct. Other sources of guidance might be professional colleagues, family members, or friends. While these sources may be valuable as a sounding board, in other cases, these perspectives may lack the necessary technical education or professional experience to provide practical feedback. In yet other cases, the guidance might be biased or prejudiced by subjective facts or circumstances.

For that reason, professional organizations, such as the National Society of Professional Engineers (NSPE), have developed codes of ethics to assist professional engineers in making decisions in their everyday professional practice and employment. Codes of ethics reflect basic established and some-times evolving norms of behavior and conduct that exist within the profes-sion, and provide general but consistent guideposts on the practice issues that professional engineers confront daily.

Except at the most basic level, professional engineering codes of ethics do not provide easy answers or solutions to ethical questions faced by most professional engineers. Most of the significant ethical dilemmas faced by professional engineers tend to be complex and textured, requiring careful and thoughtful analysis as well as an examination of multiple code of ethics provisions. At the same time, professional codes of ethics identify important guideposts that can help engineers evaluate and weigh the facts and circumstances they face, and provide a possible roadmap to addressing the ethical issues involved.

As you will note in reviewing the many NSPE Board of Ethical Review opinions contained in *Beyond the Code*, those opinions serve to illustrate that the NSPE Code is a living code that reflects significant changes in everyday professional engineering practice. In some ways, the NSPE Code of Ethics constitutes an ongoing professional engineering timeline, reflecting chan-ging professional conventions, routines, customs, practices, and patterns.

While some of the historic modifications to the code reflect a consensus of opinions within the engineering profession, other changes have essen-tially been forced on the profession. For example, in the mid-1980s, during the liability insurance crisis, many engineers who had been performing pro-fessional services in connection with hazardous waste, pollution, and other related services saw those services eliminated from their errors and omissions professional liability insurance policies. Professional liability insurance pro-tection to cover the risk of professional liability claims for hazardous waste and pollution-related services became impossible to obtain in the market. In response to this problem, many engineers sought to reduce their personal and professional risk exposures by employing contractual indemnification provisions in their professional services agreements with their public and private clients, whereby clients would agree to "defend, indemnify, and hold the engineer harmless" for the ordinary negligence of the engineer. This approach was in direct conflict with then Section III.9. of the NSPE Code, which stated:

> Engineers shall accept personal responsibility for their professional activities.

After careful review and deliberation, and in response to the growing need for guidance to engineers regarding professional liability exposure, the

NSPE Board of Directors agreed to a limited modification to Section III.9 to state:

> Engineers shall accept personal responsibility for their professional activities; provided, however, that Engineers may seek indemnification from professional services arising out of their practice for other than gross negligence, where the Engineer's interests cannot otherwise be protected.

This change illustrates the fact that the NSPE Code of Ethics is not an inalterable static document but a living document reflecting evolving circumstances that arise in professional engineering practice. It is also a recognition that a code of ethics must be adaptable to changing times, or its legitimacy and acceptance will be questioned.

In another example of adaption and change, the NSPE Code was, at one time, modified to reflect changing practice relating to the issue of conflicts of interest. NSPE Code of Ethics Section II.4.d. originally admonished engineers in public services not to participate in decisions concerning professional services solicited or provided by them or their organizations in public or private engineering practice. Because of instances in which the code was held not to apply to certain conflicts of interests involving engineers serving on quasi-governmental bodies, Section II.4.d. was later broadened in the late 1980s to add "quasi-governmental" bodies as areas of public service where engineers should avoid conflicts of interest. This change was a recognition of the proliferation, and involvement, of professional engineers on quasi-government bodies (e.g., condominium boards and not-for-profit entities) that often step into a partial governmental role, and the potential for conflicts of interest to arise.

There have also been instances where the NSPE was required, as a matter of law, to modify the code. During the 1970s, the codes of ethics of several engineering and other professional societies were challenged by the US federal government as constituting an "agreement in restraint of trade" and therefore violative of the Sherman Antitrust Act. Following litigation in the federal courts, national architectural and engineering groups, including the NSPE, were directed under penalty of law by the United States Department of Justice to modify their codes of ethics to remove provisions prohibiting (1) competitive bidding for engineering services and (2) the supplanting of one engineer by another. Later, following a civil investigative demand by the United States Federal Trade Commission, the NSPE agreed with federal antitrust officials to eliminate provisions from the NSPE Code that made it unethical to engage in certain types of promotional advertising.

Another recent change to the NSPE Code of Ethics involved recognition by the professional engineering community that professional engineers play an important role in sustainable development. As a result, in 2007, a new Section, III.2.c. was added to the NSPE Code of Ethics, stating:

> Engineers are encouraged to adhere to the principles of sustainable development in order to protect the environment for future generations.

A footnote was also added to the code at the time that defines "sustainable development" as:

> the challenge of meeting human needs for natural resources, industrial products, energy, food, transportation, shelter, and effective waste management while conserving and protecting environmental quality and the natural resource base essential for future development.

More recently, in early 2019—in an effort to highlight the importance of diversity and to encourage broader antidiscrimination efforts within society generally and the professional engineering community in particular—the NSPE was expected to approve a recommendation to add language to its Code of Ethics imploring professional engineers to treat all persons with dignity, respect, fairness and without discrimination.

Opinions of the NSPE Board of Ethical Review

While a code of ethics is an essential part of any profession's efforts to assist practitioners in matters of ethics, a code of ethics alone is insufficient to provide anything more than general guidance on specific issues that confront practicing professional engineers. Most, if not all, so-called learned professions have some type of deliberative body to consider ethical questions raised by members of the profession. The legal and medical professions have established boards and committees under their organizational bylaws and procedures to consider a wide range of ethical issues facing their members. In a similar manner, the NSPE's Board of Ethical Review serves the same role for professional engineers and engineering students. Since its founding, the Board of Ethical Review has rendered and published over 500 ethics opinions, and thousands of informal opinions interpreting the NSPE Code of Ethics in cases involving factual situations that have been submitted by members, government officials, and the public.

At the time the NSPE Code of Ethics was developed, there were continuous requests from individuals as well as state societies and local chapters for interpretations of the Code in specific circumstances. The NSPE saw this need as an opportunity for service to the profession, and in 1954 created a Board of Ethical Review. Composed of seven individuals serving three-year terms and representing various areas of professional practice (e.g., industry, government, education, private practice, construction) as well as the NSPE's six geographic governance regions, the Board is not empowered to evaluate actual ethical violation cases or take formal disciplinary action against NSPE members. Instead, the Board of Ethical Review receives factual circumstances submitted by NSPE members and others, analyzes the ethical issues involved, and renders a written advisory opinion. These decisions are published and disseminated to NSPE members solely as guidance and for educational purposes. Originally, each Board of Ethical Review decision was presented to the NSPE Board of Directors, which then determined whether the decision would be published. In 1963, the applicable governing bylaw was changed to give the Board of Ethical Review final authority regarding release and publication. Today, more than 500 NSPE Board of Ethical Review opinions are available at www.nspe.org.

The following are among the numerous ethical issues considered by the NSPE Board of Ethical Review:

- What is the role of the professional engineer in protecting public health and safety?
- When does a professional engineer have the competence to perform a particular professional engineering service?
- Are the contents of a professional engineer's report objective and truthful?
- Is a professional engineer engaged in a circumstance that constitutes a conflict of interest?
- Does a professional engineer have an obligation not to disclose certain information to another party?

The NSPE Board of Ethical Review has confronted these and countless other factual situations in response to requests from professional engineers, public officials, and members of the public.

In my legal practice of almost 40 years and as an engineering society executive, I have had the opportunity to review a range of books and publications addressing the issue of engineering ethics. In my opinion, *Beyond the Code* is singular and exceptional in the manner in which it addresses the topic of engineering ethics. The text combines the theoretical and the practical in a way that will delight readers, particularly those who, over the years, have encountered the NSPE's "You Be the Judge" and "On Ethics" articles as well as other versions of the NSPE Board of Ethical Review's opinions. The authors have created something special—highlighting the essence of the NSPE Code of Ethics and identifying key NSPE Board of Ethical Review opinions to illustrate the critical ethical concerns contained in those Code sections. I congratulate the authors on a job well done!

Fundamental Canons of the NSPE Code of Ethics for Engineers

Preamble

Engineering is an important and learned profession. As members of this profession, engineers are expected to exhibit the highest standards of honesty and integrity. Engineering has a direct and vital impact on the quality of life for all people. Accordingly, the services provided by engineers require honesty, impartiality, fairness, and equity, and must be dedicated to the protection of public health, safety, and welfare. Engineers must perform under a standard of professional behavior that requires adherence to the highest principles of ethical conduct.

I Fundamental Canons

Engineers, in the fulfillment of their professional duties, shall:

1. Hold paramount the safety, health, and welfare of the public.
2. Perform services only in areas of their competence.
3. Issue public statements only in an objective and truthful manner.
4. Act for each employer or client as faithful agents or trustees.
5. Avoid deceptive acts.
6. Conduct themselves honorably, responsibly, ethically, and lawfully so as to enhance the honor, reputation, and usefulness of the profession.

Read the full NSPE Code of Ethics for Engineers online: www.nspe.org/resources/ethics/code-ethics

Note from the Authors

We created this book in response to some frustration we, as engineering ethics instructors, had encountered in choosing texts for our courses. In the process of text selection, we noted two gaps in the set of engineering ethics literature designed for students and professionals.

First, we noted that, while there are a number of excellent textbooks on engineering ethics, there exist few anthologies. But, rather than simply creating an anthology, we sought to address what we suspected was the reason behind this lacuna. The reason, in our minds, was that engineers were not aware of the ways in which reading philosophical articles might be relevant to their professional practice. For this reason, we wanted to create a hybrid textbook/anthology that would accomplish this task.

Second, we noted that while many of the ethical concepts behind various codes of ethics (concepts such as loyalty, responsibility, risk, etc.) were discussed indirectly in various engineering texts, no text existed that spoke directly about the ethical complexities involved in applying the codes in real life.

We hope that this text will help fill these gaps. This text is not intended to replace a standard engineering ethics textbook; nor is it designed to serve as a comprehensive anthology in engineering ethics. Rather, it is a unique text designed with three goals in mind:

1. To introduce engineers to the ethical complexities involved with interpreting and applying the NSPE Code of Ethics
2. To connect engineers with academic articles from the vast literature on engineering ethics that might help them better understand these ethical complexities and begin to develop their own solutions
3. To offer students the opportunity to grapple with ethical complexities as those complexities manifest themselves in real life as represented in case studies from the NSPE Board of Ethical Review archives.

This text is by no means intended to offer the final word on any of the ethical complexities surrounding the NSPE Code of Ethics. Instead, it is meant to serve as a gateway to ethical inquiry. If we as authors have done our job well, readers should finish this book with many more questions than when they began.

Preface

Here's a fact: ethics, the study of right and wrong, is not a branch of psychology, sociology, or even law. Instead, ethics is actually a branch of philosophy. Here's another fact: engineers make great philosophers—really great ones, actually. And, what is more, once they've have been exposed to them, many engineers find they genuinely enjoy thinking about the kinds of complex philosophical issues involved in ethics.

Maybe you are an engineer who has had some exposure to the philosophical study of ethics in the past. In that case, none if this is news to you. However, to some, these facts might be surprising. To begin with, ethics does not exactly seem like a topic for philosophers. Ethics is about being good. You are either good or you aren't. How could this be a topic for philosophical investigation? Next, in the minds of some, nothing seems further from engineering than philosophy. Engineers make stuff—real, useful, important stuff. Philosophers ponder things—abstract things, not so useful, and (if we are honest), maybe not so important. What's more, ethics is just about following the rules, right? And, unless you are a bad person, following the rules is a pretty straightforward affair. This is why many engineering students think of the required ethical component of their curriculum as a waste of time. Granted, ethics is important. But most people already know what is right and what is wrong. So spending time on ethics when you could be working on that overdue project seems unnecessary at best. Many professional engineers feel similarly about professional codes of ethics. Sure, it's great we have them. No one would say that we *shouldn't* have codes of ethics. But ethical codes don't actually help us behave ethically—we already know how to do that (or we don't, in which case it's unclear how much a code of ethics would help). A code of ethics is just a thoughtful reminder to keep on the right side of the rules. Of course, we all need a reminder now and then, but there is no reason to spend too much time thinking about ethics.

Of course, as you are reading this, you'll have suspected that we, the authors of this book on engineering ethics, have a different opinion. To find out if we are wrong, you would have to read this book. If you are already skeptical, sinking time into an ethics text might not seem like such a good bet. But, before you decide, let us say a few things about why you might want to take that bet.

Ethics, it turns out, is not simply a matter of being a good person (though it might involve that). And it isn't just about learning a set of rules (though rules may be involved). It is about asking and answering (or trying to answer) fundamental questions about how we ought to live. And because we live in a world of competing needs and values, we often find ourselves confronted with situations in which it isn't at all clear what the right thing to do is. These ethical problems, as they are called, are at the center of applied ethics—the branch of ethics that asks what we ought to do in particular, real-world situations.

One reason that ethics falls under the umbrella of philosophy is that ethical problems are deeply complex and almost never admit of straightforward answers. Finding the answers to these questions matters quite a bit because they affect the most fundamental decisions we, as human beings, can make. For this reason, ethical questions are quite compelling. Philosophers are usually known as "deep thinkers" (sometimes there is a bit of an eye roll included here for the wishy-washy sound of "deep"). But what most people don't realize is that, for many philosophers, "deep thinking" translates to analytical thinking. These sorts of philosopher enjoy shifting through complex problems in a precise and reasoned way. They live to clarify a problem, offer creative and well-supported solutions, and test their solutions to that problem in a rigorous way. And if they don't solve the problem, they are more than willing to gather what they've learned from their failure, and start again.

Hopefully, for the engineers reading this preface, this process sounds familiar. Engineers are very often skilled analytical thinkers who love to carefully dissect a problem and creatively construct an answer. Engineers take pride in testing their work; tinkering and tailoring their solution until they get it right. They aren't afraid to revisit the problem, looking at it from another angle, trying a new approach. Engineers aren't afraid of complexity. They live for a challenge. And that sort of mindset is exactly what is required for moral problem solving.

Too often, engineers are asked to blindly follow various codes of professional conduct, and to pay lip service a set of ethical ideals they have never really thought about. Considering that engineers have the perfect skill set to think deeply about moral questions, this seems like a waste. What's more, it can be argued that no one, not even philosophers, are in as good a position to engage in the ethical issues surrounding the practice of engineering as engineers. True, philosophers who study ethics are often skilled moral problem solvers. However, as we will see, many of the ethical issues facing engineers are as much technical problems as they are ethical ones. Arguably, finding solutions to these problems requires both philosophical and technical competencies. As engineers, you already have the required technical knowledge. What we hope to offer you the philosophical knowledge that you need to begin to seriously engage with moral problems.

The title of this book, as you've seen, is *Beyond the Code*. This title is meant to refer in general to the code of professional ethics in engineers, of which there are many. However, it is also meant more specifically to refer to the Code of Ethics endorsed by the National Society of Professional Engineers (NSPE.) As one of the largest and most influential professional organizations for engineering in the United States, the NSPE has long been a leader in ethical engagement in the field. The NSPE offers a wealth of ethical resources for engineers including an impressive code of ethics. The six Fundamental Canons of its Code of Ethics are both inspiring and, to some extent, platitudinous. To some, these tenets, which tout abstract ideals such as honor and dedication, may even seem banal. However, in the words of David Foster Wallace, "banal platitudes can have a life-or-death significance."

This book is designed to complement the NSPE Code of Ethics by helping readers "go beyond" in their understanding of the philosophical issues bound up in the code. While reading this book, you will be confronted with various ethical dilemmas that arise as we attempt to apply the code to engineering practice. And you will be offered guidance on how to clarify these problems and how to begin working on solutions to them.

This book is also intended to fill a particular lacuna in the resources offered by the NSPE. Although the NSPE Code of Ethics is thoughtful and well-constructed, it is necessarily open to interpretation. In reality it takes substantial philosophical deliberation to be able to apply the principles articulated in the code to real-world practice. The NSPE offers a great deal of support in helping professionals interpret the code, including a huge volume of actual cases from its Board of Ethical Review (BER) which engineers can look to as examples. However, there is no substitute for personal philosophical reflection on the ethical issues that underlie the code. Such reflection is the basis for moral problem solving, and it is indispensable.

There are a great many philosophical journal articles that can aid in philosophical reflection about engineering ethics. However, engineers outside of academia rarely have any exposure to these texts. Furthermore, these texts are often aimed at academics with specialized knowledge in ethics. Unfortunately, this can act as a barrier—keeping those with the most direct connection to the issues discussed in the engineering ethics literature, the engineers, from engaging with it. Finally, because of the abstract nature of some philosophical texts, it isn't always clear to engineers how philosophical articles relate to professional codes of ethics. It's no wonder then that engineers are not usually regular consumers of the latest research in engineering ethics. They have never really been invited to be.

It is our hope that this book can help resolve some of these issues. Each of the main chapters of *Beyond the Code* is centered on one of the Fundamental Canons of the NSPE Code of Ethics. The chapters begin with an introduction designed to draw out the ethical complexities involved with interpreting and applying a particular canon. Be forewarned: our intension here is in a sense to complicate the issues, not to simplify them. The reason, as you will see, is that real life is messy and ethical matters are themselves very complicated. Because of this, it's rarely easy to perfectly apply abstract codes of conduct in real-world situations. Better to be exposed to these ethical complications now than to be blindsided by them in real life. That way, you'll have a head start in creating a game plan to deal with them. The second component of each chapter is designed to offer you some tools to create that game plan. Here we have selected excerpts from the philosophical literature on ethics and engineering ethics that offer some future insight with regard to the ethical complexities we've uncovered in the first part of the chapter. Will reading these excerpts answer all of the questions we've raised regarding how to interpret and apply the code? Absolutely not. But reading them will help you begin to develop your own answers to these questions. Next you will find a section containing cases from the NSPE BER archives that we think embody some of the ethical complexities discussed in the chapters. Along with presenting questions from the NSPE, we've included our own questions. These "Questions for a Deep Dive" are designed to help you "go beyond" the surface level of each case, and to offer a judgment in those cases that takes account of the ethical complexities. As you will see, there are no easy answers to the questions we propose. But it is our sincere belief that when faced with an ethical dilemma it's better to wisely answer "it's complicated" than to foolishly answer "it's simple." Finally, we have included a section of "Guided Further Reading." Here we have included links to articles that help take the reader to the "next level" of philosophical engagement with the underlying issues covered in each chapter. We introduce each reading and follow up with discussion questions. These more advanced readings are aimed at readers who wish to further extend their engagement in the field of engineering ethics.

Our survey of the ethical issues involved with interpreting and employing the NSPE Code of Ethics is by no means comprehensive. As a field, engineering ethics is constantly growing, evolving, and reshaping itself. We hope to offer both students of engineering and professional engineers an entryway into that field. It is our most sincere hope those reading this book will become contributing participants in the field themselves.

Introduction

The introduction discusses some of the philosophical background needed to address the problems we discuss throughout the book. We discuss normative ethics, including consequentialist and deontological theories. We discuss applied ethics, including the use of moral theories as imperfect tools, value conflicts, and the differences between legal and moral requirements. Along the way, we illustrate these applied issues with discussions of some NSPE cases. Finally, we turn to issues in metaethics and philosophy of science that sometimes get in the way of teaching applied ethics. Students are often puzzled by the possibility of moral knowledge or how morality could be objective. Students sometimes think that there is nothing puzzling about scientific knowledge, and that it is completely unproblematic to suppose that it is objective. We address these issues to clear the way for applied discussion. We make the status of moral knowledge and moral objectivity a bit less puzzling. And we make the status of scientific knowledge and scientific objectivity a bit more puzzling. The main goals of this chapter are to introduce students to ideas and methods we employ in the book—and to clear away some epistemological and metaphysical issues that sometimes raise pedagogical difficulties in ethics courses.

Chapter I

Chapter 1 begins with an examination of the first Fundamental Canon of the NSPE Code: "To hold paramount the safety, health and welfare of the public." This canon may seem straightforward, but its simplicity is deceptive. To begin with, we might wonder about what, if anything, differentiates public welfare from health and safety. We open Chapter 1 with a discussion of the nature of public welfare, which we refer to as "public wellbeing." This leads us to a much larger discussion regarding the three potential issues that engineers must address if they hope to meet their professional obligation to safeguard the public. These are: paternalism, technological mediation, and distributive justice.

As we explore these issues, we raise a number of ethical questions, including: Are there cases in which the public may not know what is in their best interest? In that case is it permissible for engineers to make decisions on behalf of the public? And might engineers be permitted to "influence" the public's choices through design? Finally, do all members of the public share a common interest? In other words, what if what is beneficial to certain members of the public comes at the expense of other members?

To help you begin to answer some of these questions, we've included two excerpts from articles belonging to the contemporary literature on engineering ethics. The first is Mary L. Cummings's "Integrating Ethics in Design through the Value-Sensitive Design Approach," in which she discusses one approach to integrating human values into engineering design: value-sensitive design. The second article, by Erin A. Cech is, "The (Mis)Framing of Social Justice: Why Ideologies of Depoliticization and Meritocracy Hinder Engineers' Ability to Think about Social Injustices." In this article, Cech identifies two potential cultural ideologies within engineering that she claims contribute to the (mis)framing of social justice issues within the engineering profession.

Chapter 2

Chapter 2 centers on the second Fundamental Canon, which insists that engineers "perform services only in their area of competence." This principle is intended mainly to prohibit engineers from engaging in technical work for which they are not properly qualified. However, its adoption raises interesting questions about the nature of competence itself. In this chapter, we ask particularly about moral competence. How does one become morally competent? What is the role of mentors in developing moral competence? How does moral competence relate to technical competence, and what does this relationship mean in engineering practice? And how do we go beyond competence—how does one progress from moral competence to moral expertise?

Here we turn to the work of Aristotle, who was the first in the Western canon to articulate the role that practical/ethical judgment plays in ethical competency. Our discussion of Aristotle makes clear the importance of exemplars or mentors in moral development. Here we connect to the work of Vivian Weil, who examines the various ethical considerations involved with mentorship. Next, we probe the relationship between technical competence and moral competence. Here we address the work of the twentieth-century philosopher Herbert Marcuse, who asks whether what he calls "technological rationality" actually compromises one's moral sense. Finally, we consider an Aristotelian inspired proposal by Jon Alan Schmidt. Schmidt argues that technical creativity holds the key to avoiding many moral dilemmas—essentially narrowing the gap between technical and moral expertise.

Chapter 3

Objectivity is a notion that relates to truth. In Chapter 3, we raise questions about truth and objectivity, and the relation that these concepts bear on both forming and reporting beliefs. We think about what it means for a belief to be "objective" and for a person to be "objective" in their thinking.

We recount some of the history of the pursuit of objectivity in relation to both science and philosophy by delving into the writings of seventeenth-century philosopher René Descartes. We view his famous search for indubitable knowledge in the context of his interest in finding a "firm foundation" for the science in a time before the scientific revolution. Taking a cue from Descartes, we look to understand some of the ways that objectivity can be corrupted. We present an article by Sven Ove Hansson which discusses a major threat to objectivity in science and engineering, "Fallacies of Risk." We give special attention here to the phenomenon of social engineering—discussing the potential moral dangers surrounding it. Next we turn to the role of scientific integrity in the public's perception of science and engineering. We argue that maintaining objectivity in these areas is essential both to maintaining public trust and to ensuring the survival of science and engineering. Here we bring in the work of Susan Haack, whose writing on scientific integrity helps illuminate the importance of objectivity in science and engineering. In the final sections of this chapter, we turn our attention to the connection between epistemic obligation—the obligation to form beliefs well—and moral obligation. As Willard van Orman Quine suggests, all rational agents, including engineers, have an epistemic obligation to resist bias in forming beliefs. However, because an engineer's beliefs inevitably affect the wellbeing of the public, might she have a special moral obligation to pursue scientific objectivity as well? We investigate an article by Sheralee Brindell that answers, "yes." She attempts to broaden the concept of scientific inquiry by arguing that requests for scientific and technical explanation reveal a set of moral criteria related to the issue of trust.

Chapter 4

In Chapter 4 we examine the topic of loyalty in the profession of engineering. We start with the case of computer engineer Edward Snowden. Snowden had various loyalties that came into conflict. There is a question about how those loyalties should be balanced, and whether Snowden made the right decision in leaking classified US National Security Agency (NSA) documents. This sort of conflict was the principal concern of Josiah Royce, a nineteenth-century American idealist who wrote *The Philosophy of Loyalty* in 1908. This book explains what degenerate loyalty (loyalties that are too exclusive or shortsighted) might look like and proposes an ideal model, which Royce calls "loyalty to loyalty." This model is helpful for readers to consider as they move toward careers in engineering because it suggests that not only do they have to be faithful to particular individuals or groups, but they also have to be loyal to an overarching ethical principle that can apply to all situation and cases. Royce is quite good in articulating this position.

Next we introduce the concept of "attitudinal loyalty" by guiding the reader through selections from Hannah Arendt that address the "banality of evil"— the idea that great evil can be perpetrated by groups of people who fail to take the appropriate moral responsibility for their actions.

Although the question of loyalty has deep roots in the history of philosophy, it emerges in the contemporary literature in the problem of whistleblowing. Does an engineer's obligation to be loyal to her employer outweigh her obligation to the public? And must an engineer's loyalty to the public outweigh her personal loyalties—for instance, obligations to family or self? We end Chapter 4 by considering Mike W. Martin's answers to these questions. Martin notes that whistleblowing has become a "preoccupation" in engineering. Because of this, he claims, engineers are in danger of ignoring personal factors when considering public obligations. Martin argues that although engineers have a strong prima facie obligation to report wrongdoing, this obligation must be weighed against personal obligations, such as the obligation to protect one's family or career. Furthermore, Martin calls attention to the public's responsibility to engineers. As he explains, the strength of an engineer's obligation to blow the whistle is partially determined by the protections put in place by the public for those who report wrongdoing.

Chapter 5

Chapter 5 aims to deepen our understating of the fifth canon, "Avoid deceptive acts." We begin by asking several questions about the nature of honesty and deception. Is honesty just a matter of following the familiar courtroom pledge "tell the truth, the whole truth, and nothing but the truth?" Or is there something more to honesty than truth. And is honesty itself always a good thing? Or are there times when honesty could be harmful or destructive? And if telling the truth is not always the best policy, what, if anything, is the real value of honesty? Furthermore, what does it mean to fail to be honest? Is lying the opposite of honesty, or can we fail to be honest even without lying? And what is the connection between lying and deception? Might one be deceptive without telling a lie, and is one worse than the other? Finally, where do issues of honesty and deception make contact with actual engineering practice?

The moral issue of deception has a long-standing place in the history of philosophy. To help orient readers to the topic, we share insights from philosopher of language Paul Grice. Grice's work on the nature of communication makes it clear that honesty cannot be a matter of just telling the truth, and that deception cannot simply be a matter of telling lies. We follow our discussion of Grice with a presentation of Jennifer Saul's work on the moral difference between lying and deception. We then turn our attention to exploring the issue of what makes honesty morally beneficial and deception morally detrimental. Here we consider what consequentialists, deontologists, and care ethicists have to say about the value of honesty. The historical discussion of truth-telling becomes especially interesting in the context of engineering, where "the truth" is often technically complex and easily misunderstood. In technical fields where there is often an expansive gap between expert and lay person, might there be cases in which it is in the public's best interest for an engineer to refrain from telling the truth in its entirety? The "Problem of Full Disclosure," as we call it, is one that Paul B. Thompson tackles in his article on truth-telling and the problem of risk. After a brief discussion of Thompson's article, we move on to two final issues of deception as it relates to engineers. While most of Chapter 5 focuses on honesty and deception with regard to the public, we close the chapter by drawing attention to two other forms of deception: deceiving one's self (self-deception) and deceiving one's peers (plagiarism).

Chapter 6

The final chapter of *Beyond the Code* offers a culmination of themes that began in Chapter 1. The sixth fundamental canon of the NSPE Code of Ethics challenges engineers to "Conduct themselves honorably, responsibly, ethically, and lawfully so as to enhance the honor, reputation, and usefulness of the profession." Here we ask if, in addition to the obligations engineers have to themselves and to the public, they also have ethical obligations to the profession itself. If so, what is the nature and extent of the responsibility engineers have for enhancing the honor, reputation, and usefulness of the profession, and how are engineers to accomplish such a weighty task? We argue that the final directive connects issues of obligation to talk of character and, in doing so, raises questions about personal and professional excellence.

We begin by considering a number of obstacles to professional responsibility. We show how the notion of responsibility can become murky for engineers when they are embedded in complex organizational structures. In situations in which engineers lack complete control over decisions regarding their work, they might tempted to eschew responsibility altogether. On this point we look to Michael Davis, who attempts to identify what role, if any, social forces play in determining the boundaries of ethical obligation in engineering. Davis offers reasons for engineers to embrace responsibility rather than finding reasons to avoid it. After gaining some clarity on the barriers to professional responsibility, we turn to the question of how to cultivate a sense of responsibility. Here we return to the themes of virtue and excellence introduced in Chapter 2. Michael Pritchard argues that, in thinking about professional responsibility, we have focused too much on wrongdoing and how to avoid it. This leads to a warped sense of what it means to take responsibility as an engineer. He suggests that we ought to focus on the positive aspects of engineering practice, including the development of virtuous character traits. By cultivating their character, Pritchard argues that engineers can move from merely doing the minimum to fulfill their obligations to going "above and beyond the call of duty." However, issues of character are inherently personal. Our view is that questions of morality and professionalism have deep existential import and cannot be addressed without appealing to issues of personal meaning. With this in mind, we conclude this book by returning to the work of Mike W. Martin. Martin emphasizes the connection between personal meaning and professional responsibility. He argues that morality requires that an engineer go beyond mere compliance with ethical codes and develop moral commitments that are rooted in her identity as a person and a professional.

Reading this book will not guarantee that engineer-ethicists come up with the right moral answers, but this has never been the way that moral deliberation works. Rather, the process of developing answers to ethical questions is something that starts out messy and vague and then, over an extended period of time, comes into greater and greater focus. Such deliberation should be natural for engineers—the engineering design process is an iterative practice, so that engineers continually refine their designs to best serve public needs. Answers concerning the common good are not cut-and-dry from the start; but they are, undeniably, worth pursuing.

Introduction
Background

We have two goals for this introduction. One is to provide you with the background needed to understand and evaluate the NSPE Code of Ethics. The code and its associated discussions make use of various ethical ideas and raise various ethical problems. Here we explain the ideas and problems that will be most important as background for the discussion ahead. We discuss normative ethics, applied ethics, metaethics, and philosophy of science. Our second goal is to eliminate some natural concerns one might have about the field of ethics. Some people worry that no ethical theory is plausible enough to be used as a tool to address ethical problems in the real world. Others worry that, in contrast to science, there is no truth about ethics to be found. Such concerns sometimes get in the way of doing ethics. We address them in this introduction. With the relevant background in place, and with the relevant worries addressed, the introduction will equip you to address the issues that arise in connection with the NSPE Code and its application to the engineering profession. (Note that we use "moral" and "ethical" interchangeably.)

Normative Ethics

Normative ethics is about actions. People who engage in normative ethics seek to discover principles that determine the moral status of actions. We can begin to understand normative ethics by considering some examples that bring out the strengths and weaknesses of various theories: Imagine there is a runaway trolley. If you do nothing, the trolley will kill five people who are tied to a track. But you are standing next to a lever. And if you pull the lever, the trolley will be diverted onto another track. The five will be saved. But there is one person tied to the alternate track. And if you pull the lever, that one person will die. What should you do? Call this example **Trolley**. Before reading on, take a few minutes to think about it.

Most people, when given just this example, tend to think that you should pull the lever. After all, you are trading one life for five. It is obvious that you should pull it. But there are always a few people who resist that judgment. If you are one of the holdouts, imagine there are six people who will die unless you divert the trolley onto the alternate track. Now imagine that there are seven ... imagine that there are 100 people on the other track. Keep increasing the number if you like. If you are still not convinced, imagine your mother is one of the many people who will die unless you divert the trolley. Eventually, almost everyone agrees that pulling the lever is the right thing to do.

Now consider a different example. Imagine again that there is a runaway trolley. This time, if you do nothing, the trolley will pass through a tunnel, come out the other end, and hit and kill five people tied to the track just outside the tunnel. However, you are standing on top of the tunnel, just over the entrance. In front of you is a large man. You can push the large man into the trolley just before it enters the tunnel. The impact will kill him. But he is so big that it will also stop the trolley before it exits the tunnel. And the five people tied up near the exit of the tunnel will be saved. Call this example **Large Man**. Take a moment to think about whether you should push the large man into the trolley or just let it pass through. Now compare it to what you wrote down about Trolley. If you thought should pull the lever in Trolley, consider what your reason for pulling tells you about whether you should push in Large Man.

Many people, when just given Large Man and not given Trolley, think you should not push the large man into the trolley. They think it is absolutely wrong. And you should just let the trolley go through the tunnel. But other people are holdouts. They think you should push the large man. Sometimes they just want to be consistent. They have already considered Trolley. They know that their reasoning in Trolley supports pulling the lever. And they recognize that that same reasoning will motivate pushing the large man. Other people might look at it this way. In Large Man you are trading one life for five. It is too bad that the large man has to die. But one life for five is too good a deal to pass up. If you are one of the holdouts, we ask you to consider another example. Imagine you are a doctor. Imagine you have five patients who will die if they do not get new organs. Let's suppose they each need different organs. You see a janitor pass by an elevator shaft. He is healthy, and you can push him down the elevator shaft in such a way that he will die but his healthy organs will be salvageable. So you have two options. You can let your five patients die. Or, you can push the janitor down the elevator shaft, harvest his healthy organs, and save your five patients. Call this example **Organ Harvest**.

Almost everyone agrees that harvesting the janitor's organs is wrong. And, after considering Organ Harvest, almost everyone agrees that pushing the large man in Large Man is wrong. And a natural thought is this: pushing the large man or the janitor is wrong because killing someone is worse than letting someone die.

So there is a puzzle. In Trolley, it seems like you should pull the lever, killing the one and saving the five. And the reason seems to be that you are trading one life for five. And that seems acceptable. But that same reasoning implies that you should push in Large Man and Organ Harvest, and that seems unacceptable. On the other hand, in Large Man and Organ Harvest it seems like you shouldn't kill the one even if doing so will save the five. And that seems to be because killing is worse than letting die. But that same reasoning implies that you shouldn't pull the lever in Trolley. And that doesn't seem correct. Call this **The Trolley Problem**. The Trolley Problem is that it seems permissible to trade one life for five in Trolley but not in Large Man. And it is difficult to see how to reconcile those two judgments.

Consequentialism

One natural reaction to Trolley and Large Man is this: if we are just given Trolley we think it is OK to pull the lever; if we are just given Large Man we think it is wrong to push. But when we put them together, it seems like there really isn't a relevant difference between pulling in one and pushing in the other. The two cases should be treated alike. After all, in each case you are trading one life for five. How could it be that we should kill in one but not in the other? The consequences are all that matters. The view that consequences are all that matters to morality is **consequentialism**.

Here we will look at just one form of consequentialism—**hedonic act utilitarianism (HAU)**. The core idea behind HAU is that pleasure is all and only what is good, pain is all and only what is bad, and wright and wrong are just determined by amounts of pleasure and pain along with some simple math.

To understand HAU, we need to introduce some jargon. Actions have consequences. Some of these consequences might include pleasure. Other consequences might include pain. The **hedonic utility** of an action is the result of subtracting the total amount of pain that is a consequence of the action from the total amount of pleasure that is a consequence of that action. For example, imagine you are at a party of five people and serve everyone pizza. The pizza is delicious, everyone enjoys it, and gets 5 units of pleasure each. But it also gives everyone bad indigestion and they get 10 units of pain each. So the total amount of pleasure that is a consequence of your action is 25. And the total amount of pain that is a consequence of your action is 50. The hedonic utility of serving everyone pizza is found by subtracting the number representing the total amount of pain (50) that is a consequence from the number representing the total amount of pleasure (25). The hedonic utility of your action is therefore −25.

Another term we need to introduce is **maximizing**. An act maximizes hedonic utility if and only if no other act has a higher hedonic utility. For example, imagine again you are at the party of five. Instead of pizza you could have served everyone hummus. While hummus isn't as tasty as pizza, and everyone would have only gotten 1 unit of pleasure from the hummus, they wouldn't have gotten indigestion and so would have received 0 units of pain. In that case, the hedonic utility of serving everyone hummus rather than pizza is 5. For simplicity, let's pretend that your only options were to serve everyone hummus (for a hedonic utility of 5) or everyone pizza (for a hedonic utility of −25). In that case, serving everyone hummus maximizes hedonic utility. Now we are in a position to understand HAU:

> HAU: An act is right if and only if that act maximizes hedonic utility.

One virtue of HAU is that it seems to provide a consistent way to evaluate Trolley and Large Man. A natural thought is that you are trading one life for five in both cases. And so the two cases are morally the same. It is plausible that letting five die so that one doesn't have to kill one in these types of cases has a lower hedonic utility than killing one to save five. Thus HAU delivers the judgment that the right thing to do in both Trolley and Large Man is to pull the lever and push the large man. And so this would provide a solution to the Trolley Problem.

One problem for HAU is that it doesn't seem to get Organ Harvest right. It might very well turn out that doctors could maximize hedonic utility by killing people and harvesting their organs. But it still doesn't seem like doctors should do so. So there is room to doubt that only consequences matter. And if consequences aren't the only thing that matters, then maybe there really is a difference between what we should do in Trolley and what we should do in Large Man.

Deontology

Once we see the problems faced by HAU and other consequentialist approaches, a natural reaction is to revisit our initial thought about Trolley and Large Man. Recall, the initial thought was that in each case you are trading one life for five. So the cases should be treated in the same way. If it's OK to pull then it's OK to push. And if it's wrong to push then it's wrong to pull. We might start to think that something more than consequences matters in evaluating the morality of our actions. And this is an approach adopted by deontological theories of morality.

Here we will look at just one form of **deontology**—the **Doctrine of Double Effect (DDE)**. DDE is less ambitious than HAU. While HAU tries to explain all of good and bad and right and wrong, DDE tries to address just one question: When is it OK to do something that will lead to an evil? So DDE isn't a general theory about right and wrong and good and bad. It is a theory about one way in which it can be acceptable to do something you know will lead to an evil.

Like HAU, this theory uses some jargon. So we should say a bit to clarify it. First, the theory distinguishes between **intending and foreseeing**. Imagine you are arguing with a friend about a controversial topic. As you do so, there are certain things you intend. For example, you intend to make certain sounds needed to speak the English language. You intend to convince your friend that you are right and he is wrong. You intend to make a good case for your position. You intend to have fun. All of these are things that you are trying to make happen. But there are other things that you make happen during the course of your conversation that you to do not intend. For example, as you speak, your breath will move air particles around. And as you speak, you may have various verbal tics or hand gestures that you know you will make but don't intend to make. In these cases, you foresee that as a result of arguing with your friend such things will happen. But you don't intend for them to happen. You wouldn't bother arguing with your friend if none of the things you were trying to accomplish, like having fun or convincing them, had any chance of happening. But you would still argue with your friend if you didn't move air particles around when you talked or if you didn't have unusual verbal tics and hand gestures. That is why you intend to have fun and convince your friend. But you merely foresee that you will move air particles around and make unusual unconscious hand gestures.

Second, the theory distinguishes between **ends and means**. Imagine you have a videogame console. Imagine you walk up to it and hit the power button. If you are like us, you don't hit the power button just to hit the power button. You do so in order to play a game. In this case, you intend to hit the power button. But you do so only as a means to something else. In this case, hitting the power button is a means to playing a game. This is different from intending an end. Suppose you want to hit the power button and play a game in order to have fun. In that case, you might be playing the game or having fun as an end. So hitting the power button is intended as a means. And playing the game and having fun is intended as an end.

Third, the theory talks about having **proportionally grave reason** for permitting the evil. This just means that the good thing you intend really outweighs the bad thing that you foresee. For example, imagine again there is a runaway trolley. If you do nothing, it will hit and destroy your videogame console that is tied to the track. But if you divert the trolley onto another track, it will hit and kill one person who is tied to the alternate track. In this case, there is no proportionally grave reason to kill the person in order to save your videogame console. As valuable as it might be to you, the videogame console doesn't outweigh the life of the person you could kill. Now we are in a position to state DDE.

> DDE: A person may permissibly perform an action that is foreseen to cause an evil if:
>
> (i)   the good effect is intended,
> (ii) the evil effect is not intended (either as an end or as a means),
> (iii) there is proportionally grave reason for permitting the evil, and
> (iv) the action performed is not wrong in itself.

DDE, if true, would vindicate our initial judgments about Trolley and Large Man. The key difference between the two cases concerns condition (ii) of DDE. In Trolley, you do not pull the lever intending to kill the man on the other track. You merely foresee that he will die. If he were not on the track, you would still divert the trolley. In Large Man, you push the man intending to kill him. You are using his death as a means of saving the five. So, if DDE is true, then it is OK to pull the lever in Trolley and wrong to pull the lever in Large Man.

One problem with DDE is that there are variations of Large Man that it seems to get wrong. Imagine that it is not five people at stake if you fail to push the large man. Imagine instead that if you fail to push him all of New York, Texas, and their inhabitants will be destroyed. Everyone in the states will suffer a slow and painful death. Many people have the intuition that it is OK to push the large man in this case. But DDE implies that it is not—for you are using the large man's death as a means to save New Yorkers and Texans from horrible deaths. And DDE maintains that that is forbidden.

Applied Ethics

Sometimes the Trolley Problem, and the theories in normative ethics we have used it to motivate, are written off as merely theoretical and of no interest to those of us who care about the real world. One reason to dismiss the Trolley Problem is that Trolley-like problems rarely, if ever, happen. A reason to dismiss normative ethical theories is that they are sometimes difficult to apply, and each theory we have discovered has serious problems. The task of applied ethics is to identify and make progress on real-world moral problems. Engineering ethics is a branch of applied ethics. And those of us who work in engineering ethics seek to identify and make progress on the real problems faced by professional engineers.

So we really do owe an explanation of how all of what we have discussed is relevant to applied ethics in general and engineering ethics in particular. We will explain by way of example. The question the Trolley Problem forces us to ask is this: When is it OK to kill someone in order to save others? Doctors really could save lives by killing people and harvesting their organs. And that seems wrong. Some people will die from being vaccinated. But more people will be saved if vaccinations are widespread. And adopting the policy of widespread vaccinations seems like the right thing to do. So adopting a policy of killing people and harvesting their organs would save lives. And so would adopting a policy of widespread vaccinations. Both policies will cause people to die. Both will save lives overall. So why is it that we are horrified by one of them but find the other acceptable?

Some philosophers and engineers have thought that reflection on the Trolley Problem can illuminate the problem about how to program the artificial intelligence (AI) that runs autonomous vehicles. Some think the Trolley Problem helps in a very direct way. There will be some cases in which autonomous vehicles face a Trolley-like problem. And in those cases we should program the autonomous vehicle to do the right thing. We are skeptical of this particular application of the Trolley Problem to the problem of autonomous vehicles. But, even so, we recognize that the Trolley Problem is relevant in a deeper and less direct way. In particular, reflection on the Trolley Problem can teach us about when it's OK to kill a few people to save a lot of people. And that question is of broad relevance to the problem of self-driving cars and many other dimensions of an engineer's work, for although they will rarely be in an exact Trolley-type scenario, their design decisions will inevitably cause some to die and others to live.

All of these issues about whether and how to apply the Trolley Problem and normative ethics to the real world are exercises in applied ethics. Applied ethics is concerned with taking the tools of theoretical ethics and using them to evaluate real-world moral problems. These include the problem of how to program autonomous vehicles and the problem of why it is permissible to adopt a policy of widespread vaccination but not organ harvesting that were just discussed. But they also include many more. What should be bought and sold? How should society be organized? Is abortion permissible? When is sex permissible? How much am I obligated to give to the poor? These and many other questions compose the field of applied ethics.

Moral Theories as Imperfect Tools

There is a natural worry one might have here. In our discussion of normative ethics, we saw that we haven't really figured out what the best normative
theory is. Consequentialism and deontology each have their strengths. But
they are each also problematic in various ways. It doesn't seem plausible that
either sort of theory captures the whole truth about morality. One might
reasonably wonder, then, how normative ethics could be useful to real-world
problems.

We think this worry can be addressed by looking at how physicists use
their theories. The best two theories in physics are General Relativity and
Quantum Mechanics. General Relativity is good at explaining the behavior
of big things like planets and stars. It has implications for the behavior of
very small things like subatomic particles. But it is much less reliable in that
domain. Quantum Mechanics is very good at explaining the behavior of
subatomic particles. It has implications about the behavior of big things like
planets and stars. But it is less reliable than it is about big things.

General Relativity and Quantum Mechanics are inconsistent with one
another. They describe the universe in radically different ways. Physics uses
both theories but for different purposes. No one has been able to unify them
into a single theory even though they have tried. In light of such failure,
physicists simply use each theory where it is strongest.

Some philosophers have suggested that we should think about moral
theories in the way that physicists think about their theories. None of our
moral theories are good enough to count as the One True Moral Theory.
But we have consequentialist theories that are pretty good at explaining
some aspects of morality. And we have deontological theories that are pretty
good at explaining other aspects of morality. If we are interested in applied
ethics, we should just use each theory where it is most successful. Moral
theories are useful tools. But no single moral theory perfectly captures
morality.

Value Conflicts in Applied Ethics

Throughout this book we will discuss various cases in which values come
into conflict in engineering practice. Value conflicts occur when we try to
apply the NSPE Code of Ethics to real-world situations. For example, the
fifth Fundamental Canon tells us to avoid deceptive acts. But the fourth fundamental canon tells us to be faithful to our employers and clients. However,
in some cases our employers and clients want us to deceive. So, depending
on how we understand these canons, a conflict arises. Normative and applied
ethics give us the tools to understand the canons, and, if a value conflict
arises, to make progress in navigating the conflict and deciding what to do.

Let us be clear: we are not once and for all solving these dilemmas. That's not what happens in applied ethics. Failing to find a single answer to moral problems does not mean we are not making progress on the issues, and it does not mean that the problems are intractable. In some cases we may be left with more than one reasonable answer. But we will have cleared away a number of bad answers in the process.

This illustrates a standard method in applied ethics. We take on board certain moral principles and examine real-world cases in which they conflict. Then we try to figure out how best to resolve those conflicts. A standard set of such principles employed by applied ethicists is what we might call the four basic principles of applied ethics. Often employed in discussion of healthcare ethics, these principles may offer guidance to those of us in other public service professions such as engineering as well. The principles are:

1. Non-maleficence: Do not harm.
2. Beneficence: Act in such a way that the person benefits.
3. Autonomy: Honor the person's right to self-determination—to formulate and follow a life plan of her own making.
4. Justice: Distribute goods and services in a way that is fair.

In some cases, the application of these principles is unproblematic. But there are other cases in which the principles come into conflict. When such conflict occurs, engineering ethicists can look for the view that best balances these principles. For example, in some cases the principle of beneficence and the principle of autonomy come into conflict. We want to act in a way that benefits a person. We want to act in a way that respects their autonomy. But sometimes people do not choose what is best for them. When, if ever, is it acceptable to override a person's autonomy in order to secure an outcome that is best for them? In 2016 *Rust*, a multiplayer survival videogame, included an update. The update served to select the race and gender of the player. So the game would pick a race and gender for a player. And that player's account would be correlated with that race and gender for good. There was no changing it. One the one hand, this decision on the part of the game designers yielded a cost in autonomy. Players couldn't just pick whatever race or gender they wanted. On the other hand, it might be eye-opening to see the world as a character of a particular race or gender rather than whatever race or gender one wants to pick. It might make for a more interesting game in certain ways. Here the relevant issue is finding the right balance between benefiting the player and preserving the player's autonomy.

For another example, let us return to the issue of self-driving cars. Consider the following case submitted to the NSPE Board of Ethical Review (BER).

Public Health, Safety, and Welfare—Driverless/Autonomous Vehicle

Case 16-5
Year: 2016
Facts:

Engineer A is a professional engineer working as a consultant to an automobile manufacturer that is considering the development of a driverless/autonomous vehicle operating system. Engineer A is assigned to an engineering risk assessment team whose members are being asked to make a recommendation relating to potential situations that could arise in connection with the operation of driverless/autonomous vehicles. The following scenario is among the situations that are being considered by the engineering risk assessment team: In the event of an unavoidable crash, does the vehicle's system choose the outcome that will likely result in the greatest potential for safety for the vehicle's passengers or does the vehicle's software system instead choose an option in which the least amount of potential harm is done to any of those involved in an accident, such as having the car crash into a stationary object (e.g., telephone pole, etc.) with the probability of causing some passengers serious but non-life-threatening injuries instead of striking and potentially causing a fatal injury to a pedestrian, cyclist, or motorcycle rider?

This is a case in which our values come into conflict. Whatever Engineer A's team decides, someone will be harmed. When an accident of the relevant sort occurs, either the passengers will suffer non-fatal harm *or* others involved in the accident will face the possibility of fatal harm. So both options will lead to a violation of the principle of non-maleficence. But the option that has the car crash into a stationary object does better with respect to adhering to non-maleficence than the option of having the car prioritize the safety of the passengers above all else. For in that case, although the passengers are harmed, no one is killed. As it turns out, however, most customers would prefer to purchase a car that prioritizes their safety over the safety of others. So Engineer A's team would do better with avoiding violation of the principle of autonomy for its customers by programming the car to prioritize passenger safety. For in that case, the wishes of the customers would be respected in a way that they are not if the car is programed in such a way as to prioritize the safety of all involved in a crash. In engineering ethics, we seek to find the best way to balance the relevant principles when they come into conflict in cases like these. And these are the sort of issues that we examine in this book.

Morality and Law

When we do applied ethics, it is important to distinguish between what is moral and what is legal. For example, segregation was legal but not moral. More relevant to engineers will be cases in which there is no law, and yet there might be a moral obligation. In the Chapter 1 "Cases for Discussion" we include BER Case 18-9. In that case, an engineer is a part of a residential development project in a coastal city. There is no building code in place. So the team has a great deal of flexibility about how to proceed with the project. But the engineer has access to information and an algorithm that together make the engineer think the project should be built with a 100-year storm surge in mind. No law states that the engineer's team is required to do this. But legally, it is arguable that the engineer's team should do it. (We will return to this in Chapter 1.) Another potential point of divergence between legality and morality that is of special importance to engineers are cases of whistleblowing. Especially in the recent past, the laws in United States did not favor whistleblowers. Nonetheless, engineers still might have an obligation to blow the whistle even when doing so would be illegal. (We will return to this topic in Chapter 4.) So in these cases looking to the laws does not settle the moral questions we are interested in.

Metaethics

There is another worry one might have about the project of applied ethics. Not only might one be concerned with the fact that we haven't found the whole truth about normative ethics. And so our tools are not up to the task. One might have an even deeper worry. One might think there is no truth in morality. Or, if there is, one might think that we have no way to know what that truth is. These sorts of issues belong to the field of metaethics. We find that whenever we teach applied ethics, these sorts of issues come up. Students reasonably ask how we can know whether a moral claim is true.

One way to understand metaethics is by considering different theories about the truth and falsity of **moral statements**. Consider a list of such statements:

- Abortion is right.
- Abortion is wrong.
- Slavery is wrong.
- Mother Teresa was good.

- Hitler was good.
- Hitler was evil.
- Pleasure is good.
- Pain is bad.

Some of these statements, such as "Hitler was evil," are agreed to be true by almost everyone. Others, such as "Hitler was good," are widely thought to be false. Still other moral statements, such as the statements about abortion, are surrounded by widespread disagreement. But whatever we think of the truth or falsity of these particular moral statements, it seems that some moral statements are true and others are false. Metaethical theories may be divided according to how they answer the question: "What makes moral statements true?"

Some who doubt that morality is objective accept the **error theory**. According to this theory, no moral statements are true. All moral statements are false. Humans typically make moral statements, and in doing so think they are saying something true. But they are mistaken. When one person says "Abortion is wrong" and another person says "Abortion is right" they are both saying something false. An error theorist is like an atheist about morality. An atheist might think that both "God is loving" and "God is hateful" are false because she believes God does not exist. So there is nothing in the world to make such theological statements true. Similarly, an error theorist believes that moral statements are all false because there is nothing in the world to make them true. There is no such thing as goodness, badness, rightness, or wrongness to make such statements true.

The error theory is a very strange view. If it were true, it would mean that humans are radically mistaken about what the world is like. For this reason, one might wonder why anyone would believe such a theory. What could possibly motivate such a radical view? One important motivation for the error theory is the **argument from explanation**. According to this argument we should not believe in goodness, badness, rightness, or wrongness because they are not needed to explain any observations.

There are two premises of this argument. First, one should only believe in something if it is needed to explain what one sees and hears. Perhaps as you read this book you are studying in the school library. You look around and see other students studying. You see tables, chairs, bookshelves, and lights. Now consider a list of things you might think are in the library. You might think there are:

- Other people
- Tables
- Chairs

- Bookshelves
- Lights
- An invisible and silent leprechaun.

The first five items on the list seem like things you should believe in. But it would be absurd to believe that there is an invisible leprechaun in the library, hanging upside down from the ceiling, silently staring at you. What is the difference between the leprechaun and the other items on the list above? A natural answer is that you need people, tables, etc. to explain what you see and hear. But you don't need the leprechaun to explain anything. If there were no people, for example, you wouldn't see anyone. But if there were no invisible silent leprechaun? In that case things would appear exactly as they would if there were such a leprechaun. The leprechaun is not needed to explain what you see and hear. The other items on the list are. That is why you should believe people, tables, etc. but not the leprechaun. It would be a different story if the leprechaun became visible, hopped down from the ceiling onto your shoulder, and whispered in your ear "Don't steal my pot of gold." In that case, the leprechaun would make a difference to what you see and hear, and perhaps you should believe in it. But as long as the leprechaun remains invisible and silent, you should not believe in it. You are just tacking on something extra that you don't need to explain anything. This lends support to the first premise of the argument from explanation.

The second premise of the argument is that moral properties are not needed to explain what you see and hear. Think about something that seems obviously evil. Imagine you see an innocent child killed with a man's bat swing. What is needed to explain what you have seen and heard? You need physical things. There must be the matter that makes up the child and the man and the bat. You might need beliefs and desires to explain why the man swung the bat. But once you accept that there is the physical and there is the mental, it seems that everything about the death of the innocent child has been explained. As evil as the event seems, supposing that what happened was evil is not needed to explain what you have seen and heard. If there were no such thing as evil, the event would appear to you just as it would if there were. It is just tacking on something extra to suppose evil exists. It is just like believing in the leprechaun. And just as believing in the leprechaun is absurd, believing in goodness, evilness, rightness, and wrongness is absurd.

A challenge for anyone who wants to defend this argument concerns the first premise. The explanation for why you should not believe in the leprechaun is too demanding. There are things that we obviously get to believe, but the first premise would imply that we should not believe. We can see this by considering some of the skeptical scenarios discussed by Descartes and other philosophers later in this chapter. Go back to the story about you in the library looking around and taking in your environment. It is true that the leprechaun is not needed to explain what you see and hear. But it is also true that other people, tables, chairs, bookshelves, and lights are not needed to explain what you see and hear. Suppose, for example, that you are a sleeping caveman dreaming about the library. All other humans have been killed. If the caveman story is true, then you would see and hear exactly what you see and hear now. But there would be no other people, no tables, etc. Imagine that only two things exist—you (a brain in a vat) and a computer hooked up to your brain with electrodes. The computer zaps your brain in one way and you see other people. It zaps your brain in another way and you hear the quiet hum of a library air conditioner. If the brain in a vat story is true, you would see and hear exactly what you see and hear now. But there would be no other people, no tables, etc.

Finally, suppose the only things that exist are you (a disembodied soul) and an omnipotent evil demon. The demon waves its demony hands in one way and it appears to you that you have a body and are in a library and that there are other people. If that were true, then you would see and hear exactly what you see and hear now. But you would have no body and no other people would exist. If you should only believe what is needed to explain what you see and hear, then you should not believe in other people or that you have a body. For stories about dreaming, and demons, and brains in vats also explain what you see and hear. That is a bit extreme. We don't have to take such wild stories seriously. But the first premise of the argument from explanation insists that we do. So the first premise is false. If we are looking for a theory about what we should believe, we need to go back to the drawing board. The challenge for the error theorist that wants to motivate her theory, then, is to come up with a better account of what we get to believe, one that makes morality come out as like the leprechaun, but not other beliefs such as the belief that other people exist or that I have a body.

Another doubt concerning the objectivity of morality stems from the thought that morality works in the way that taste is sometimes thought to work. This theory, **subjectivism**, holds that a moral statement is true for a person if and only if that person sincerely believes it. Consider the following:

- I like buffalo wings.
- I do not like buffalo wings.

If your friend says "I like buffalo wings" and you reply "No I don't, I hate buffalo wings," your reply would be based on a confusion. All you are talking about when you say you don't like buffalo wings is you. You aren't making a claim about what everyone likes. You are just making a claim about what you like. "I like buffalo wings" can be true for your friend but false for you.

To argue about whether it is true would be as silly as arguing about whether a bank is a financial institution or sloped ground along a body of water. You would just be using "bank" to talk about different things. Similarly, the subjectivist thinks that when your friend says "Abortion is wrong" and you say "Abortion is not wrong" you are just talking about different things. Your friend isn't making the claim that abortion is wrong, period, and for everybody. She is just claiming that abortion is wrong for her. It is true *for her* that abortion is wrong. But it is still true *for you* that abortion is not wrong.

It is important to note here that subjectivism and error theory are motivated in different ways. The error theorist recognizes that morality seems to exist to us. And it seems to work a certain way. She recognizes that to defend her view she needs to give us a reason to doubt how morality appears to us. Subjectivism is defended in a very different way. The error theorist tells us that our moral intuitions and appearances are mistaken, and that the argument from explanation shows that they are mistaken. Such beliefs are guilty until proven innocent. On the other hand, the subjectivist tells us that our moral intuitions and appearances are innocent until proven guilty. The reason we should believe subjectivism is because it matches the way morality seems to us. The error theorist tells us to doubt that morality is the way it appears to be. The subjectivist tells us to accept that morality is the way it appears to be. Start with the way morality seems before you were thinking about metaethics. Build your metaethical theory out of that. The subjectivist tells us that, if we do so, then we will see that subjectivism matches the way morality seems to us. And that is why we should believe it.

One challenge for subjectivism is the **argument from absent disagreement**.

Imagine you are finishing up a night of drinking in the bar district. You walk back to campus with your friends and in your dorm you start talking about abortion. Your friend says that abortion is wrong. She gives reasons and arguments for why she thinks it's wrong. You argue that abortion is not wrong. You give reasons and arguments for your position. At around 3am things get heated. Your friend yells out 'Abortion is wrong!' You yell back 'No it's not true that abortion is wrong!' Suddenly there is a knock at the door. You open the door and see a sleepy-looking subjectivist. She tells you that the two of you are confused. When your friend says 'Abortion is wrong' all she means is that abortion is wrong for her. When you say 'It's not true that abortion is wrong' all you mean is that abortion is not wrong for you. Neither of you, the subjectivist insists, is making claims about the other. You are just making claims about yourself. It can be true for your friend that abortion is wrong even if it is not true for you. It is as if the two of you are arguing about whether 'I like buffalo wings' is true or about whether a bank is a financial institution. You are just talking past each other. It is just a confusion. In light of this, you can quiet down so the subjectivist can go back to his room and sleep.

It seems that the subjectivist is mistaken. You and your friend really do seem to be arguing. When your friend says 'Abortion is wrong!' she isn't just making a claim about what is true for her. She is claiming that abortion is wrong (period!), and for everyone. And when you say 'It's not true that abortion is wrong!' you are making a claim about everyone and not just yourself. You are really disagreeing. Think about when people yell at each other on cable news about abortion or some other issue. It seems like they really do disagree. It doesn't seem like they are just talking past one another. Finally, remember the whole reason we were supposed to accept subjectivism in the first place. The suggestion was that we should trust the way morality appears to us. The claim was that subjectivism would match that appearance. But morality papers do allow for disagreement. So subjectivism doesn't really match how morality appears to us. And so now we have no reason to accept it.

Moral objectivism is the view that some moral statements are true, some are false, and that whether they are true or false doesn't depend on what anybody believes. This view takes moral statements to work in the same way that other statements such as historical and scientific statements are supposed to work. Do you think it's true that '2 + 2 = 5'? OK. But you're wrong. Do you think it's true that 'Caesar never existed'? If so, you're wrong. Similarly, if you think it's true that 'eating babies just for fun is permissible'? Sorry. You're wrong. It isn't.

As we have seen, people sometimes doubt that morality is objective because they are attracted to the error theory and the argument from explanation. Or they are tempted to think that morality is subjective. Another doubt about moral objectivism is **the argument from widespread moral disagreement**. Humans have been arguing, for example, about abortion for a long time. It doesn't look like we'll come to a consensus about it any time soon. The lack of consensus about morality suggests that it isn't tracking anything objective.

In raising objections to skepticism about moral objectivism we do not mean to suggest that moral objectivism faces no problems. We only mean to help you see past the naïve assumption that morality is *obviously* subjective or non-existent. And, we think it is worth noting, there are skeptical problems faced by science itself.

Philosophy of Science

Consider combustion, a process that is central to many engineering processes: combustion reactions are critical for chemical transformations in chemical engineering; combustion of fossil fuels provides energy; and the combustion engine generates mechanical power by combustion of a fuel. Combustion is so dominant in engineering that the words "engine" and "engineering" derive from the same root. Think about the last time you started a fire. Maybe you were camping during winter and wanted to make sure everyone was warm after nightfall. You lit a match, tossed it in with some kindling and some wood, and then the fire got going. This process, combustion, is so familiar that it seems unremarkable. Nevertheless, it is a source of puzzlement. While contemporary scientists agree that combustion occurs because of oxidation, long ago scientists accepted the **theory of phlogiston**. According to this theory, combustible objects contain phlogiston particles. Combustion occurs when such particles leave an object. If there really are phlogiston particles one might think that when an object is burnt it will lose weight. After all, particles have weight, burning an object causes it to lose phlogiston particles, so combustion results in weight loss. This prediction is borne out in most cases, like with the wood and kindling in your campfire. But it turns out that some metals gain weight when they are burnt. Reflection on the history and demise of the theory of phlogiston serves to illustrate a number of doubts philosophers have had about the objectivity of science.

One source of doubt is the **underdetermination problem**. We might think there is an easy argument from the story above to the falsity of phlogiston theory. The argument would be that phlogiston theory predicts that burning something causes it to lose weight. But burning certain metals causes them to gain weight. So phlogiston theory is false. Scientists at the time remained unconvinced, however. Some thought the relevant experiments simply showed that phlogiston particles have negative weight! We might laugh at this now. But what is wrong with the phlogiston theorists' reasoning here? We have an observation: some metals gain weight when burnt. The theory of oxidation predicts that observation. But so does the theory according to which phlogiston particles can have negative weight. The only good reason to believe one scientific theory rather than another is a difference in their ability to successfully predict observations. So it provides no reason to believe one theory rather than the other. Some philosophers of science believe that what is true of oxidation theory, phlogiston theory, and the observation that some metals gain weight when burnt is true of *all* scientific theories and *any* set of observations. In particular, for any scientific theory that correctly predicts any set of observations, there are an infinite number of other, incompatible, scientific theories that also correctly predict those observations. Successful prediction of observations is the only reason to prefer one scientific theory over another. So we have no reason to believe any scientific theory at all.

One way to try to address the underdetermination problem is by denying that consistency with observations is the only good reason to believe a scientific theory. Perhaps there are theoretical virtues, such as simplicity, that can be used, along with observational adequacy, to rule out theories. And perhaps that will allow us to settle on some scientific theories. A challenge for this sort of view is to explain why we should think theoretical virtues such as simplicity track the truth, and whether such virtues are really sufficient to narrow down the number of incompatible scientific theories enough to support objectivism about science.

Another source of doubt about the objectivity of science is **pessimistic induction**. Eventually phlogiston theory gave way to oxidation theory. The two theories posited different unobservable entities. Oxidation theory, we are supposing, was a better theory. So scientists eventually went with it and the unobservables it posited. But notice that the history of science is littered with stories like this. We've got a theory that posits certain unobservable entities that is pretty good at predicting observations. Then we get a theory that is even better at predicting observations but that posits completely different unobservable entities. Every scientific theory before our current ones gave way to a better scientific theory that posited completely different unobservable entities. So our current scientific theories will probably suffer the same fate. And therefore, we have no good reason to believe in the unobservable entities posited by our current and best scientific theories. All the stuff scientists are telling us about quantum entities? Don't believe it. Eventually we'll get an even better theory that tells us that something completely different exists.

One way to try to deal with pessimistic induction is to appeal to the idea of approximate truth. It is true that all previous scientific theories have been replaced by better ones. And it is true that our current scientific theories will be replaced by still better ones. Nevertheless, earlier theories were approximately true. And current scientific theories are even closer to the truth. And future theories will be still closer to the truth. That is enough to support objectivism about science. A challenge for anyone holding this view is to address the worry that previous theories were not even approximately true. Phlogiston theory, for example, posited entities which simply don't exist at all. It made predictions about combustion that were approximately true. But the entities it posited were nowhere near the truth. In the same way, when our current theories are replaced by better theories, it will remain the case that our theories make approximately true predictions about some phenomenon. But the entities that our best scientific theories posit will be shown to be completely non-existent and replaced with totally alien entities.

Another source of doubt about the objectivity of science is **descriptivist relativism**. You might think that if two people associate different descriptions with a word, then they are talking about different things when they use that word. Imagine you are at a financial institution withdrawing some money. You associate the word "bank" with financial institution. Imagine your friend is near the ocean standing on land that borders the water with sloped ground. He associates "bank" with sloped ground along a body of water. Since you associate "bank" with different descriptions, you are talking about different things when you talk about banks. This natural thought has led some to think that supporters of distinct scientific theories are talking about different things. Oxidation theorists, for example, associate one description with "burning." Phlogiston theorists associate a different description with "burning." So they must be talking about different things when they talk about burning. And, just as you inhabit one world and your friend next to the ocean inhabits another world, so too do the proponents of phlogiston theory inhabit a different world than the proponents of oxidation theory.

One problem for descriptivist relativism is that it is unclear why the fact that people talk about different things would imply that they inhabit different worlds. Why isn't it just that they exist in the same world in which the same stuff exists but that one, the oxygen theorist, is talking about something that exists and another, the phlogiston theorist, is talking about something that doesn't exist? Another problem is that it is unclear why associating different descriptions with a phenomenon is sufficient, by itself, to make us talk about different things. Why isn't it just that phlogiston theorists and oxygen theorists are talking about the same thing but simply have radically different theories about that thing? Maybe what it takes to talk about something isn't to correctly describe it, but to instead have the right sort of causal connection to it. Surely, before the development of chemical theory, people were able to talk about water even if they had no idea that it was composed of H_2O and even if they had no theory about it whatsoever. Similarly, it seems that phlogiston theorists were talking about burning. It's just that they had a mistaken theory about what burning consists of.

It is important to recognize some differences between the underdetermination and pessimism problems, on the one hand, and the argument from descriptivist relativism on the other. Even if they are correct, the underdetermination and pessimism problems do not show that there is no objective scientific truth. At most they just show that we are too dumb to figure out what the objective scientific truth is. On the other hand, descriptivist relativism, if correct, would show that scientific truths are not objective. This should provide some comfort for the objectivist. The underdetermination and pessimism problems have at least *some* plausibility. But we think descriptivist relativism, though historically important, doesn't really have much going for it for the reasons discussed above. So, at best, the arguments of this section show that we are just too dumb to know what the objective scientific truths are.

Another important thing to note is that there are still some objective scientific truths we can know even if the underdetermination and pessimism problems turn out to be sound. In particular, such problems do not threaten the idea that we can rule out a bunch of scientific theories because they conflict with observation. And we can know which of the theories match observation and which don't. Maybe that is not all that the objectivist about science would hope for. But it is not trivial either.

In presenting some doubts about the possibility of knowledge of scientific truths, we are not suggesting that such doubts are in the end well-founded. We just want to help you see past the naïve, knee jerk idea that science is the ONE TRUE OBJECTIVE THING and that there are no important challenges to scientific objectivism. Life is puzzling. Just as philosophers have found puzzling things about every other area of life, they have found puzzling things about science. Such puzzles are not exclusive to morality.

Why Metaethics and Philosophy of Science?

If we're interested in the applied problems faced by professional engineers, why bother with metaethics and philosophy of science? We find that unless we address these issues at the beginning of class, students wonder how we could have any moral knowledge. And, without such knowledge, they sometimes think it is pointless to discuss applied ethics. So, in addressing moral epistemology, and in identifying some common problems about moral knowledge and scientific knowledge, we can then move on to more applied issues.

Introduction Key Terms and Concepts

Trolley
Large Man
Organ Harvest
The Trolley Problem
Consequentialism
Hedonic Act Utilitarianism (HAU)
Hedonic Utility
Maximizing
Deontology
Doctrine of Double Effect (DDE)
Intending and Foreseeing
Ends and Means
Proportionally Grave Reason

Moral Statements
Error Theory
The Argument from Explanation
Subjectivism
The Argument from Absent
    Disagreement
Moral Objectivism
The Argument from Widespread
    Moral Disagreement
The Theory of Phlogiston
Underdetermination Problem
Pessimistic Induction
Descriptivist Relativism

Introduction: End of Chapter Reading

Guided Core Reading   22

Core Reading I.1: 'An ethical framework for evaluating experimental technology' by Ibo van de Poel (excerpts)

Core Reading I.2: 'Why ethics matters for autonomous cars' by Patrick Lin (excerpt)

Guided Further Reading   33

Further Reading I.1: 'Thinking like an engineer: The place of a code of ethics in the practice of a profession' by Michael Davis

Further Reading I.2: '"Things that went well—no serious injuries or deaths": Ethical reasoning in a normal engineering design process' by Peter Lloyd and Jerry Busby

Further Reading I.3: 'Metaethics in context of engineering ethical and moral systems' by Lily Frank and Michał Klincewicz

Tip: If you can't use the QR codes, use the hyperlinks found on the book's webpage instead: www.routledge.com/9781138183865.

Guided Core Reading

Core Reading I.1: 'An ethical framework for evaluating experimental technology' by Ibo van de Poel (excerpts)

Preparing to Read

In this reading van de Poel addresses the control problem for experimental technologies. On the one hand, it is difficult or impossible to predict the consequences of introducing experimental technologies to society. On the other hand, once an experimental technology has been introduced, it is difficult to take it back. Van de Poel suggests dealing with this problem by adopting an experimental incremental approach to introducing new technology to society. Drawing on ideas from bioethicists, van de Poel appeals to principles of non-maleficence, beneficence, respect for autonomy, and justice to construct an ethical framework to guide societal experimentation with new technologies.

Excerpted from: Van de Poel, I. (2016). An ethical framework for evaluating experimental technology. *Science and Engineering Ethics*, 22, 667–686. doi.org/10.1007/s11948-015-9724-3. © The Author 2015, reprinted by permission of Springer Nature. Internal references generally omitted.

Introduction

Swarm robots. Human enhancement. Algae based on synthetic biology. Automated driving vehicles. What these new technological possibilities have in common is that they may seriously impact society. What they also have in common is that the exact impacts on society are currently largely unknown and are very hard to predict beforehand.

    ...

    The difficulties in dealing with experimental technologies go back to the control dilemma formulated by Collingridge .... This says that in early phases of new technology, when a technology and its social embedding are still malleable, there is uncertainty about the social effects of that technology. In later phases, social effects may be clear but then often the technology has become so well entrenched in society that it is hard to overcome negative effects.

    ...

New Technologies as Social Experiments

One way to conceptualize the introduction of technology is to conceive of the introduction as a social experiment. A 2007 report by the *European Expert Group on Science and Governance* stressed the importance of the notion. They noted, "we are in an unavoidably experimental state. Yet this is usually deleted from public view and public negotiation" (Felt et al. 2007: 68) And they continue: "If citizens are routinely being enrolled without negotiation as experimental subjects, in experiments which are not called by name, then some serious ethical and social issues would have to be addressed" (Felt et al. 2007: 68).

Towards an Ethical Framework for Experimental Technology: Informed consent

When a technology is introduced it amounts to a social experiment because even if all reasonable efforts to anticipate consequences haven been undertaken, there will be unanticipated consequences. This can be turned into a more deliberate and responsible experimentation by following Popper's idea of piecemeal social experiments.

Martin and Schinzinger … have proposed *informed consent* to judge the acceptability of social experiments with new technology. The application of this principle is problematic. It may be hard to identify individuals potentially affected by the introduction of technology. To deal with this, Martin and Schinzinger propose the following specification of informed consent for situations in which individuals cannot be readily identified:

> Information that a rational person would need, stated in understandable form, has been widely disseminated. The subject's consent was offered in a proxy by a group that collectively represents many subjects of like interests, concerns, and exposure to risk (Martin and Schinzinger 1996: 87).

It remains unclear whether they understand the second condition to require unanimous consent by the representative group or only a majority decision. In the first case, the requirement of informed consent might be too strict. In the second case, it may be doubted whether what they propose is still a form of informed consent. Also, the first condition is problematic. Risks and benefits of experimental technologies may not only be hard to estimate, sometimes they are unknown.

Table 3 An ethical framework for experimental technology

1	Absence of other reasonable means for gaining knowledge about risks and benefits
2	Monitoring of data and risks while addressing privacy concerns
3	Possibility and willingness to adapt or stop the experiment
4	Containment of risks as far as reasonably possible
5	Consciously scaling up to avoid large-scale harm and to improve learning
6	Flexible set-up of the experiment and avoidance of lock-in of the technology
7	Avoid experiments that undermine resilience
8	Reasonable to expect social benefits from the experiment
9	Clear distribution of responsibilities for setting up, carrying out, monitoring, evaluating, adapting, and stopping of the experiment
10	Experimental subjects are informed
11	The experiment is approved by democratically legitimized bodies
12	Experimental subjects can influence the setting up, carrying out, monitoring, evaluating, adapting, and stopping of the experiment
13	Experimental subjects can withdraw from the experiment
14	Vulnerable experimental subjects are either not subject to the experiment or are additionally protected or particularly profit from the experimental technology (or a combination)
15	A fair distribution of potential hazards and benefits
16	Reversibility of harm or, if impossible, compensation of harm

Developing an Ethical Framework

I propose to start from the broader and more general set of ethical principles that have been articulated in bioethics: non-maleficence, beneficence, respect for autonomy, and justice (Beauchamp and Childress 2013). Table 3

Conditions for Responsible Experimentation in the Context of Experimental Technology

Non-maleficence

One ought not to (intentionally) inflict harm (Beauchamp and Childress 2013). Conditions 1 through 7 in Table 3 can be seen as a specification of the principle of non-maleficence for social experiments with technology. Condition 1 requires that before a technology is introduced, other reasonable means to gain knowledge about risks, like lab tests or field tests, have been exhausted. Conditions 2 and 3 require that that if harm occurs the experiment be stopped or can be adapted to avoid harm. Condition 4 states that harm should be contained. For reasons explained above, a complete avoidance of harm is usually not possible for experimental technologies. Conditions 5 through 7 all aim at achieving non-maleficence through the strategy of incrementalism (rather than anticipation) that was explained above. Condition 5 follows from Popper's (1945) idea of piecemeal social experiments and is intended to avoid large-scale harm and to increase what is learned from the experiment. Condition 6 is based on the idea of Collingridge ... that incrementalism requires flexibility. Condition 7 follows Wildavsky's ... idea that in order to deal with the risks of new technology we should not solely depend on containment of expected risks, but also on resilience in order to be able to deal with unexpected risks.

Beneficence

We should not only avoid harm but also do good. Introducing possible but unknown harm would only be permissible if it is reasonable to expect at least some benefits from the experiment. This is what is expressed in condition 8. For experimental technologies, we often do not know the potential benefits and drawbacks well enough to list all possible effects. Therefore condition 8 is formulated in terms of whether it is reasonable to expect social benefits from the experiment. Balancing risks and benefits requires accurate knowledge of risks and benefits and the point of experimental technology is that such knowledge is usually lacking. It seems better to use a criterion that requires less anticipatory knowledge of social impacts. Condition 9 was developed as an alternative specification that something is learned from the experiment that benefits society. The learning is not scientific learning but rather trial-and-error learning about an on-going intervention through the experimental introduction of a technology into society. This learning is enabled by some of the already mentioned conditions like condition 2 (monitoring) and condition 5 (gradually scaling up to enable learning).

Respect for Autonomy and Justice

Conditions 10 through 13 are intended to safeguard the moral principle respect for autonomy. Condition 10 covers the 'informed' part of informed consent. But rather than requiring individual consent, condition 11 requires a form of collective consent by approval by a democratically legitimized body. A potential problem of such collective consent is that it may lead to a tyranny of the majority, requiring unacceptable sacrifices from individuals for the collective good. Conditions 12 and 13 and the conditions 14 through 16, which address the moral principle of justice, can be seen as a way to avoid such exploitation. They guarantee that experimental subjects have a say in the set-up of the experiment (condition 12), and are able to withdraw from the experiment (condition 13). They also guarantee that vulnerable people are either additionally protected or are not subjected to the experiment (condition 14) and risks and benefits are fairly distributed (condition 15). The last two conditions are especially important in the light of the moral principle of justice. In the case of clinical experiments usually three main groups can be distinguished: the experimental group undergoing the intervention, the control group (undergoing another intervention or no intervention), and the larger population that might profit from the results (including vulnerable groups within this larger population). In the case of technologies, risks and benefits may be distribution over a larger number of groups and distribution effects may be more complicated. While in medicine the main effects are health effects for individuals, some technologies may also shift the power relations between groups and so have complicated distribution effects. Condition 16 that states that irreversible harm should be avoided, which can be seen as a specification of non-maleficence and when irreversible harm nevertheless occurs, compensation should be offered.

References

Beauchamp, T.L., & Childress, J.F. (2013). *Principles of biomedical ethics*. New York: Oxford University Press.

Felt, U., Wynne, B., Callon, M., Gonçalves, M.E., Jasanoff, S., Jepsen, M., Joly, P.-B., Konopasek, Z., May, S., Neubauer, C., Rip, A., Siune K., Stirling, A., & Tallacchini, M. (2007). *Taking European knowledge society seriously. Report of the expert group on science and governance to the Science, Economy and Society Directorate, Directorate-General for Research, European Commission*. Brussels: Directorate-General for Research, Science, Economy and Society.

Martin, M.W., & Schinzinger, R. (1996). *Ethics in engineering* (3rd ed.). New York: McGraw-Hill.

Guided Reading Questions

1. What is the control problem? What examples from your own exposure to engineering illustrate this problem?
2. In what ways does van de Poel think anticipation-based solutions to the control problem are deficient? Do you think he is right about this? Or do you think his criticisms are exaggerated? Why?
3. What is the incremental and experimental approach that van de Poel proposes? Do you think that it is a viable solution to the problem? Does it do a better job than the anticipation-based solutions? If so, why? If not, why not?
4. What is the informed consent principle for introducing experimental technology? What, according to van Poel, are its problems?
5. What are the four general moral principles for experimental technology? How do they give rise to the conditions of van de Poel's framework? Do you think his principles are helpful?

Read the Full Article (optional)

You can read the full article online by scanning the QR code or following the link below. The article is available **Open Access** and no subscription or login is required.

www.link.springer.com/article/10.1007%2Fs11948-015-9724-3

Core Reading I.2: 'Why ethics matters for autonomous cars' by Patrick Lin (excerpt)

Preparing to Read

If motor vehicles are to be truly autonomous and able to operate responsibly on our roads, they will need to replicate—or do better than—the human decision-making process. But some decisions are more than just a mechanical application of traffic laws and plotting a safe path. They seem to require a sense of ethics, and this is a notoriously difficult capability to reduce to algorithms for a computer to follow.

Excerpted from: Lin, P. (2016). Why ethics matters for autonomous cars. In M. Maurer, J. Gerdes, B. Lenz, & H. Winner (Eds.), *Autonomous Driving.* Berlin and Heidelberg: Springer. doi.org/10.1007/978-3-662-45854-9_4. © The Author 2015, reprinted by permission of Springer Nature. Internal references omitted.

4.1 Why Ethics Matters

To start, let me offer a simple scenario that illustrates the need for ethics in autonomous cars. Imagine in some distant future, your autonomous car encounters this terrible choice: it must either swerve left and strike an eight-year old girl, or swerve right and strike an 80-year old grandmother …. Given the car's velocity, either victim would surely be killed on impact. If you do not swerve, both victims will be struck and killed; so there is good reason to think that you ought to swerve one way or another. But what would be the ethically correct decision? If you were programming the self-driving car, how would you instruct it to behave if it ever encountered such a case, as rare as it may be?

Striking the grandmother could be the lesser evil, at least to some eyes. The thinking is that the girl still has her entire life in front of her—a first love, a family of her own, a career, and other adventures and happiness—while the grandmother has already had a full life and her fair share of experiences. Further, the little girl is a moral innocent, more so than just about any adult. We might agree that the grandmother has a right to life and as valuable a life as the little girl's; but nevertheless, there are reasons that seem to weigh in favor of saving the little girl over the grandmother, if an accident is unavoidable. Even the grandmother may insist on her own sacrifice, if she were given the chance to choose.

But either choice is ethically incorrect, at least according to the relevant professional codes of ethics. Among its many pledges, the Institute of Electrical and Electronics Engineers (IEEE), for instance, commits itself and its 430,000+ members "to treat fairly all persons and to not engage in acts of discrimination based on race, religion, gender, disability, age, national origin, sexual orientation, gender identity, or gender expression" …. Therefore, to treat individuals differently on the basis of their age, when age is not a relevant factor, seems to be exactly the kind of discrimination the IEEE prohibits ….

Age does not appear to be a relevant factor in our scenario as it might be in, say, casting a young actor to play a child's character in a movie. In that movie scenario, it would be appropriate to reject adult actors for the role. Anyway, a reason to discriminate does not necessarily justify that discrimination, since some reasons may be illegitimate. Even if we point to the disparity of life experiences between the old and the young, that difference isn't automatically an appropriate basis for different treatment.

Discriminating on the basis of age in our crash scenario would seem to be the same evil as discriminating on the basis of race, religion, gender, disability, national origin, and so on, even if we can invent reasons to prefer one such group over another. In Germany—home to many influential automotive companies that are working to develop self-driving technologies—the right to life and human dignity is basic and set forth in the first two articles of the very first chapter in the nation's constitution …. So it is difficult to see how German law could even allow a company to create a product that is capable to making such a horrific and apparently illegal choice. The United States similarly strives to offer equal protection to all persons, such as stipulated in the fourteenth amendment of its constitution.

If we cannot ethically choose a path forward, then what ought to be done? One solution is to refuse to make a swerve decision, allowing both victims to be struck; but this seems much worse than having only one victim die, even if we are prejudiced against her. Anyway, we can force a decision by modifying the scenario: assume that 10 or 100 other pedestrians would die, if the car continued forward; and swerving would again result in only a single death.

Another solution could be to arbitrarily and unpredictably choose a path, without prejudice to either person .... But this too seems ethically troubling, in that we are choosing between lives without any deliberation at all—to leave it to chance, when there are potentially some reasons to prefer one over the other, as distasteful and uncomfortable as those reasons may be. This is a dilemma that is not easily solvable and therefore points to a need for ethics in developing autonomous cars.

4.1.1 Beyond Crash-Avoidance

Many readers may object right away that the dilemma above, as well as others that follow, will never occur with autonomous cars. It may be suggested that future cars need not confront hard ethical choices, that simply stopping the car or handing control back to the human operator is the easy path around ethics. But I will contend here that braking and relinquishing control will not always be enough. Those solutions may be the best we have today, but if automated cars are to ever operate more broadly outside of limited highway environments, they will need more response-options.

Current research already makes this case as a matter of physics ..., but we can also make a case from commonsense. Many ordinary scenarios exist today in which braking is not the best or safest move, whether by human or self-driving car. A wet road or a tailgater, for instance, may make it dangerous to slam the brakes, as opposed to some other action such as steering around the obstacle or simply through it, if it is a small object. Today, the most advanced self-driving cars cannot detect small objects such as squirrels ...; therefore, they presumably cannot also detect squirrel-sized rocks, potholes, kittens, and other small but consequential hazards can cause equipment failure, such as tire blowouts or sensor errors, or deviations from a safe path.

In these and many other cases, there may not be enough time to hand control back to the driver. Some simulation experiments suggest that human drivers need up to 40 s to regain situation awareness, depending on the distracting activity, e.g., reading or napping—far longer than the 1–2 s of reaction time required for typical accident scenarios .... This means that the car must be responsible for making decisions when it is unreasonable to expect a timely transfer of control back to the human, and again braking might not be the most responsible action.

One possible reply is that, while imperfect, braking could successfully avoid the majority of emergency situations a robot car may find itself it, even if it regrettably makes things worse in a small number of cases. The benefits far outweigh the risks, presumably, and the numbers speak for themselves. Or do they? I will discuss the dangers of morality by math throughout this chapter.

Braking and other responses in the service of crash-avoidance won't be enough, because crash-avoidance is not enough. Some accidents are unavoidable—such as when an animal or pedestrian darts out in front of your moving car—and therefore autonomous cars will need to engage in crash-optimization as well. Optimizing crashes means to choose the course of action that will likely lead to the least amount of harm, and this could mean a forced choice between two evils, for instance, choosing to strike either the eight-year old girl or the 80-year old grandmother in my first scenario above.

4.1.2 Crash-Optimization Means Targeting

There may be reasons, by the way, to prefer choosing to run over the eight-year old girl that I have not yet mentioned. If the autonomous car were most interested in protecting its own occupants, then it would make sense to choose a collision with the lightest object possible (the girl). If the choice were between two vehicles, then the car should be programmed to prefer striking a lighter vehicle (such as a Mini Cooper or motorcycle) than a heavier one (such as a sports utility vehicle (SUV) or truck) in an adjacent lane ....

On the other hand, if the car were charged with protecting other drivers and pedestrians over its own occupants—not an unreasonable imperative— then it should be programmed to prefer a collision with the heavier vehicle than the lighter one. If vehicle-to-vehicle (V2V) and vehicle-to-infrastructure (V2I) communications are rolled out (or V2X to refer to both), or if an autonomous car can identify the specific models of other cars on the road, then it seems to make sense to collide with a safer vehicle (such as a Volvo SUV that has a reputation for safety) over a car not known for crash-safety (such as a Ford Pinto that's prone to exploding upon impact).

This strategy may be both legally and ethically better than the previous one of jealously protecting the car's own occupants. It could minimize lawsuits, because any injury to others would be less severe. Also, because the driver is the one who introduced the risk to society—operating an autonomous vehicle on public roads—the driver may be legally obligated, or at least morally obligated, to absorb the brunt of any harm, at least when squared off against pedestrians, bicycles, and perhaps lighter vehicles.

The ethical point here, however, is that no matter which strategy is adopted by an original equipment manufacturer (OEM), i.e., auto manufacturer, programming a car to choose a collision with any particular kind of object over another very much resembles a targeting algorithm .... Somewhat related to the military sense of selecting targets, crash-optimization algorithms may involve the deliberate and systematic discrimination of, say, large vehicles or Volvos to collide into. The owners or operators of these targeted vehicles bear this burden through no fault of their own, other than perhaps that they care about safety or need an SUV to transport a large family.

4.1.3 Beyond Harm

The problem is starkly highlighted by the following scenario ...: Again, imagine that an autonomous car is facing an imminent crash, but it could select one of two targets in adjacent lanes to swerve into: either a motorcyclist who is wearing a helmet, or a motorcyclist who is not. It probably doesn't matter much to the safety of the car itself or its occupants whether the motorcyclist is wearing a helmet; the impact of a helmet into a car window doesn't introduce that much more risk that the autonomous car should want to avoid it over anything else. But it matters a lot to the motorcyclist whether s/he is wearing a helmet: the one without a helmet would probably not survive such a collision. Therefore, in this dreadful scenario, it seems reasonable to program a good autonomous car to swerve into the motorcyclist with the helmet.

But how well is justice and public policy served by this crash-optimization design? Motorcyclists who wear helmets are essentially being penalized and discriminated against for their responsible decision to wear a helmet. This may encourage some motorcyclists to not wear helmets, in order to avoid targeting by autonomous cars. Likewise, in the previous scenario, sales may decline for automotive brands known for safety, such as Volvo and Mercedes Benz, insofar as customers want to avoid being the preferred targets of crash-optimization systems.

Some readers may want to argue that the motorcyclist without a helmet ought to be targeted, for instance, because he has acted recklessly and therefore is more deserving of harm. Even if that's the correct design, notice that we are again moving beyond harm in making crash-optimization decisions. We're still talking about justice and other such ethical considerations, and that's the point: it's not just a numbers game.

Programmers in such scenarios, as rare as they may be, would need to design cost-functions—algorithms that assign and calculate the expected costs of various possible options, selecting the one with the lowest costs— that potentially determine who gets to live and who gets to die. And this is fundamentally an ethics problem, one that demands much more care and transparency in reasoning than seems currently offered. Indeed, it is difficult to imagine a weightier and more profoundly serious decision a programmer would ever have to make. Yet, there is little discussion about this core issue to date.

Guided Reading Questions

1. Lin considers a case in which your autonomous vehicle must either kill an elderly woman or a little girl. He considers reasons why it should target the elderly woman and reasons why it should not. Where do you stand on this? Do you think the right thing to do is to kill the elderly woman? The little girl? Both? Or randomly pick which one dies? Why?

2. Some people complain that automated cars will never be, or at least need not be, in the kind of situation discussed in question 1. Lin has a response to this. What is his response? Do you agree with it? Or do you side with the view that this problem need not arise?

3. Lin considers the idea that maybe the autonomous vehicle should run over the young girl. The idea is that an autonomous car should protect its occupants first and foremost. And they are less likely to be hurt if they hit the little girl than they are if they hit the elderly woman. What do you think of this? Should the car target the girl? What do you think of the more general point that maybe a car should be programmed to prioritize the safety of its occupants?

4. What do you think about Lin's helmet example? Should the car be programed to swerve into the motorcyclist wearing a helmet? What problems might such programming cause? Can you think of any other puzzling examples in light of Lin's points?

Read the Full Chapter

You can read the full chapter online by scanning the QR code or following the link below. The chapter is available **Open Access** and no subscription or login is required.

www.link.springer.com/chapter/10.1007/978-3-662-45854-9_4

Guided Further Reading

Further Reading I.1: 'Thinking like an engineer: The place of a code of ethics in the practice of a profession' by Michael Davis

Find the Article

Davis, M. (1991). Thinking like an engineer: The place of a code of ethics in the practice of a profession. *Philosophy and Public Affairs*, 20(2), 150–167. www.jstor.org/stable/2265293.

Read the article online by scanning the QR code or following the link below. Your college library will need to subscribe to the journal, and you may need to login via your library's website or use campus wifi to get access.

www.jstor.org/stable/2265293

Preparing to Read

Beyond the Code is premised in part upon the idea that, on their own, engineering codes of conduct are not enough to ensure engineers understand how to fulfill their obligations. We, the authors have argued, that engineers must "go beyond" the code in the sense that they must understand the various moral complexities that arise when trying to apply the code in real life. However, this is not to say that engineering codes of ethics—the NSPE Code of Ethics in particular—are not invaluable resources for engineering ethics. For this reason, before we go "beyond the code" it is worthwhile taking a moment, as Michael Davis does in this article, to examine the role of professional codes of ethics in engineering.

Guided Reading Questions

1. What was the decision Lund made? What was your initial reaction upon learning of it? Was Lund wrong? Was what he did permissible? Do you think it can be permissible for an engineer to think like a manager?

2. Davis considers two ways in which we might understand the contrast between 'thinking like an engineer" and "thinking like a manager." One way concerns expert knowledge and skill. The manager deals with people and understands problems in terms of people. The engineer deals with things and understands problems in terms of them. What was Davis's criticism of this way of understanding what Lund was asked to do? Do you agree with Davis about this? Why or why not?

3. Davis argues that a professional code has advantages over personal conscience. Part of his argument involves a comparison of a professional code with the rules of a game like baseball. Among other things, a code allows an engineer to know what to expect of other engineers. Do you think the analogy is apt? Even if it is apt, do you think that it is enough to support the use of a code? Can you think of ways engineers could know what to expect of one another without a code?

4. According to Davis, engineers should follow their code of ethics because its content makes it worthy of being followed. He considers a hypothetical example in which there is no code that is

widely followed by engineers. He argues that it would be too easy to fire a particular engineer for taking a moral stand in such a case. Do you buy this argument? Do you agree that a code helps protect individual engineers from getting fired for doing the right thing? If you do, why? If not, why not? Davis thinks this also provides an explanation for how Lund could reject the exhortation to "think like a manager rather than an engineer." Do you think Davis is right about that? Or is he mistaken?

5. Davis argues that the code, if Lund had followed it, would have prevented him from thinking like a manager. Do you think he is right about this?

Further Reading I.2: "'Things that went well—no serious injuries or deaths": Ethical reasoning in a normal engineering design process' by Peter Lloyd and Jerry Busby

Find the Article

Lloyd, P., & Busby, J. (2003). 'Things that went well—no serious injuries or deaths': Ethical reasoning in a normal engineering design process. *Science and Engineering Ethics*, 9, 503–516. doi.org/10.1007/s11948-003-0047-4.

Read the article online by scanning the QR code or following the link below. Your college library will need to subscribe to the journal, and you may need to login via your library's website or use campus wifi to get access.

https://link.springer.com/article/10.1007/s11948-003-0047-4

Preparing to Read

At the beginning of this chapter, we briefly introduced the reader to the role of ethical theories in the study of ethics. In the following chapters, however, we will not make direct use of these theories in our exploration of the ethical complexities behind the fundamental canons of the NSPE Code of Ethics. Likewise, with the exception of Chapter 2 (when we discuss virtue ethics), we will not usually appeal to a particular ethical theory when offering suggestions for how to approach these complexities. However, it is important to note that many of those working in engineering ethics do make explicit use of ethical theories such as deontology, consequentialism, and virtue ethics, both as a framework for understanding ethical issue in engineering and as a basis for addressing moral issues in engineering. For this reason, we have included this article by Peter Lloyd and Jerry Busby, which makes explicit use of ethical theory in discussing ethical reasoning in the engineering design process.

Guided Reading Questions

1. Lloyd and Busby consider the practice of treating engineering ethics as a sub-problem of engineering design. One concern they have about this approach is that it leads to individualized specialization on very specific moral problems. Do you agree that this is a problem for the approach? Why would such focus and specificity be problematic?
2. Lloyd and Busby give three reasons for thinking that engineering ethics should be consequentialist rather than deontological. First, engineering ethics is based on the outcome of processes. Second, engineering as a profession aims to change the world. Third, engineering ethics has a link between decisions and outcomes. Do you agree with this? Based on what we learned about deontology earlier in this chapter, do you think that being concerned with outcomes or linking decisions to outcomes should suggest that only outcomes matter? If you agree, why? If you disagree, why?
3. Consider two questions: First, how do engineers reason about morality? Second, how should engineers reason about morality? Lloyd and Busby are primarily concerned with the first question. Do you think providing an answer to the first question can help us

find an answer to the second? Or do you think the two questions are largely independent?

4. One issue that comes up in Lloyd and Busby's paper is the value of simplicity. It seems that many engineers think a simple design is more beautiful, and for that reason to be preferred to an unduly complicated design. Do you agree that there is a connection between beauty and simplicity? When can the value of simplicity be overridden in design? Can simplicity ever make something ugly?

Further Reading I.3: 'Metaethics in context of engineering ethical and moral systems' by Lily Frank and Michał Klincewicz

Find the Article

Frank, L, & Klincewicz, M. (2016). Metaethics in context of engineering ethical and moral systems. Association for the Advancement of Artificial Intelligence (AAAI) Spring Symposium Series.

Read the article online by scanning the QR code or following the link below. Select the title from the contents—*no subscription or login is required.*

www.aaai.org/Library/Symposia/Spring/ss16-04.php

Preparing to Read

As a branch of applied ethics concerned with the concrete and practical side of ethics, engineering ethics seldom concerns itself with the more abstract topics of metaethics. Lily Frank and Michał Klincewicz, however, argue that when it comes to certain applied topics—in particular the issue of moral development in AI—our metaethical issues are relevant to applied projects.

Guided Reading Questions

1. Frank and Klincewicz contrast a moral microscope AI with a simulation AI. They think the moral microscope is plausible only if moral realism is true. But the simulation AI could be made whether moral realism or anti-realism is true. Do you agree with this? In particular, they hold that a moral microscope AI could detect things we are insensitive to and be free of cognitive distortions. Do you think these things would be helpful and possible even if moral anti-realism is true? Or do you think the authors are correct in holding that they are helpful only if moral realism is true.

2. Frank and Klincewicz distinguish between strong and weak ambitions for moral AI. There is disagreement, they think, about what humans do when they make moral judgments. Depending on which metaethical theory is true, and depending on whether AI can be conscious, AI may not even be able to make moral judgments. And so engineering or modeling human moral judgments must be preceded by settling the relevant philosophical questions. Do you agree with this? Contrast this with judgments of taste. For example, can AI usefully model human judgments about what is tasty even if it is unable to make such judgments itself? If so, what might this reveal about whether AI can model human judgments about morality if anti-realism is true? If not, why not?

3. What is the distinction between motivational internalism and motivational externalism? Which of the two views do you think is right? What implications would this have for building moral AI?

4. Frank and Klincewicz compare the project of building conscious AI with the project of building AI that makes moral judgments. They claim that the two projects are not that different. Do you agree with them about this? Or do you think the two projects are very different?

5. The authors suggest building moral AI in such a way that assumes the least demanding metaethical theory. What do they mean by demandingness? What do you think about this strategy for building moral AI? Is it really the best strategy? Or can you think of a better one?

Bibliography

Aquinas, T. (1988). *Summa Theologica* II-II, Q. 64, art. 7, 'Of Killing.' In W. P. Baumgarth & R. J. Regan (Eds.), *On Law, Morality, and Politics* (pp. 226–227). Hackett.

Awad, E., S., Dsouza, R., Kim, J., Schulz, J., Henrich, A., Shariff, J.-F., Bonnefon, F., & Rahwan, I. (2018). The Moral Machine experiment. *Nature*, 563, 59–64.

Bonnefon, J. F., Shariff, A., & Rahwan, I. (2016). The social dilemma of autonomous vehicles. *Science*, 352(6293), 1573–1576.

Brennan, J. (2007). *The Best Moral Theory Ever: The Merits and Methodology of Moral Theorizing* [Dissertation]. University of Arizona.

Brennan, J., William English, John Hasnas, & Peter Jaworski. (2020). *Business Ethics for Better Behavior*. Oxford University Press.

Chakravartty, A. (2017). Scientific realism, In E. N. Zalta (Ed.), *The Stanford Encyclopedia of Philosophy* (Summer). https://plato.stanford.edu/archives/sum2017/entries/scientific-realism.

Davis, M. (1991). Thinking like an engineer: The place of a code of ethics in the practice of a profession. *Philosophy & Public Affairs, 20*(2), 150–167.

Feldman, F. (1978). *Introductory Ethics*. Prentice-Hall.

Foot, P. (1978) The problem of abortion and the doctrine of the double effect, in *Virtues and Vices*. Blackwell.

Frank, L. & Klincewicz, M. (2016). Metaethics in context of engineering ethical and moral systems [Paper presentation]. Association for the Advancement of Artificial Intelligence (AAAI) Spring Symposium Series.

Furey, H., & Hill, S. (n.d.). MIT's Moral Machine project is a psychological roadblock to self driving cars [Unpublished manuscript].

Harris, J. (1975). The survival lottery. *Philosophy*, 50, 81–87.

Lin, P. (2016). Why ethics matters for autonomous cars. In M. Maurer, J. Gerdes, B. Lenz, & H. Winner (Eds.), *Autonomous Driving*. Springer, doi.org/10.1007/978-3-662-48847-8_4.

Lloyd, P., & Busby, J. (2003). 'Things that went well—no serious injuries or deaths': Ethical reasoning in a normal engineering design process. *Science and Engineering Ethics*, 9, 503–516. doi.org/10.1007/s11948-003-0047-4.

McIntyre, A (2019). Doctrine of double effect, In E. N. Zalta (Ed.), *The Stanford Encyclopedia of Philosophy* (Spring). https://plato.stanford.edu/archives/spr2019/entries/double-effect.

Mill, J. S. (1963–1991). *The Collected Works of John Stuart Mill* (33 vols.). Gen. Ed. J. M. Robson. University of Toronto Press.

Niiniluoto, I. Scientific progress. In E. N. Zalta (Ed.), *The Stanford Encyclopedia of Philosophy* (Winter). https://plato.stanford.edu/archives/win2019/entries/scientific-progress.

Oberheim, E., & Hoyningen-Huene, P (2018). The incommensurability of scientific theories, In E. N. Zalta (Ed.), *The Stanford Encyclopedia of Philosophy* (Fall). https://plato.stanford.edu/archives/fall2018/entries/incommensurability.

Reiss, J., & Sprenger, J. (2017). Scientific objectivity. In E. N. Zalta (Ed.), *The Stanford Encyclopedia of Philosophy* (Winter). https://plato.stanford.edu/archives/win2017/entries/scientific-objectivity.

Shafer-Landau, R. (2003). *Whatever Happened to Good and Evil?* Oxford University Press.

A. Shariff, A., Bonnefon, J.-F., & Rahwan, I. (2017). Psychological roadblocks to the adoption of self-driving vehicles. *Nature Human Behaviour*, 1(10), 694–696.

Sinnott-Armstrong, W. (2019). Consequentialism. In E. N. Zalta (Ed.), *The Stanford Encyclopedia of Philosophy* (Summer). https://plato.stanford.edu/archives/sum2019/entries/consequentialism.

Temkin, L. (2012). *Rethinking the Good: Moral Ideals and the Nature of Practical Reasoning.* Oxford University Press.

Thomson, J. (1976). Killing, letting die, and the trolley problem. *The Monist*, 59(2), 204–217.

Van de Poel, I. (2009). Values in engineering design. In Meijers, A. (Ed.), *Philosophy of Technology and Engineering Sciences* (pp. 973–1006). Handbook of the Philosophy of Science, Vol. 9. Elsevier.

Van de Poel, I. (2016). An ethical framework for evaluating experimental technology. *Science and Engineering Ethics*, 22, 667–686. doi.org/10.1007/s11948-015-9724-3.

Public Wellbeing

"Hold paramount the safety, health, and welfare of the public."

While an engineer's obligation to protect the public is seldom questioned, it is worth pausing to ask what underlies this responsibility. One answer is that the work of engineers has far-reaching consequences with regard to public health, safety, and **wellbeing**. Technology allows us to transcend many of the limitations nature has placed on us. It brings with it the potential for great good and also great harm. Engineers, as creators of technology, must always keep in mind the people affected by the products they create. This is the basis for an engineer's **professional responsibility**. Professional responsibility refers to moral obligations by virtue of being a member of the profession in addition to whatever obligations one has simply in virtue of being a human being. Although protecting the public welfare may appear almost platitudinous, it is not as straightforward as it may seem. In this chapter, we will discuss three potential issues that engineers must address if they hope to meet their professional obligation to safeguard the public. These are paternalism, technological mediation, and distributive justice.

Public Welfare

What is public welfare? The concept itself is rather more complex than it appears. First of all, is there more to wellbeing than just health and safety? Presumably the NSPE's answer to this question is "yes" if they've gone to the trouble of listing it even after pointing out an engineer's obligation to hold paramount health and safety.

The term "welfare" as it's used in this context is more or less synonymous with what philosophers call "wellbeing." Within the philosophical literature, there is a rich and complex discussion of what constitutes human wellbeing. For our purposes, we will make three important assumptions:

1. Human wellbeing is made up of a variety of values.
2. Sometimes these values conflict within another when we attempt to realize them in a given situation. Therefore, these values must be weighed against one another.
3. The way in which these values contribute to individual wellbeing is not the same for every individual. In that case, there is no hard and fast rule for how conflicting values ought to be weighed against one another in a given situation.

The realization of values such as health and safety can certainly contribute to human wellbeing. These values are obviously ones that engineers can have direct influence over, which is perhaps why they are placed front and center in the NSPE's code of ethics. However, health and safety aren't the only values relevant to human wellbeing. What other values matter? One value that is particularly relevant to professional ethics is individual **autonomy**. Autonomy is the ability of an individual to make decisions in accordance with their own values.

What sorts of things might compromise individual autonomy? There are some obvious candidates. For instance, if a doctor were to force a particular treatment on a patient against the patient's will, this would obviously be a violation of the patient's autonomy. However, there are other less direct ways of violating a person's autonomy. For instance, we might compromise someone's autonomy by interfering with their ability to make an informed choice. Consider the following hypothetical situation:

> Imagine you are on an international flight. The attendant asks if you would like chicken or beef for your meal. As a vegetarian, you would prefer not to have either. But your blood sugar is incredibly low, so you opt for the chicken just to make sure you don't go into hypoglycemic shock on the trip. What if it turned out there was a vegetarian option the flight attendant purposely failed to mention because they had an overstock of chicken and beef meals? Is it true that you freely chose to eat chicken over a vegetarian meal? In one sense of the word "freely" yes, you did choose the chicken. After all, no one forced that choice. You could have eaten nothing and taken your chances that you would go into shock. But in another sense, your choice was compelled because your options were artificially limited.

This example is one in which your autonomy is compromised because the flight attendants are looking out for themselves. Arguably, flight attendants have a responsibility to prioritize the needs of the passengers over, say, a negligible financial gain for the airline. In that case, it was not ethically acceptable for the attendants to mislead their passengers by omitting information that was relevant to the passengers' needs. There are other cases, however, that are much less clear-cut. In these cases the ethical conflict involves a tradeoff between obligations to another person—for instance a conflict between the duty to inform and the duty to protect.

Paternalism

You're back on a plane. You've just tucked away your laptop in an overhead compartment after finally finishing some important work during the flight. Unknown to you, the pilots have just detected a serious mechanical problem--one that the pilots know will force a crash landing of the plane. The pilots intend to alert the passengers so that they can prepare themselves for the landing. However, in order to avoid the potential chaos of a mass panic, they intend to hold off on alerting passengers until the last possible second. After a successful, though frightening landing, all of the passengers escape the plane—though not with enough time to retrieve their belongings. Here again, you didn't choose to leave your laptop because you were never offered the choice to retrieve it. And yet the pilots' decision to withhold information from passengers in this case seems very different than the flight attendants' decision discussed in the previous case. In this situation, the pilots only compromised passenger autonomy in order to secure passenger safety. Philosophers call this **paternalism**. A **paternalistic action** is one that interferes with an individual's autonomous decisions *for that individual's own good*. Although employing paternalistic actions may have clear benefits with regard to health and safety, it is not clear that doing so also "holds paramount" public welfare. Consider the following case submitted to the NSPE BER.

Duty to Report Unsafe Conditions/Client Request for Secrecy

Case 98-9
Year: 1998
Facts:

Engineer A, a structural designer of a large commercial building, incorporates new and innovative design concepts. After construction is complete and the building is occupied, he finds an omission in his calculations that could result in its collapse under severe, but not unusual wind conditions. The collapse would not only jeopardize the occupants and their immediate surroundings but could possibly cause a "domino" effect threatening a much larger area.

Engineer A advises the architect and client of the problem. After consultation with the architect, the client, and the city engineer, all agree upon remedial construction, which can be accomplished over the next few months. A storm monitoring system and contingency evacuation plan for the building and surrounding neighborhood are developed for the time before construction is complete.

Both the client and architect strongly agree that the situation should be kept secret, with construction accomplished during the evening hours when the building is unoccupied. Engineer A is confident that the construction will completely rectify any structural concerns and that the evacuation plan has a reasonable chance of success.

Engineer B, the city engineer, has concern for the public, especially the office workers in the building and their right to know, but the architect and the client maintain that right is superseded by the consequences of a possible public panic resulting from any notification.

In this case, community members weren't forced to stay despite the danger. However, they did not choose to stay either. And that's because they weren't aware that there was a choice to be made. So clearly, members of the public would suffer a violation of autonomy should Engineer B decide to keep the project a secret.

Ordinarily, members of the public have a right to know if they might be at risk. And it would take a great deal to suspend this right. Let's assume there is a strong possibility that giving them that information may ultimately compromise their safety (for instance, perhaps the instigation of a mass panic could cause injury or delay the remedial construction). Even so, it is difficult to imagine that risks would be grave enough in this case to justify such a serious compromise of autonomy. In that case, the suggestion to employ secrecy, though perhaps driven by paternalistic motivations, is not morally justified. However, it's not difficult to imagine a case in which acting to fully inform the public could generate serious risks to health and safety. In these cases, it's an open question, morally, whether paternalistic actions might be justified. There are cases in which paternalistic action seems much more acceptable from a moral point of view. For example, the creation and enforcement of seatbelt laws, though not uncontroversial, are arguably examples of the justifiable use of paternalism.

But "more acceptable" instances of paternalism such as seatbelt laws are, again, not totally uncontroversial. This is particularly true in situations in which the individual or group subject to the paternalistic interventions places a high value on freedom. It's hardly surprising, for instance, that paternalistic laws requiring motorcyclists to wear helmets face much more pushback than seatbelt laws. Part of the draw of riding a motorcycle for some is the idea of the freedom that comes with it. For some riders, the risk involved with riding a motorcycle itself is part of its appeal. In such cases, it's not clear whether politicians have the moral authority to restrict autonomy by passing helmet laws.

Engineers, however, are not typically policy makers in the same way politicians or the heads of corporations are. Politicians often directly influence people's choices via legal directives while, more often than not, engineers indirectly shape the public's choices through design. How so? It's not usually within the purview of an engineer (as an engineer) to create a law that restricts an individual's freedom "for her own sake." However, an engineer can design a product that accomplishes the same end. Consider, for instance, a cell phone that is designed to block incoming and outgoing texts while inside a moving vehicle. This kind of technology might be more effective at curtailing distracted driving than a law that banned texting on the road. And yet the public, in cases in which their choices are being shaped indirectly through design, are probably far less cognizant that their choices are being "manipulated." This brings us to the next issue engineers must address if they hope to uphold their obligation to hold paramount the safety, health, and welfare of the public—the issue of technological mediation.

Technological Mediation

Arguably, through technological design engineers have the power to influence how we perceive the very space of possibilities for action. For example, a study conducted by a team led by Collin Payne, an assistant professor of marketing at New Mexico State University, showed that the design of a shopping cart could significantly influence a customer's buying habits. By simply partitioning grocery carts into sections, with a section specifically for fruit and produce, Payne's research team found that shoppers increased their purchase of fruits and vegetables by 102 percent. Certainly, this case shows that a small change in design can make a significant change in action.

Peter-Paul Verbeek calls the phenomenon in which engineers and scientists are able to shape the public's actions and decisions through technology **technological mediation**. Verbeek argues that technology itself is not **value neutral** in the sense that it is a mere tool designed to help each user pursue his or her own purposes. Rather, the way an object is designed can either inhibit or encourage certain actions. Chairs, for instance, encourage us to "sit" because they are designed for that purpose. Arguably, the designer's values and intensions are "built" into the design itself, making the technological object **value laden**. Because of the value-laden nature of technology, engineers have the power to influence not only practical decisions but moral ones as well. No doubt, iPhone users will have noticed that Apple's App Store not only screens out applications that it considers to be a potential technical threat (such as apps that contain bugs or virus), but ones which it considers to be moral threats as well (for instance, apps that contain pornography or violence.) **Moral autonomy**—the ability to make one's own moral decisions—is at the very heart of individual freedom, and because of this we are (and should be) fiercely protective of it. Where is the line between benign influence and undue coercion? It's hard to say. But even the gentlest methods of influencing the public's decisions warrant reflection. As we've seen, sometimes the influences that we are not consciously aware of are the most powerful of all. Of course, not all instances of technological mediation are the result of active deliberation on the part of the engineer. In fact, many, if not most, are unintentional. However, even unintentional actions can have serious consequences. Through decision-shaping designs, engineers pass along their values to the public, whether they mean to or not. It is therefore up to engineers to consider what kind of world they are shaping.

At this point, we are brought face-to-face with a question at the very heart of paternalism in engineering: who is in the best position to know what sort of world is best? Until now, we have been assuming that engineers, as technical experts, are sometimes in a better position than the public themselves to determine what is in the public's best interest. But is this assumption warranted? Certainly engineers have more technical expertise than most members of the public. However, does having the relevant technical expertise put engineers in a privileged position with regard to knowing what is in the public's best interest? Perhaps not. Questions concerning risk and benefit are not only **epistemic** questions—questions about technical *knowledge*—they are questions about **value** as well. Arguably, engineers are in a better position than most members of the public to determine the risks of a particular technology. However, as we've already discussed, risk must be weighed against the other values that make up individual wellbeing. And it's not at all clear how this balancing act ought to play out. Two people might agree about the facts regarding the risk involved with particular technology, while radically disagreeing as to whether the risk is worthwhile. Here we might worry that because of an engineer's focus on technical matters, she might be in an especially bad position to determine what the layperson values. Perhaps highly technical knowledge puts an engineer in danger of being out of touch with what is important to the ordinary person. Furthermore, we might worry, as Erin Cech, an assistant professor of sociology at the University of Michigan does, that by emphasizing the development of technical skills rather than interpersonal ones, engineering education makes engineers less capable of empathizing with the public's concerns.

One way of addressing this worry is through utilizing **value-sensitive design** (VSD). As Mary Cummings puts it, "The primary goal of VSD is to influence the design of technology by explicitly attending to which human values are taken into consideration and integrated into and throughout the design process" (2006, p. 701). In the excerpt from her article included in this chapter, Cummings explains the method and process of value-sensitive design, and notes how it can be used to augment existing approaches to design in engineering to better incorporate a wide variety of human values.

Distributive Justice

The importance of engineers being in touch with the public's concerns leads us to the final issue that must be discussed with regard to the first Fundamental Canon in the NSPE Code of Ethics. This is the issue of distributive justice.

"Acting in the interest of the public" sounds like an intrinsically egalitarian concept. However, the "public" is not a homogenous whole in which all of its members have the very same interests and vulnerabilities. When considering public wellbeing, engineers must ensure that distribution of risk and benefit is both just and appropriate. This doesn't happen as naturally as one might think—even in a field that touts its connection to human wellbeing. The development of new vaccines or devices that provide access to clean drinking water is guided by the aim of making humanity *as a whole* better off. However, the job of bettering humanity cannot be accomplished by treating humanity as a whole. This is because, in our imperfect world, human beings do not have equal access to opportunities, wealth, and privileges. For this reason, an equal distribution of goods or harms may result in a morally unjust distribution of those entities. For instance, the development of a cutting-edge vaccine may seem like great news for humanity. However, such vaccines are often so expensive that they become inaccessible to those that need them most. These realizations about the connections between inequality and justice are at the heart of distributive justice. One conception of **distributive justice** is that it concerns the morally just distribution of benefits and harms in our actual world rather than an ideal world. In an ideal world, where all members of humanity were playing on an equal playing field, it might be perfectly just to distribute benefits and harms equally among individuals. In the actual world, however, we must account for existent inequities between individuals or groups of individuals in order to get a just distribution of benefits and harms.

Issues of distributive justice are further complicated in engineering by the fact that "bettering humanity as a whole" is not always what drives the development of new technologies. To a large extent, the ideals that drive the development of new technology are entirely divorced from the impetus to improve the lives of those in most in need of improvement. Many technologies are developed to cater to the needs (or further the interests of) an elite few. Sometimes this restriction is merely an issue of access. For instance, Henry Ford designed the Model T such that even workers on the assembly line could afford it. However, to many even a mass-produced technology like the automobile is still out of reach. Other times, we get exclusion by design. Consider, for instance, the Vertu—a custom-made, luxury cell phone with a built-in concierge. This kind of elite technology is hardly designed with all members of the public in mind. This is not to say that designing such products is necessarily wrong. However, it is important to acknowledge that, for better or worse, a large swath of engineering practice reflects the values of modern capitalism. For this reason, engineering products can accentuate the social and economic inequalities.

Even when technology is developed with an eye towards justice, often it is not implemented that way. In practice, certain technologies benefit some citizens at the expense of others. This is because many inequalities are structural—baked into the very foundations of our societal framework. The result is that certain individuals or groups of individuals will automatically be more vulnerable to the risks of engineering products and far less likely to enjoy the benefits of such products. The technique of fracking, for instance, offers relatively easy access to natural gas, making it an economically attractive option for energy companies. These companies stand to benefit significantly from the use of the technology. However, there are substantial risks involved with fracking, including environmental contamination, increased seismic activity, and sundry public health hazards. These risks are serious moral matters. Adding substantially to this concern is the fact that such risks are often taken on exclusively by individuals who may receive little or no benefit from the use of the technology. Other technologies are potentially morally problematic by being insensitive to the fact that what is beneficial for one group is detrimental to another. Arguably, in a war zone, lining the streets with tracked armored vehicles and grenade launchers might count as an appropriate show of force. However, as President Obama noted in 2015, when placed in the hands of police during a civilian demonstration, "militarized gear can sometimes give people a feeling like there's an occupying force, as opposed to a force that's part of the community that's protecting them and serving them." Such examples serve to remind us that acting in the public's interest must involve recognition of the many social complexities that contribute to wellbeing.

How should engineers go about addressing these complexities? The first step is acknowledging their existence. This step may seem small, but it's not an easy one to take. Because social and economic inequalities are so firmly engrained in human societies, it can be difficult to recognize and respond to them. Furthermore, because we've become so accustomed to inequality, we've developed a wide array of unconscious biases regarding the nature and sources of inequality. These biases can sometimes act as psychological defenses against feelings of guilt or anxiety for those of us in positions of relative privilege within society. The result is that we often fail either as individuals or a society to acknowledge and address concerns regarding distributive justice.

In the excerpt from her article included in this chapter, Erin A. Cech argues that certain aspects of engineering culture actually contribute to a misconception that concerns regarding justice, in particular social justice, are not relevant to engineering practice. She claims that cultural ideologies within engineering might lead to fundamental misunderstandings concerning social justice issues. In particular, she argues that the cultural framework within professional engineering fosters the misconception that engineering work cannot be separated from the social world. She attempts to correct this misconception by drawing our attention to the ideological mechanisms that perpetuate these misunderstandings.

Wrapping Up

Where does this discussion of public wellbeing leave us with regard to satisfying the ethical imperatives articulated in the first Fundamental Canon? The short, and possibly frustrating, answer is that there are no hard and fast rules as to how to hold paramount the safety, health, and wellbeing of the public. This position of uncertainty with regard to public wellbeing is hardly unique to engineering ethics. Medical ethicists, for instance, have been debating this issue for years. A quick Google Scholar search on "medical paternalism" will show you just how extensive and complicated this debate is. A search of "distributive justice" will yield similar results.

Professionally, occupying a position of uncertainty with regard to one's professional duty is uncomfortable to say the least. But it is far better than being in a position of ignorance with regard to the moral complexities of those obligations. In occupying a position of ignorance we risk applying overly simplistic solutions to moral dilemmas—ones that may prove ineffective and perhaps even detrimental to public wellbeing. Unlike academics who specialize in engineering ethics, engineers as practitioners do not have the luxury of taking the time to dive headlong into such debates. However, it is essential that engineers be aware of them. We hope to have shed some light on those complexities, and to have offered at least some starting points for engineers to develop more robust solutions to the moral issues regarding wellbeing.

Chapter I Key Terms and Concepts

Wellbeing

Professional Responsibility

Autonomy

Paternalism

Paternalistic Action

Technological Mediation

Value Neutral

Value Laden

Moral Autonomy

Epistemic

Value

Value-Sensitive Design (VSD)

Distributive Justice

Chapter 1: End of Chapter Reading and NSPE Board of Ethical Review Cases

Guided Core Reading   52

Core Reading 1.1: 'Integrating ethics in design through the value-sensitive design approach' by Mary L. Cummings (excerpt)

Core Reading 1.2: 'The (mis)framing of social justice: Why ideologies of depoliticization and meritocracy hinder engineers' ability to think about social injustices' by Erin A. Cech (excerpts)

NSPE Board of Ethical Review Cases   61

Case 17-7: Public Health Safety and Welfare—Engineering Standards (2018)

Case 18-9: Public Health and Safety—Building Codes to Address Environmental Risk (2018)

Case 16-10: Public Health, Safety and Welfare—Former Employee's Participation in a Public Safety Standards Hearing (2016)

Guided Further Reading   66

Further Reading 1.1: Technological paternalism: On how medicine has reformed ethics and how technology can refine moral theory' by Bjorn Hofmann

Further Reading 1.2: 'How artefacts influence our actions' by Auke J. K. Pols

Further Reading 1.3: 'Engineering social justice into traffic control for self-driving vehicles?' by Milos N. Mladenovic and Tristram McPherson

Tip: If you can't use the QR codes, use the hyperlinks found on the book's webpage instead: www.routledge.com/9781138183865.

Guided Core Reading

Core Reading 1.1: 'Integrating ethics in design through the value-sensitive design approach' by Mary L. Cummings (excerpt)

Preparing to Read

One way to tackle the issue of paternalism in engineering is for engineers to adopt approaches to design which take factor in human values beyond health and safety. In this excerpt, Cummings explains the method and process of value-sensitive design (VSD), and notes how it can be used to augment existing approaches to design in engineering to better incorporate a wide variety of human values.

Excerpted from: Cummings, M. L. (2006). Integrating ethics in design through the value-sensitive design approach. *Science and Engineering Ethics*, 12, 701–715. © Springer 2006, reprinted with permission. Internal references and notes omitted.

Value-Sensitive Design

The primary goal of VSD is to influence the design of technology by explicitly attending to which human values are taken into consideration and integrated into and throughout the design process. ...VSD highlights the way in which technology both shapes society and is shaped by social factors. ... Thus complex sociotechnical systems involve intertwined interactions between humans and technology and cannot be designed in a value vacuum. The formalized VSD methodology consists of a three-pronged iterative approach, which includes investigation of conceptual, empirical, and technical issues specific to a particular design.

The conceptual investigation consists of an analysis informed by the philosophy of those value constructs relevant to the design in question. When applying the VSD approach, twelve specific human values have been determined to have ethical import that should be considered in the design process: human welfare, ownership and property, privacy, freedom from bias, universal usability, trust, autonomy, informed consent, accountability, calmness, identity, and environmental sustainability. While neither independent not [*sic*] exclusive, these values were selected in the development of VSD because they represent the broad values generally discussed in technology and ethics literature, as well as those that have become more important with the increasing use of computer technologies in everyday life. ... The conceptual investigation focuses on how the relevant human values are either supported or diminished by a particular design. For example, in the design of a system that monitors employee use of the Internet and e-mail, the human values of privacy and informed consent are central ethical issues to be considered.

The conceptual investigation phase not only identifies those basic human values that could be both supported and diminished by technology, but also considers how the technology could both socially benefit and negatively impact stakeholders. … During the conceptual analysis phase, it is important for the designer to consider both direct and indirect stakeholders. Direct stakeholders are defined as those who interact directly with a technology, while indirect stakeholders are those who are peripherally connected to the technology. In the case of an employee Internet and e-mail monitoring device, while the direct stakeholders are the employees and the management that monitors the employees, indirect stakeholders include those people outside the company who send and receive e-mail messages without realizing the extent of the monitoring activity, as well as other organizations that could gain access to sensitive employee information.

For engineering professors and students, this conceptual phase is likely the most difficult due to the abstract and philosophical nature of values. In a design class, discussions about which of the twelve values students think are most important and why, would be an effective starting point for the conceptual investigation. In addition, identifying possible benefits and harms for potential stakeholders as a result of the technology under consideration would likely raise awareness of how any of the twelve values would either be supported or diminished.… The goal in this phase for an engineering design project would be to identify one or two values of central interest that could be viewed as a common thread throughout the project. It is likely that through the course of the project, this list could be updated so that new values take the place of earlier ones. This iterative approach is critical to the fundamental engineering design process as requirements, both technical and social, often change as designs become better defined.

The second phase of VSD is empirical investigation, which focuses on quantitative and qualitative measurements to evaluate the design from both a technical and value assessment approach. A primary consideration in this phase of analysis is investigating how design trade-offs affect perceptions, behaviors, and prioritization of competing values, and furthermore, how the designer can support or detract from value conflict. For example, a common design tradeoff that can directly impact human values is the issue of usability. … However, while usability is an important design consideration that can impact human performance, higher levels of usability can actually compete with human values of ethical import. For example, a website that provides users with easy-to-access personal information could inadvertently allow third-parties easy access as well, thus potentially diminishing the human value of privacy.

The last phase of the VSD approach concerns the investigation of technical issues. In this phase, technical designs are analyzed to assess how they support particular values, and how values identified in the conceptual investigation could be best supported by different design possibilities. While the technical and empirical investigations seem similar, they are different in that the technical phase focuses on the technology while the empirical phase focuses on the human interaction with the technology....

VSD is not a design approach that is fundamentally different from or replaces other systems engineering and design approaches. Rather it is a tool that can be used to augment an already established design process, either in practice or in the classroom. Typical systems engineering approaches (e.g., the waterfall model... and the spiral model...) begin with conceptual design phases, then include stages for design and development, similar to VSD's technical investigation phase, and are typically followed with test and evaluation phases similar to that of the VSD empirical investigation stage. Applying VSD does not require a fundamentally different approach to design. Because VSD generally falls along engineering design principles of conceiving an idea, designing an artifact, and then testing this design, it can be incorporated into already established design processes, particularly in the classroom. VSD is a structured approach for incorporating ethical concerns into the design process and thus it can be integrated with instructional design projects with clear objectives and goals that can be communicated to students. Most importantly from an instructional standpoint, VSD provides a road map for instructors on how to include ethical considerations into design projects, even if they are not trained in philosophy or ethics. This ease of integration into design projects is critical because a major roadblock to the widespread inclusion of ethics in engineering curricula is the lack of dedicated resources (such as engineering ethics professors and funding).

Discussion Questions

1. Earlier in this chapter, we introduced the idea of a cell phone that would block incoming and outgoing texts while drivers were inside a moving vehicle in order to promote safe driving. Imagine you are designing a product that is intended to promote safe driving by either inhibiting or encouraging certain actions

or choices made by the driver. What sort of product would you design and how would it function?

2. Who would be the direct and indirect stakeholders for your product?

3. What are the specific conceptual issues relevant to the design of your product with regard to human values? To answer this question, give examples of issues that may arise with regard to the following: human welfare, ownership and property, privacy, freedom from bias, universal usability, trust, autonomy, informed consent, accountability, calmness, identity, and environmental sustainability. How could each of these values be supported or diminished with regard to your design?

4. What are the specific empirical and technical issues relevant to the design of your product?

5. Now that you have completed the initial round of the VSD process, how would you modify the design of your product (or design a new product) to address the issues you uncovered during the process?

Read the Full Article (optional)

You can read the full article online by scanning the QR code or following the link below. Your college library will need to subscribe to the journal, and you may need to login via your library's website or use campus wifi to get access.

https://link.springer.com/article/10.1007%2Fs11948-006-0065-0

Core Reading 1.2: 'The (mis)framing of social justice: Why ideologies of depoliticization and meritocracy hinder engineers' ability to think about social injustices' by Erin A. Cech (excerpts)

Preparing to Read

In order to meet the requirements of their responsibility with regard to distributive justice, engineers must be sensitive to the social factors that underlie many of those inequalities. However, our understanding of social issues is shaped by our own experiences and values—sometimes for the worse. In this excerpt from her article, Cech identifies two potential cultural ideologies within engineering that she claims contribute to the (mis)framing of social justice issues within the engineering profession: depoliticization and meritocracy. Cech explains how these two ideologies work in tandem to produce a misconception among engineers that issues of inequality and injustice are not relevant to engineering practice. Cech argues that these interlocking ideologies are deeply ingrained in engineering culture. Engineering students become acculturated to these ideologies during the process of professional socialization within their engineering programs. Later they reproduce these ideologies outside of their programs. Cech claims that, in order to make space for social justice concerns in engineering, engineers must directly confront these ideologies early on in their educational development.

Excerpted from: Cech E.A. (2013). The (mis)framing of social justice: Why ideologies of depoliticization and meritocracy hinder engineers' ability to think about social injustices. In J. Lucena (Ed.), *Engineering Education for Social Justice.* Philosophy of Engineering and Technology, vol. 10. Springer. © Springer Science+Business Media Dordrecht 2013, reprinted with permission. Internal references omitted.

Depoliticization of Engineering

The first important ideology within the culture of engineering is the notion that engineering is a purely "technical" domain, and thus asocial and apolitical. Because science and mathematics knowledge is understood to be the basis of engineering expertise, engineering work is assumed to be carried out objectively and without bias. … As presumed "neutral" actors, engineers defer to the objectivity and value neutrality that are assumed to be part of these methods ….

However, as decades of Science and Technology Studies research has demonstrated, even the most seemingly objective and neutral realms of engineering practice and design have built into them social norms, culturally-informed judgments about what counts as "truth," and ideologically-infused processes of problem definition and solution .... Engineering work is necessarily heterogeneous and "technological" work can never be separated from its social or political influences .... Indeed, prioritizing certain "technical" features (faster, smaller, cheaper vs. quality or sustainability) over others is a social and political choice at its core. Thus, the notion that engineering work can somehow be separated from the social world is *itself* a cultural frame for understanding what engineering is.

Connected to the understanding that engineering work can be separated from the social is the ideological belief that it *should* be separated from the social. I call this the ideology of *depoliticization*—the belief that engineering work, by definition, should disconnect itself from social and cultural realms because such realms taint otherwise pure engineering design methodologies. Through the frame of depoliticization, the political and social foundations of all engineering work are culturally invisible in the meaning systems surrounding that work. More importantly, the ideology of depoliticization means that aspects of social life that have to do with conflicting perspectives, cultural values, or inequality are cast as "political" and thus irrelevant—perhaps even dangerous—to "real" engineering work .... As a result, these concerns are defined as illegitimate to engineers' day-to-day work by the very culture of the profession. Engineering's status as a profession depends on its relevance to society, and depoliticization allows engineers to carry on with their socially important work (e.g. food and medicine production) without having to grapple with the messiness that comes with actually engaging with questions of the effects of engineering work on society.

The ideology of depoliticization is deeply rooted in engineering. Early engineers sought to ground their new profession in math and science knowledge to increase engineering's status as a profession. Thus, early notions of engineering design drew from similar enlightenment notions about the potential for "purity" in scientific inquiry, isolated from religious, social, or political influence .... From the mid-nineteenth century on, a key facet of engineers' privileged status in society was their assumed ability to make decisions from purely technical considerations. Engineers and scientists were called upon in the 1920s to help instill technocratic decision-making procedures into public policymaking. Technocratic rule was supposed to diminish emotion, corruption and "politics" in public administration .... Today, most engineers continue to conceptualize and portray their work as generally above any emotional, social or political messiness.

Depoliticization means that "social" issues, which encompass considerations of social justice and equity, are considered inappropriate within engineering contexts. Engineering students learn early through professional socialization that justice issues are "social" and "political" and thus irrelevant to serious classroom and study group conversations.

...

The majority of students take on the dominant depoliticized worldview that is core to the professional culture into which they are being socialized. In a study of engineering students at several universities, I found that social justice concerns (e.g. "understanding the consequences of technology," "improving society," and "professional and ethical responsibilities") became less important to engineering students over the course of their undergraduate careers, and that the cultural ideologies promoted by their engineering programs had a direct influence on the decreased importance of social justice issues to students ....

...

But what happens if social justice issues do make it to the floors of engineering classrooms, labs and workplaces? I argue that a second ideology in engineering, the ideology of meritocracy, frames the very existence of social inequality as the result of just and fair processes, and thus simply not of concern to engineers.

The Ideology of Meritocracy

The ideology of meritocracy is, broadly, the belief that success in life is the result of individual talent, training, and motivation, and that those who lack such characteristics will naturally be less successful than others .... The meritocratic ideology is deeply engrained in the popular belief in the "American Dream" (success comes to those who work hard and dream big) and is resonant in the popularity of stories about individuals who pull themselves up by their "bootstraps" .... The meritocratic ideology is not just a way of interpreting the outcomes of successful people, however. It is often deployed as an individual-level explanation for sweeping wealth, gender, and racial/ethnic inequalities in the U.S. It is "a theory of justice in which distribution of rewards is expected from the distribution of individual talents" .... This ideology is also a *moral* judgment—meritocracy legitimates the unequal distribution of rewards as the outcome of morally acceptable and fair processes ....

The meritocratic ideology is the most prominent explanation of social inequalities in the U.S. .... Because discrimination based on religion, class, gender, age, etc. is formally illegal, most Americans believe that inequality of outcomes is based on fair mechanisms. This belief relies on several assumptions: (a) that the opportunity for personal achievement is widespread; (b) that individuals are personally responsible for their position in society, and (c) that the overall system of opportunities and rewards is equitable and fair .... But, of course, over a century of social science research has demonstrated that all three of these foundational assumptions are false: the opportunity for personal achievement is severely restricted by the quality of education one's family can afford, processes of discrimination prevent equal access to opportunities for women and minorities, and other structural and cultural processes sharply curtail opportunities for those who are not wealthy, heterosexual, white men ....

...

It becomes difficult, therefore, for Americans to cognitively reconcile the structural reality of injustices with the belief that the social system is equitable and just. However, the very framing of inequalities as the result of individual outcomes resulting from a meritocratic system allows Americans to square the visible differences in opportunities and outcomes for women, racial/ethnic minorities, and the poor with the general societal belief in equality. If the system is seen as fair, social injustices arising from that system are seen as legitimate.

...

The meritocratic ideology is deeply engrained in the culture of engineering. To the extent scholars have been able to trace the history of the culture of engineering, this ideology has been central to the worldview promoted in engineering for at least a century .... The maverick view of engineering innovation (exemplified by Thomas Edison and Steve Jobs) promotes a romanticized notion of success where individual hard work, talent, and dedication can lead to pathbreaking engineering designs even out of home garages ....

The meritocratic worldview is widespread among engineers working in both industry and academia .... It is also a central ideology in the professional socialization within engineering education .... As students learn to become engineers, they adopt as their own the dominant worldviews of their future profession .... Thus, the socialization of engineering students often reorients or reinforces their framing of social inequalities as the result of fair, meritocratic processes.

...

Why is the meritocratic ideology such a compelling frame within the culture of engineering for understanding social injustice? For one, this frame denies the structural foundations of inequality—foundations that may include the work of engineers. ... If inequality is the result of individual failings, then the profession of engineering neither plays any role in that inequality, nor has any responsibility to attempt to rectify it.

Secondly, the meritocratic ideology frees engineers from the responsibility to design accessible or inexpensive products that alleviate social problems but may have little profit potential (e.g. slower, less expensive internet connections that would allow more people to access the internet). … Again, the popularity of this ideology within engineering is not the result of uncaring or naive individual engineers, but rather the outcome of a cultural frame that eliminates these social complexities from problem definition and solution.

Guided Reading Questions

1. Cech claims that one ideology in engineering is the view that technical concerns are distinct from social concerns. How does this claim relate to the concept of technological mediation discussed in this chapter?
2. Cech argues that "Engineering students learn early through professional socialization that justice issues are 'social' and 'political' and thus irrelevant to serious classroom and study group conversations." Can you think of any examples from your own experience in an engineering program that either confirm or disconfirm Cech's claim?
3. Specifically, what sorts of "social complexities" do you think may be being ignored within engineering education and professional practice? Can you give any examples from your own experience in the classroom or the field?
4. How, specifically, might the ideology of meritocracy effect design decisions within engineering?
5. Assuming depoliticization and meritocracy exist and function in engineering culture the way Cech argues they do, what can be done to combat these ideologies?

Read the Full Article (optional)

You can read the full article online by scanning the QR code or following the link below. Your college library will need to subscribe to the journal, and you may need to login via your library's website or use campus wifi to get access.

https://link.springer.com/chapter/10.1007%2F978-94-007-6350-0_4

NSPE Board of Ethical Review Cases

All Cases Copyright © National Society of Professional Engineers (NSPE), www. nspe.org. All rights reserved. To request permission to reproduce any NSPE Board of Ethical Review Case, please contact the NSPE Legal Department (legal@nspe.org).

Case 17-7: Public Health Safety and Welfare—Engineering Standards

Public Health Safety and Welfare—Engineering Standards

Case 17-7
Year: 2018
Facts:

A proposed amendment to a local ordinance that is being promoted by a city citizen's group has been brought forth by a city council member. The proposed change to the ordinance is contrary to established engineering standards. The changes would install traffic engineering infrastructure that many within the local engineering community, including Engineer A, consider unsafe, believe does not satisfy current standards and best practices, and is contrary to a state law that requires an engineering study before proceeding with the change. The city attorney attempted to explain these factors to the members of the city council in a recent public forum, but the city council voted to proceed with the proposed change to the ordinance.

Question from the NSPE:
What are Engineer A's obligations under the circumstances?

Going Beyond—Our Questions for a Deep Dive

1. In what way does the situation above embody the problem of "paternalism" discussed early in this chapter?

2. Could the value-sensitive design (VSD) process described by Cummings be of use in helping engineers identify the ethical values at issue in this case beyond safety? If so, how could the identifying instances of these values help engineers address this case? For instance, could value identification help engineers offer an attractive alternative solution to the citizens' group? Could it help engineers explain the risks of adopting the proposed solution?

3. Considering the fact that the city council voted to proceed with the changes even after being advised to do otherwise by the city attorney, do the engineers involved have any additional obligation to try to convince the council not to go through with the project?

4. Do the engineers involved have any obligation to try to "override" the city council's decision? If so, how might the engineers go about fulfilling this obligation?

5. The fact that the city council decided to proceeded with the project even after being advised to do otherwise might indicate that their constituents prioritized other concerns over safety. What concerns might these be? Is it possible, as Cech suggests, that because Engineer A belongs to a professional culture that prioritizes safety, he or she was unaware of some potential social issues that were relevant to members of the community?

6. Is it permissible for an engineer to take on a job that she or he considers "high risk" if she or he is sure that the stakeholders are fully informed of the risk?

7. When, if ever, is it permissible for an engineer to refuse to do work that members of the public have asked him or her to do?

Read the Board's Discussion and Conclusion

To read the discussion and conclusion of this case by members of the NSPE Board of Ethical Review, go to: www.nspe.org/resources/ethics/ethics-resources/board-ethical-review-cases/public-health-safety-and-welfare-0.

Case 18-9: Public Health and Safety—Building Codes to Address Environmental Risk

Public Health and Safety—Building Codes to Address Environmental Risk

Case 18-9
Year: 2018
Facts:

Engineer A is an engineer in private practice. Engineer A is retained by Client A, a developer, to perform hydrodynamic modeling and coastal risk assessment in connection with potential climate change and sea level rise for a residential development project near a coastal area. The geographic area in which Client A is planning to build the project currently has no building code in place. Based on newly released information as well as a recently developed algorithm that includes newly identified historic weather data, Engineer A believes the residential development project should be built to a 100-year projected storm surge elevation, due to public safety risks even at lower projections of future surge level rise. Because of the increased cost, Owner refuses to agree that the residential development project be built to a 100-year projection storm surge elevation.

Question from the NSPE:
What are Engineer A's obligations under the circumstances?

Going Beyond—Our Questions for a Deep Dive

1. Is Engineer A's primary obligation to Client A or to the future residents of the project?
2. Because they are in a vulnerable economic position, low-income communities are at greater risk of suffering serious harm from natural disasters. Should Engineer A take into account social or economic realities of future residents when considering her obligations in this situation?
3. The future residents of this development will undoubtedly assume that there were some building codes in place at the time of construction. Furthermore, they will most likely assume that, as residents, they are not at risk so long as the parties responsible for construction followed those codes. Finally, unless given reason to think otherwise, residents will naturally assume that the codes have been followed. Are members of the public such as the residents in this case entitled to make these sorts of assumptions?
4. Suppose that the public is entitled to some extent to make certain assumptions about their health and safety. In this case, how would the failure to account for the possibility of a 100-year storm in the design of the complex serve as a violation of the future residents' autonomy?

Read the Board's Discussion and Conclusion

To read the discussion and conclusion of this case by members of the NSPE Board of Ethical Review, go to: www.nspe.org/resources/ethics/ ethics-resources/board-ethical-review-cases/public-health-and-safety-building-codes.

Case 16-10: Public Health, Safety and Welfare—Former Employee's Participation in a Public Safety Standards Hearing

Public Health, Safety and Welfare—Former Employee's Participation in a Public Safety Standards Hearing

Case 16-10
Year: 2016
Facts:

Engineer A works for Company X in connection with the design and manufacturing of a new consumer product. During and following the company's standard safety testing process (which has been completed and has demonstrated that the new consumer product is within acceptable safety parameters), Engineer A observes what Engineer A believes are inconsistent product performance issues that in Engineer A's opinion raise unique safety concerns. Engineer A recommends to Supervisor B that Company X conduct a new series of tests to determine whether the new consumer product will be operated safely by consumers. Current national product safety standards do not yet address the new product or its potential impact on consumer safety. Currently, there are no governmental or industry standards relating to this new consumer product other than general and standard product safety-testing policies and procedures. Because of the potential cost and the delay that may result due to additional testing, Company X rejects Engineer A's recommendation that it perform additional safety testing. Later, Engineer A resigns from Company X. One year later, the relevant government agency announces a public safety standard hearing in connection with a series of new consumer products, including the new product developed by Company X and ones developed by its competitors. Engineer A is considering participating as a witness at the public safety standards hearing.

Question from the NSPE:
Would it be ethical for Engineer A to participate as a witness at the public safety standard hearings?

Going Beyond—Our Questions for a Deep Dive

1. To what extent are engineers obligated to anticipate the potential risks of new and emerging technology in cases where current regulations have not "caught up" with new technologies?
2. Suppose Engineer A concludes that the new product manufactured by Company X is safe if used properly, but discovers that there is risk of harm to a consumer if he or she intentionally misuses the product. To what extent, if any, are the engineers at Company X ethically obligated to discourage misuse of the product through their design?
3. Few technologies are completely safe, and most involve a tradeoff between potential risks and benefits. Should it be up to engineers to decide when a risk is "worthwhile" or should such decisions be up to companies, policy makers, or the public?
4. To a large extent, the public trusts that the new products which are made available to them are "safe." However, in cases in which the use of a product comes with unavoidable risk, to what extent are engineers obligated to communicate that risk to the public?

Read the Board's Discussion and Conclusion

To read the discussion and conclusion of this case by members of the NSPE Board of Ethical Review, go to: www.nspe.org/resources/ethics/ethics-resources/board-ethical-review-cases/public-health-safety-and-welfare-former.

Guided Further Reading

Further Reading 1.1: 'Technological paternalism: On how medicine has reformed ethics and how technology can refine moral theory' by Bjørn Hofmann

Find the Article

Hofmann, B. (2003). Technological paternalism: On how medicine has reformed ethics and how technology can refine moral theory. *Science and Engineering Ethics*, 9, 343–352. doi.org/10.1007/s11948-003-0031-z.

Read the article online by scanning the QR code or following the link below. Your college library will need to subscribe to the journal, and you may need to login via your library's website or use campus wifi to get access.
https://link.springer.com/article/10.1007/s11948-003-0031-z

Preparing to Read

As we have seen, paternalism is an important moral issue in engineering ethics. However, paternalism has received far more attention in medicine than in engineering. In this article, Bjørn Hoffman uses insights gained from discussions of "medical paternalism" in modern medicine to help illuminate the concept of technological paternalism in modern technology.

Guided Reading Questions

1. Why do you think that, historically, the issue of paternalism has received so much more attention in medical ethics than in engineering ethics? Is the lack of attention justified in your opinion?
2. As Hoffman notes, opinions among the majority of medical ethicists regarding the justifiability of paternalism in medicine have shifted back and forth throughout the years. What are your views about the morality of paternalistic intervention in medicine—is it ever morally justified for doctors to compromise

an individual's autonomy "for their own good"? What about paternalistic actions in engineering? In your opinion, is it ever morally permissible for engineers to compromise an individual's autonomy, for instance through product design, for that individual's "own good"?

3. Hoffman argues that the widespread use of technology introduces a unique variety of paternalism: technological paternalism. Do you agree with Hoffman that technological paternalism presents moral issues that cannot be captured under the traditional conception of paternalism?

4. Hoffman offers a "four-fold" conception of technological paternalism using examples from the medical field to illustrate. Can you think of examples from engineering that would be analogous to the examples Hoffman provided from medicine?

5. Assume for a moment Hoffman is correct in thinking that technological paternalism exists. Is there as much potential for technological paternalism to arise in engineering as there is in medicine?

***

Further Reading 1.2: 'How artefacts influence our actions' by Auke J. K. Pols

Find the Article

Pols, A.J.K. (2013). How artefacts influence our actions. *Ethical Theory and Moral Practice*, 16, 575–587. doi.org/10.1007/s10677-012-9377-0.

You can read the article online by scanning the QR code or following the link below. The article is available **Open Access** and no subscription or login is required.

https://link.springer.com/article/10.1007/s10677-012-9377-0

Preparing to Read

In our discussion of technological paternalism, we explored the idea that artifacts can influence our actions to some extent. However, we have yet to devote much time to explaining *how* artifacts might influence our actions. In his article, Auke Pols develops an account of how artifacts influence our actions and compares his view with two notable alternative views.

Guided Reading Questions

1. Pols argues that artifacts affect human actions in two main ways: (1) by changing the number or quality of actions available to us; and (2) by increasing the likelihood that an individual will perform or abstain from certain actions. Can you think of examples, other than the ones given in the text, of artifacts that fit each of these categories?

2. Do all artifacts come with "scripts" or are some "script-less." Try to think of an artifact that does not come with a script.

3. Pols claims that artifacts can affect what we will do because facts about them alter our reasons for action. Do you agree? Looking back, have you ever had an experience where, even if you weren't aware of it at the time, an artifact influenced your actions by altering your reasons?

4. Pols argues that his "reasons account" of moralized technology can explain why sometimes technology fails to influence a user's actions even in cases where the artifact is intentionally designed to influence a user's actions. Think of an example from your experience of a technology that was purposely designed to influence a user's actions in a particular way but which failed to do so. Apply Pols's account to your example. Can his account explain the failure?

5. Pols offers a potential counterargument to his account of the way in which artifacts influence actions. He then responds to this counterargument. Do you think his response is convincing? Can you think of any other potential counterarguments to his view? How might Pols respond to the counterargument(s) you have raised?

Further Reading 1.3: 'Engineering social justice into traffic control for self-driving vehicles?' by Milos N. Mladenovic and Tristram McPherson

Find the article

Mladenovic, M. N., & McPherson, T. (2016). Engineering social justice into traffic control for self-driving vehicles? *Science and Engineering Ethics*, 22, 1131–1149. doi.org/10.1007/s11948-015-9690-9.

Read the article online by scanning the QR code or following the link below. Your college library will need to subscribe to the journal, and you may need to login via your library's website or use campus wifi to get access.

https://link.springer.com/article/10.1007/s11948-015-9690-9

Preparing to Read

In this chapter we briefly discussed how issues of justice arise in engineering ethics. And, in her article excerpted in this chapter, Erin Cech identified some possible sources of systemic misunderstanding regarding social justice in engineering. In this article, Milos Mladenovic and Tristram McPherson demonstrate how social justice concerns arise even in an area of engineering that may seem immune to concerns of justice: traffic control technology. In doing so, they demonstrate the importance of considering questions regarding social justice in even seemingly "objective" areas of engineering.

Guided Reading Questions

1. Mladenovic and McPherson argue that we have reason to think traditional traffic controls (C1) will be replaced by a next-generation traffic control (C2) that utilizes computing, sensing,

and communication technologies. They argue that one danger of C2 is that it might be "shaped by private interests to the detriment of social justice." Can you think of specific ways in which various private interests might shape C2 in this way?

2. Mladenovic and McPherson compose a list of desiderata for traffic control design with regard to social justice. These are: safety, sustainability, privacy, efficiency, and equality of access. For the sake of manageability, they focus on efficiency and equity in their article—setting the other desiderata aside. Can you think of ways in which social justice concerns might arise in connection with the development of C2 with regard to safety, sustainability, and privacy?

3. Mladenovic and McPherson note that equity of access can be affected by a wide variety of technologies—congestion pricing or route guidance, for instance. Can you think of particular ways in which the use of technologies such as congestion pricing or route guidance could result in social injustice?

4. Mladenovic and McPherson argue that intersection traffic control faces a dilemma between sacrificing equity of access and compromising efficiency. They then offer a possible solution to this dilemma. Do you think their solution is successful?

5. Can you think of any alternative solutions to the dilemma that Mladenovic and McPherson raise for intersection traffic control?

Bibliography

Cech E. A. (2013). The (mis)framing of social justice: Why ideologies of depoliticization and meritocracy hinder engineers' ability to think about social injustices. In J. Lucena (Ed.), *Engineering Education for Social Justice*. Philosophy of Engineering and Technology, vol. 10. Springer.

Cech, E. A. (2014). Culture of disengagement in engineering education? *Science, Technology, & Human Values*, 39(1), 42–72. doi.org/10.1177/0162243913504305.

Cummings, M. L. (2006). Integrating ethics in design through the value-sensitive design approach. *Science and Engineering Ethics*, 12, 701–715.

Diekmann, S., & Peterson, M. (2013). The role of non-epistemic values in engineering models. *Science and Engineering Ethics*, 19(1), 207–218.

Dworkin, G. (1972). Paternalism. *The Monist*, 56(1), 64–84.

Eisenhower, D. (1960). Annual message to the Congress on the State of the Union [Speech, Washington DC]. www.eisenhower.archives.gov/all_about_ike/speeches/1960_state_of_the_union.pdf.

Guntzburger, Y., Pauchant, T. C., & Tanguy, P. A. (2017). Ethical risk management education in engineering: A systematic review. *Science and Engineering Ethics*, 23(2), 323–350.

Hofmann, B. (2003). Technological paternalism: On how medicine has reformed ethics and how technology can refine moral theory. *Science and Engineering Ethics*, 9(3), 343–352.

Kant, I. (2016). *Fundamental Principles of the Metaphysic of Morals* (The Project Gutenberg EBook of Fundamental Principles of the Metaphysic of Morals). www.gutenberg.org/cache/epub/5682/pg5682.txt.

Mill, J. S. (2004). *Utilitarianism* (The Project Gutenberg EBook of Utilitarianism). www.gutenberg.org/files/11224/11224-h/11224-h.htm.

Mladenovic, M. N., & McPherson, T. (2016). Engineering social justice into traffic control for self-driving vehicles? *Science and Engineering Ethics*, 22, 1131–1149. doi. org/10.1007/s11948-015-9690-9.

Morrow, D. R. (2013). When technologies make good people do bad things: Another argument against the value-neutrality of technologies. *Science and Engineering Ethics*, 20(2), 1–15.

Moynihan, T. (2014, June 4). What it's like to use a $10k phone with a real-life personal assistant. *Wired*. www.wired.com/2014/06/vertu-signature-touch.

Obama, B. (2015, May 18). Remarks by the President on community policing. https://obamawhitehouse.archives.gov/the-press-office/2015/05/18/remarks-president-community-policing.

Payne, C. R., Niculescu, M., Just, D. R., & Kelly, M. P. (2015). Shopper marketing nutrition interventions: Social norms on grocery carts increase produce spending without increasing shopper budgets. *Preventive Medicine Reports*, 2, 287–291. doi. org/10.1016/j.pmedr.2015.04.007.

Pols, A. J. K. (2013). How artefacts influence our actions. *Ethical Theory and Moral Practice*, 16, 575–587. doi.org/10.1007/s10677-012-9377-0.

Rawls, J. (1971). *A Theory of Justice*. Belknap Press of Harvard University Press.

Rosen, R. J. (2011, September 3). So, was Facebook responsible for the Arab Spring after all? *The Atlantic*. www.theatlantic.com/technology/archive/2011/09/so-was-facebook-responsible-for-the-arab-spring-after-all/244314.

Rozenfeld, M. (n.d.). Do engineers need empathy? http://theinstitute.ieee.org/members/profiles/do-engineers-need-empathy.

Russell, B. (1982). On the relation between psychological and ethical egoism. *Philosophical Studies*, 42(1), 91–99.

Spier, R. E. (2015). On dealing with the innovations of the future. *Science and Engineering Ethics*, 21(2), 267–270.

Teachout, T. (2013, November 21). What Bill Gates is blind to. *Wall Street Journal*. www.wsj.com/articles/what-bill-gates-is-blind-to-1385074096.

Van de Poel, I. (2016). An ethical framework for evaluating experimental technology. *Science and Engineering Ethics*, 22(3), 667–686. doi.org/10.1007/s11948-015-9724-3.

Vargas, J. A. (2012, February 17). How an Egyptian revolution began on Facebook. *New York Times*. www.nytimes.com/2012/02/19/books/review/how-an-egyptian-revolution-began-on-facebook.html.

Verbeek, P.-P. (2008). Morality in design: Design ethics and the morality of technological artifacts. In P. Kroes, P. E. Vermaas, A. Light, & S. A. Moore (Eds.), *Philosophy and Design: From Engineering to Architecture* (pp. 91–103). Springer. doi.org/10.1007/978-1-4020-6591-0_7.

Wiens, K. (2015, April 21). We can't let John Deere destroy the very idea of ownership. *Wired*. www.wired.com/2015/04/dmca-ownership-john-deere.

Competence

"Perform services only in their area of competence."

The second NSPE canon serves as prohibition against engineers assuming jobs that are beyond their technical experience or expertise. There could be a number of reasons why an engineer is tempted to transgress the bounds of his or her competence. Perhaps a client doesn't have the resources to hire several engineers with multiple specialties. Perhaps a young engineer who just earned her degree is pressured on the job to take on more **responsibility** than she is ready for. Whatever the reason, it's not difficult to see why pushing the limits of your experience or qualifications in engineering can have serious consequences. Consider, for instance, the 2011 fatal collapse of the six-story Canterbury Television (CTV) building during an earthquake near Christchurch, New Zealand. An investigation of the incident revealed that the collapse was caused by the fact that elements intended to protect the building from seismic force were under-engineered. The design engineer in charge of these elements lacked the relevant experience for the job. He had never designed a building over two stories; nor did he have any experience with asymmetrical designs of the type the client requested. Had the engineer had the relevant experience, he would certainly have been familiar with the type of computer analysis required by the New Zealand building code. Had he been familiar with the software required to run these tests, he might have thought to account for an important limitation in the software's analysis. As it was, the engineer completed the analysis without realizing its product was inadequate for a building with an asymmetrical shape. During the earthquake, all six stories of the CTV building collapsed, taking with it a TV studio, a language school, and various other commercial tenants.

After the investigation, the design engineer and the principal engineer both tried to shift blame for the incident. The design engineer argued that he assumed the principal engineer was reviewing his work. Meanwhile, the principal engineer argued that he had assumed that, because the design engineer held a senior position at his firm with ten years' experience in the field, he was competent for the job. It was up to the design engineer, the principal argued, to speak up if this was not the case. While it may be difficult to assign blame in cases where more than one party is responsible for a project (a topic we will return to in Chapter 6), it's not difficult to point to what caused the problem. In this case, it seems clear that lack of competency was the issue. And we have every reason to think that if either party had taken steps to verify whether the design engineer had the relevant experience for the particular job, the disaster might have been avoided.

Complications for Determining Competence

From this case, we might assume that meeting the requirements of the second canon is simply a matter of making the effort to verify an engineer's qualifications and level of experience. Unfortunately, it is not so simple. The reason is that, in many cases, it is not exactly clear what experience is relevant, how much experience is relevant, and whether this experience must be directly linked to one's qualifications or area of specialty. Consider the following case from the NSPE BER archives:

Providing Prime Professional and Design Services

Case 89-1
Year: 1989
Facts:

Engineer A is a professional engineer with a degree in mechanical engineering. For 20 years she worked for various design firms including several years with a major architectural firm. While Engineer A took no course work in architecture during her undergraduate years, she gained a significant amount of knowledge about the practice of architecture as a result of her working in the mechanical engineering area with architects in private practice and managing various design projects.

Engineer A has now established her own engineering firm which employs no architects. A developer asks Engineer A to serve as the prime professional contract holder for the design of an office building complex. Engineer A agrees and retains Engineer B to perform the structural design, Engineer C to perform the electrical design, but does not retain an architect to perform the architectural design aspects of the work. Instead, Engineer A performs those design services personally, drawing upon the knowledge gained while practicing alongside architects.

Engineer A is not an architect. However, it doesn't follow from this that she is not fully capable of performing architectural services in a competent manner. In that case, is it possible for us to include architecture as part of Engineer A's area of competence? Engineer A did have a great deal of relevant experience with architecture. Is this experience enough to make her competent? And, if so, is it permissible for her to render the kinds of services that would normally be accomplished by an architect? More generally, should an engineer's "area of competence" be determined by her specialty alone or as a matter of her experience?

These are difficult questions. Regardless of what answers we give them, it may be wise to "err on the side of caution" and take the more narrow interpretation of "area of competence"—the one that would require that engineers not perform services outside of their area of specialization (regardless of their experience). Whatever competence amounts to, it might simply be safer to require a specialist on the job. However, taking a narrow interpretation of the code may not answer every moral conundrum relating to issues of competency. Many specialties in engineering have a great deal of overlap. Furthermore, it isn't always clear what specialty is most relevant to every task or job. In that case, taking area of competency to mean "specialty" might prove needlessly restrictive or make the code very difficult to employ. Though erring on the side of caution may provide a stop gap in certain cases, it can't be the final answer to moral questions regarding competence. For those sorts of questions, there is no easy answer.

Ethical Competence

As with the obligation to hold paramount the safety health and welfare of the public, there is no hard and fast rule as to how to apply the second canon. Instead, each case must be assessed individually. When making such assessments, it can be enormously helpful, as the NSPE BER does, to compare and contrast a questionable case with more clear-cut cases. However, this practice doesn't yield easy answers. That's because, in reality, almost no two cases are exactly alike in all of the relevant moral respects. That means there is an essential element of **ethical judgment** involved in determining moral rightness in each case—an **ethical competence** as it were. Ethical judgment, in our opinion, involves much more than knowledge of morality. The ancient Greek philosopher **Aristotle** believed that ethical judgment is rather like a skill—one that takes a lifetime of practice to fully develop. In that sense, ethical competence is closely related to technical competence with regard to how it is developed and employed. Ethical judgment is most accurately thought of as a deeply ingrained disposition to respond appropriately when faced with ethical decisions. As ethical judgment develops in a person, it allows them to more easily navigate the moral complexities of novel ethical situations.

Our goal in the remainder of this chapter is to help familiarize you with the Aristotelian approach to developing the sort of ethical judgment that is constitutive of ethical competence. We will begin by introducing you to Aristotle's notion of **practical judgment**: *phronesis*. We will then explore his suggestions for developing ethical competence. Finally, we will briefly address the way that technical skill might stand in tension with moral competence. It is our hope that, by the end of the chapter, you will have gained some insight into how to better support the further development of ethical judgment in both your personal and professional life.

Practical Judgment

In any practical profession, such as engineering, the goal is to make good decisions amidst difficult circumstances. Aristotle, author of *Nicomachean Ethics*, claims that good decisions require practical judgment, a capacity that he terms *phronesis*. *Phronesis* is often translated as "ethical judgment," reflecting the fact that Aristotle is after the elusive ability to judge *rightly*—in the technical, prudential, and moral senses of the word. One could, for example, choose the correct drive shaft in designing a specific new car (this would be a technical decision), choose a shaft that is the easiest to manufacture for your employer (this would be a prudential decision), or choose a shaft that lessens fuel emissions for the sake of future generations of consumers (this would, arguably, be a moral decision). *Phronesis* includes all of these ways of understanding appropriate judgment; and, obviously, the competence of engineers turns on their ability to not only perform technical tasks, but to perform these tasks well in the aforementioned ways. *Phronesis* also refers to the **sensitivity** and **attunement** to the particularities of a specific problem, rather than merely enacting a general rule or algorithm to address all similar cases.

Moral Exemplars

But how does one foster *phronesis*? This is not a particularly easy question. Aristotle is famous for founding one of the three ethical schools of thought: **virtue ethics** (the other two being utilitarianism and deontology). He argues that *phronesis* is the **virtue of all virtues** because it allows one to organize and prioritize the other virtues—such as courage, temperance, modesty, and wittiness. For Aristotle, developing that most important of virtues, phronesis, is not a matter of accepting and enacting an abstract moral code; he says it develops more organically than that. He claims that virtue can be fostered by engaging in activities whose completion involves virtue. In short, we develop virtue by working at it. This, at first glance, seems like no help at all. Are we just supposed to work at a task and then magically develop the virtue to master it?

Aristotle suggests that virtue is cultivated most effectively when students are placed in problematic situations with **mentors** who have an established track record of virtuous behavior. In this way, students can emulate the behavior of their models and avoid the behavior that their mentors avoid. This points in the direction of an apprentice model of engineering, one that obtains in many sub-disciplines of the profession. Engaging with mentors, much in the way that the Socratic method was described by Plato, will give students first-hand experience at completing a task, and force them to evaluate and hone their abilities in the process.

In an article entitled "Where Are Today's Engineering Heroes?" G. Pascal Zachary explains that the presence of notable **exemplars** helps draw new talent in the field and ensures public support from the discipline. Exemplars from underrepresented groups are especially important because they are essential to combating many of the social injustices we referenced at the end of Chapter 1. For instance, Zachary quotes Ruth Schwartz Cowan saying, "Every woman engineer is essentially heroic" because "women engineers break two [stereotypes]: the stereotype for a 'good woman' and the stereotype for a 'good engineer'." If engineers are going to fight for social justice while securing the public good, then it will help to start by promoting equity in their own ranks.

Zachary worries that, although there is no shortage of virtuous engineers worthy of our respect, there is very little **public recognition** of these individuals. He claims that this is in part because of the ultra-specialized technical knowledge that characterizes engineering (see below); the public doesn't truly understand or relate to the work of engineers. He notes that there is no Nobel Prize for engineering; nor is there anything comparable to this kind of honor in the field. If public recognition is key to supporting the existence of engineering role models, and recognition requires understanding, then perhaps engineers have a responsibility to educate the public about what they do. Considering the role that exemplars play in moral education, creating a **public competence** with regard to knowledge of the discipline of engineering may play an important role in fostering the ethical competence of engineering professionals.

Aristotle held that, by emulating the behavior of a virtuous person, a student has the opportunity to practice virtue even before understanding what virtue entails. The student learns to recognize and internalize virtuous behavior by experiencing what virtue "feels like" rather than trying to ascertain what it is. It is important to note that this is a very different kind of knowledge than so-called **propositional knowledge**: *knowledge-that*. Instead, what we learn from emulation is a *knowledge-how*. This sort of knowledge is one that can seep into the very foundation of the discipline—changing the expectations for moral competency at the most fundamental level. Examples determine "the way things are done." The existence of role models helps create a **culture of ethics** in engineering, where right action is the norm rather than the exception. Their very presence raises the bar for what counts as the "minimal requirements" for ethical behavior.

Failure to promote a culture of ethics in engineering can have devastating effects. On April 20, 2010, the BP *Deepwater Horizon* oil rig exploded and sank in the Gulf of Mexico; it was the largest accidental oil spill in the history of petroleum engineering. Eleven people went missing and were never found, and the sea-floor oil gusher continued for 87 days until finally being capped on July 15, 2010. In its investigation into the catastrophe, the RAND Center for Catastrophic Risk Management highlighted the cultural deterioration within BP:

> It is the underlying "unconscious mind" that governs the actions of an organization and its personnel. Cultural influences that permeate an organization and an industry and manifest in actions that can either promote and nurture a high reliability organization with high reliability systems, or actions reflective of complacency, excessive risk-taking, and a loss of situational awareness.
>
> (quoted in Kelly-Detwiler, 2012)

The report noted a lack of exemplars within BP, as well as a lack of critical self-examination, stating that "management's perspective failed to recognize and accept its own fallibilities despite a record of recent accidents in the U.S." (Kelly-Detwiler, 2012). The flow of oil from the spill has never been completely contained. The *Deepwater Horizon* case illustrates that disasters almost never occur due to one faulty engineering decision in isolation; a deficiency of culture, mentoring, exemplars, and role models enables and even encourages lapses in ethics. Over time, seemingly small ethical violations become normalized and build into even larger violations, until the results are disastrous and irreversible.

Mentorship

Exemplars are important. Still, role models, as Vivian Weil suggests, are different from mentors. She notes that the word "mentor" has its roots in Homer's *Odyssey*, in which Odysseus, when leaving for the war, entrusts the care of his son Telemachus to the goddess Athena. Athena acts as almost a surrogate parent to Telemachus while Odysseus is away—guiding and protecting him as she would her own son. Weil argues that this sort of intimate, personal relationship captures the essence of mentorship. Mentors are different from **role models**: someone who acts as an example but may not be personally engaged. They are also distinct from **advisors**: someone who merely dispenses advice without any particular attachment. Mentorship involves a long-term relationship that is developed on the basis of mutual respect and concern. Good mentors are invested in their mentees—viewing the success of the mentee as inseparable from their own. The influence of a "toxic" or indifferent mentor can be devastating to an engineer's moral development. Choosing a mentor, then, is one of the most important steps in an engineer's education.

All this talk of relationships might seem out of place. Engineering is often thought of as an impersonal discipline—one that values technical acuity over connection with other human beings. However, it should be clear by now that relationships are central to the successful practice of engineering. Learning how to develop robust and healthy relationships is a skill in and of itself. It is one that must be carefully developed over time with someone who is worthy of our trust. Perhaps unexpectedly then, social competency turns out to be as essential to engineering competency as technical knowledge.

Ethical Engagement

In *Nicomachean Ethics*, Aristotle claims that the transition from childhood (which is governed by desires, impulses, and habits) to adulthood (which is ideally governed by right conduct and virtue) happens when a student is engaged in a task in a particular way. This unique engagement is called *energeia* and is literally "being-at-work." For Aristotle, this is not simply an issue of going through the motions of a job, but rather *immersing* oneself in an engrossing task. Before this gets too confusing or abstract, let's get down to a concrete example: Can you think of something you do that you are genuinely good at and passionate about? We suspect that this activity—maybe playing an instrument or a sport—is something you at first had no idea how to do and slowly developed your abilities over time. If you can think of this sort of activity, you are tapping into an experience that Aristotle says might give us some insight into the nature of *energeia*.

Now compare this sort of energetic experience to the experience of dragging yourself through a textbook that you struggle with and despise. What is the difference? Aristotle suggests that when we are engaged in the first, energetic, way we find meaning in an activity and develop a personal and non-instrumental stake in the outcome. The activity becomes something that we deem intrinsically valuable, and we begin to build our character, and not merely our financial future, on our participation in the task that we undertake. Here, we might return to the discussion of Socratic wisdom and the way it encourages one to actively participate in ever-deeper forms of investigation. In this case, one is personally involved in the learning process and derives lasting meaning from one's involvement in it. Indeed, engineering is often considered an engaging and all-encompassing task, one that requires creativity and skill, and engenders passion and commitment. "Don't drag the engine, like an ignoramus, but bring wood and water and flame, like an engineer," urged antislavery activist Maria Weston Chapman of her followers in the nineteenth century.

Technological Rationality

At this point in the book, it is hopefully clear that one of our primary objectives is to emphasize the inescapably human character of engineering practice. It is integrated with norms and moral values that cannot be reduced to mere technical abilities. The discussion of *phronesis* points in this direction since *phronesis* depends on being responsible in specific contexts and sensitive to the demands of a unique project in real time. There are, however, a variety of factors that may push the coming generation of engineers to neglect *phronesis* and supplant it with the technological expertise that defines many disciplinary-specific engineering classes. Expert technological knowledge is undoubtedly necessary in engineering practice; but it does not exhaust the definition of "being competent," and we fear that to fetishize the acquisition of this knowledge may, at certain points, distract us from the ongoing need to claim responsibility for our professional lives. Herbert Marcuse, a German-American philosopher and sociologist writing in the 1940s, expressed this worry in "Some Social Implications of Modern Technology" (1941), where he claims that technological rationality jeopardizes the moral sense that is required in ethical judgments.

By 1940, and with increasing speed in the wake of World War II, the modern university began to gravitate toward STEM disciplines (science, technology, engineering, and math). Funding and staffing resources were dedicated to fields that taught students to invent and produce cutting-edge technologies. This was a good thing for engineering departments, but Marcuse argues that it deprived students of the more general humanistic competencies that had long defined college education. For example, students received little training in thinking through different ways to live a good life. Marcuse maintains that today's culture is dominated by what he called **technological rationality**, a near obsession with fully calculable results and instrumental progress. For an example of technological rationality, think about the way many math and physics classes (courses that underpin engineering curricula) are arranged around information that students are required to memorize verbatim, and then geared toward standardized tests that objectively evaluate the acquisition of this information. The questions in these exams often have exactly one right answer that is set out in advance by an instructor. Every student needs to give exactly the same answer in order to receive full credit. Now, there is nothing particularly wrong with this sort of pedagogy in developing a certain type of expert knowledge: many engineers need to know how to solve certain differential equations, and there is a set way to solve them correctly. The problem, according to Marcuse, arises when one assumes that this sort of technological rationality is the most important or, more radically, the *only* type of human reasoning.

Marcuse is concerned that our fixation on convenient and immediate results will obscure our judgments about truly good ones. It may lead us either to have an inflated sense of our competencies when considering a potential engineering goal or it will encourage us to choose engineering goals that are not morally or prudentially appropriate. In the following passage from "Some Social Implications of Modern Technology," Marcuse asks us to ponder the dangers of technological rationality by considering a very simple technical task: driving a car. He suggests that most of us think the point of driving a car is to get to a destination as quickly as possible. Given this goal, an entire system of infrastructure (signs, roads, parking spaces) has been put in place to get us to our destination in the shortest amount of time. But Marcuse suggests that something has been lost in this technically efficient system:

> Let us take a simple example. A man who travels by automobile to a distant place chooses his route from the highway maps. Towns, lakes and mountains appear as obstacles to be bypassed. The country-side is shaped and organized by the highway. Numerous signs and posters tell the traveler what to do and think; they even request his attention to the beauties of nature or the hallmarks of history. Others have done the thinking for him, and perhaps for the better. Convenient parking spaces have been constructed where the broadest and most surprising view is open. Giant advertisements tell him when to stop and find the pause that refreshes. And all this is indeed for his benefit, safety and comfort; he receives what he wants. Business, technics, human needs and nature are welded together into one rational and expedient mechanism. He will fare best who follows its directions, subordinating his spontaneity to the anonymous wisdom which ordered everything for him ... The decisive point is that this attitude—which dissolves all actions into a sequence of semi-spontaneous reactions to prescribed mechanical norms—is

not only perfectly rational but also perfectly reasonable. All protest is senseless, and the individual who would insist on his freedom of action would become a crank.

(Marcuse, 1998, p. 46)

What is particularly wrong or objectionable about this description? The driver has dutifully followed the traffic guidelines and avoided any obstacle or hindrance to arriving at her destination. And the quicker the better, right? Well, not always. What is missed, at least according to Marcuse, is that the driver has subordinated her spontaneous thought and moral responsibility in the course of the journey, allowing the system of infrastructure—what Marcuse calls "the anonymous wisdom that orders everything"—to control her movements and her mind.

To return to our discussion about engineering competency, it is tempting to think that competency is the minimum ability to perform a task in accord with a given set of definite rules (much like going from New York to Boston using a pre-established system of infrastructure). All you have to do is not break the laws, and you are competent enough to make the drive. This, we would argue, is deeply misguided. In marked contrast to pushing autopilot and going through the motions, competency requires taking personal responsibility for your actions and for the abilities that you have at your disposal. Establishing competency is not for the sole purpose of avoiding being sued for neglect (98 percent of all engineering accidents are attributed to incompetency). Rather, the point of being competent is to take credit for the fine-tuned distinctions about the technical, prudential, and moral aspects of an engineering assignment. A sophisticated robot can read a map and follow orders. But only humans can make truly competent judgments.

The distinction between human judgment and robotic judgment has been tragically demonstrated in the case of self-driving vehicles. On February 14, 2016, a Google self-driving car collided with a bus when the vehicle incorrectly assumed that the bus would slow or stop to let the car through. This first incident caused by an automated self-driving car resulted in no injuries, but it was a harbinger of things to come. A few months later, on May 7, the first fatal self-driving car crash occurred. A Tesla Model S on Autopilot mode collided with a tractor-trailer. In this case, the software failure was not one of decision-making but rather one of detection; the computer vision failed to distinguish between a white truck and a bright sky. As early as 2009, the Institute of Electrical and Electronics Engineers' (IEEE) *Spectrum* magazine cautioned against automation in a feature titled "Automated to Death." A paradox of automation, the feature warned, is that it can actually diminish human judgment and competency: "the more reliable the automation, the less the human operator may be able to contribute to that success ... and when the human operator can't detect the system's error, the consequences can be tragic" (Charette, 2009).

Engineers themselves can be responsible for overhyping the benefits of technology. Then Tesla CEO Elon Musk had described the Tesla Autopilot feature in glowing terms: "It's almost twice as good as a person." Such claims can encourage humans to put too much trust in technology. Even if self-driving cars could be made perfectly safe (a technological impossibility), there may be less obvious second-order and third-order effects of automated driving on society:

- How will automated travel affect the distribution of populations and resources?
- How might automated travel impact the disparities between well-traveled areas and more remote areas?
- What are the potential impacts on public visits to parks, rest areas, and open spaces?
- What are the effects on employment patterns?

For every engineering decision, the desire for efficiency and convenience, driven by technological rationality, must be balanced by a moral consideration of unintended social consequences.

In the field of engineering ethics, this point is raised by Mike Martin in his critique of Samuel Florman's position on the obligations of engineers. Florman claims that competent engineers have the obligation to follow the established laws of their profession, but have little or no obligation to "[filter] their everyday work through the sieve of ethical sensitivity" (Martin, 2000, p. 122). He adds that professionals only have the duty to fulfill the expectations of their clients and employers. We agree with Martin when he critiques this position, and would add that such a position is a product of the dangerous form of technological rationality described by Marcuse. In Martin's words (p. 122)—ones that we also support—"In an important sense [this ethical] filtering is exactly what should be expected of engineers in exercising their professional judgment," and determining the scope of competency.

Excellence and Expertise

What then, does moral competency involve if not merely technical rationality? To answer this question, we must return to Aristotle. For many of us, the word "virtue" brings to mind a particular set of (rather dull and restrictive) character traits such as piety, sobriety, modesty, chastity, and the like. The virtuous person, we think, is nothing if not "well behaved."

This sort of picture is not particularly inspiring. In that case, it's hard to see how we could be driven in to becoming virtuous in the sense of *energeia*. However, when Aristotle implores us to be virtuous, he has an entirely different notion in mind. Aristotle's concept of virtue is much closer to the concept of "excellence" than it is to a Victorian picture of propriety. What is it to be excellent at something? It depends on what you are doing and, as Aristotle thought, on what you are. According to Aristotle, everything (both natural and man-made) has a particular function; what he called a **telos**. A thing's *telos* is a sort of purpose that is particular to that thing. For instance, the function of a plant is to grow, and the function of a glass is to hold liquid. But what is the unique function of human beings? What separates them from the world of animals and inanimate objects? According to Aristotle, it is the ability to reason.

Of course, something can be better or worse at fulfilling its function. A harpist is someone who plays the harp, but an excellent harpist is someone who plays the harp well. Likewise, human beings can be better or worse at fulfilling their function as people. What makes something a person may be their ability to reason. However, what makes someone an *excellent person*, says Aristotle, is the ability to reason well. What does it mean to reason well? To answer this question, it helps to ask what it means to do anything well.

Think of the last time you heard a truly excellent musician play. Robert Krulwich (2014) describes a film recording of musical virtuoso Glenn Gould at home with his piano:

> Through the window, you catch snatches of his back yard. It's a windy day and he's got a coffee cup sitting on the piano top. He's working on a Bach partita, not just playing it, but singing along in his swinging baritone. As he plays, he gets so totally, totally lost in the music that suddenly (1:57 from the top), smack in the middle of a passage, with no warning, for no apparent reason, his left hand flips up, touches his head; he stands up, and walks in what looks like a trance to the window. There's an eerie silence. Then, in the quiet, you hear the Bach leaking out of him. He's still playing it, but in his head, he's scatting the beats. Then he turns, wanders back, sits down, and his fingers pick up right where his voice left off, but now with new energy, like he's found a switch and switched it. What just happened? I'm not sure. But I think this is a rare vision of what it's like to be so in your head you leave your body, or at least the moving parts of your body, totally behind.

Gould is enraptured. He carries us along with him as he leaves everything else behind. Music had become so second nature to him that playing was inseparable from any domestic activity. It was not something he was just good at, or even a "part of him." It was who he was.

Getting it Right

No doubt you've experienced such a performance—one in which a musician could get lost in the moment because music had become second nature. How did they get there? Gould was a musical prodigy—someone who is born with robust musical ability. However, you don't necessarily need to be a prodigy to become a musical virtuoso. Most musicians had to work very hard to get to the point of effortless abandon. When they began playing a musical instrument, chances are it felt far from natural (and was less than enchanting for their audiences). At first, they had to be conscious of, say, where to place their hands on the keys, and how to apply just the right pressure at the right time. On their first try, they may have pressed the keys too softly, making the music almost inaudible. Then perhaps, when corrected, they overcompensated by banging out the notes with too much force. They had to learn how to read music—possibly mapping out the scales alongside the notes. Keeping all of this in mind was no doubt confusing and frustrating at first. It must have been hard to imagine what it would feel like to get it right, never mind getting it "just right." But with enough practice, the right guidance, and the right circumstances, they can develop their natural ability—gradually transforming from beginner to expert.

Excellence of any kind, according to Aristotle, is not only a level of achievement; it is a skill—and one that takes a great deal of effort to perfect. Aristotelian perfection involves not over- or under-reacting, but getting it "just right." This has come to be known as Aristotle's **Doctrine of the Mean**. Virtues, on this account, are "midway points" between extremes. This is not to say that one should always behave moderately, but rather that one should always react appropriately, doing the right thing, in the right way, towards the right people, and for the right reasons. Since the "appropriate response" will vary from situation to situation, it's hard to describe exactly what it is. But, like a perfectly executed symphony, you know it when you see it (or rather, hear it). **Moral expertise** is no different in kind from any other type of expertise, and we become morally excellent in the same way we become excellent at anything else.

Jon Alan Schmidt points out that the kind of **moral know-how** Aristotle is advocating is not so different from the technical skills truly excellent engineers already employ in their professional practice. When she first begins, the engineering novice strictly follows the rules and applies the formulas she's gathered from textbooks and lectures. Gradually, she advances to the point where she can make on-the-spot adjustments using general rules of thumb to account for situational complexities. As she progresses, she learns that sometimes there is no hard-and-fast rule that can be applied to solve a technical problem. Instead, she must apply creativity and discernment to find the best solution. With enough guidance and experience, the competent engineer develops the kind of ease and familiarity with technical problem solving that allows her to move easily through complex tasks. If all goes well, this sort of well-calibrated judgment becomes second nature. She becomes the kind of expert that others look to model themselves after. In the end, this process, though long and involved, is well worth it. The kind of satisfaction an engineer gets from preforming at the highest level is second to none. It becomes one of the most significant rewards of the profession.

Technical and Moral Expertise

If this is the path to technical expertise, Schmidt asks, then why should the road to moral expertise be so very different? To become excellent at anything we need some natural ability, true. But, more importantly, we need good examples to learn from, the right circumstances to grow, sufficient opportunity to practice, and the good sense to learn from our mistakes. There is no mystery, then, to becoming a virtuous person. We learn to be good people in the same way we learn to be good at anything else. Schmidt (2014) argues that engineers ought not to think of their technical training as somehow distinct from their moral education. "Ethical competence," he writes, "should be seen as an essential component of technical competence, such that it is impossible for an engineer to be both competent and unethical at the same time." Here Schmidt insists that moral excellence is just "part of the job description" for engineers. Why is this? If excellence, as Aristotle suggests, is relative to a goal, then we must consider the goals of engineering. The mandate to "hold paramount the safety and wellbeing of the public" makes engineering an inherently "others-focused" profession. This focus on others, as we've said, is at the center of morality. In that case technical and moral competence go hand in hand.

Perhaps then it is not technical rationality per se that is the problem. It's just that we have a very narrow notion of what it takes to be technically competent. It's not just about blind rule following, or algorithmic decision-making. True, these are important steps on the road to competency, but they are not constitutive of truly excellent practice. True excellence, be it technical or moral, involves an internalized skill—one that is so much a part of who you are that employing it becomes almost effortless. This sort of expertise isn't gained quickly or easily. It isn't gained without failure. We will make lots of mistakes along the way—over- and under-correcting while we calibrate our moral instincts. But that's just part of the process.

Chapter 2 Key Terms and Concepts

Responsibility
Ethical Judgment
Ethical Competence
Aristotle
Practical Judgment
Phronesis
Sensitivity
Attunement
Virtue Ethics
Virtue of all Virtues
Mentor/Mentorship
Public Recognition/Public
    Competence

Propositional Knowledge
Culture of Ethics
Role Models
Advisors
Energeia
Technological Rationality
Technical Expertise
Excellence
Telos
Doctrine of the Mean
Moral Expertise/Moral
    Know-How

Chapter 2: End of Chapter Reading and NSPE Board of Ethical Review Cases

Guided Core Reading   *89*

Core Reading 2.1: 'Mentoring: Some ethical considerations' by Vivian Weil (excerpts)

Core Reading 2.2: 'Changing the paradigm for engineering ethics' by Jon Alan Schmidt (excerpts)

NSPE Board of Ethical Review Cases   *97*

Case 17-7: Public Health Safety and Welfare—Engineering Standards (2018)

Case 18-9: Public Health and Safety—Building Codes to Address Environmental Risk (2018)

Case 16-10: Former Employee's Participation in a Public Safety Standards Hearing (2016)

Guided Further Reading   *102*

Further Reading 2.1: 'The good engineer: Giving virtue its due in engineering ethics' by Charles E. Harris Jr.

Further Reading 2.2: 'Regulation or responsibility? Autonomy, moral imagination, and engineering' by Mark Coeckelbergh

Further Reading 2.3: 'Engineering and the problem of moral overload' by Jeren Van den Hoven, Gert-Jan Lokhorst, and Ibo van de Poel

Tip: If you can't use the QR codes, use the hyperlinks found on the book's webpage instead: www.routledge.com/9781138183865.

Guided Core Reading

Core Reading 2.1: 'Mentoring: Some ethical considerations' by Vivian Weil (excerpts)

Preparing to Read

In this reading, Weil defends an understanding of "mentor" that is honorific. In particular, to be a mentor is to be a good, successful mentor. And those supervisors who fail to live up to the standards of a good mentor are not themselves mentors. This generates a puzzle. People sometimes use terms like "toxic mentor" and describe mentors as problematic in certain ways. Weil addresses this puzzle. She then turns to the ancient story of Athena, where she finds lessons for mentors in graduate and science education.

Excerpted from: Weil, V. (2001). Mentoring: Some ethical considerations. *Science and Engineering Ethics*, 7, 471–482. doi.org/10.1007/s11948-001-0004-z. © Springer Nature 2001, reprinted by permission. Internal references omitted.

There is a popular notion of a mentor. It is the notion of "someone who serves as a career role model and who actively advises, guides, and promotes another's career and training." No special activity on the part of the mentor is required, not even explaining to students what they should notice and why they should emulate the behavior. Swazey and Anderson argue for distinguishing role models from mentors. ... Their point is that merely presenting a model of appropriate conduct is not adequate. Role models are valuable, but mentoring includes much more than modeling appropriate conduct. A mentor engages in various instructional activities—including coaching and offering criticism—and in a range of nurturing activities that amount to "giving special protection". To be a mentor is to be involved in a relationship. The relationships are informal, fully voluntary for both members, but at least initially and for sometime thereafter, characterized by great disparity of experience and wisdom. The mentoring relationship is usually thought of as gradual, evolving, long-term, and involving personal closeness.

...

[I]t is a distinctive feature of mentoring that it is voluntary. Mentoring cannot be mandated or assigned. Even if departments assume a collective responsibility for the guidance of graduate students, they cannot insure that each student has a mentor in the honorific sense. ... A related distinctive feature of mentoring in the honorific sense is that it is not subject to monitoring. Mentoring generally brings mentor and mentee into a relatively intimate relationship, not entirely public or available for observation. It is an ongoing relationship rather than a process with structure and predictability.

...

Mentoring is too "chancy" a phenomenon, too much a matter of factors which cannot be predicted and controlled, to be allowed to be critical to success in graduate study. It is dangerous for any institution to rely heavily on luck. It is foolhardy to depend upon mentors' establishing long-term relationships with students to transmit ethical standards and to give guidance critical for students' success.

...

[G]raduate students must cope with risks and uncertainties that arise in large part from conventions and arrangements devised within institutions. Because procedures and requirements in institutions are modifiable, there is a prospect for making changes that reduce uncertainty and mitigate dangers. Modifying institutional practices is not free of risk, but when the transmission of appropriate standards is at stake, the risk seems acceptable.

...

The first step is to assume collective responsibility for determining the needs of graduate students. The next step is to devise arrangements to meet the needs that have been identified. Instead of counting on individuals to step forward on their own to form relationships with individual students that somehow meet a set of needs that have not been well articulated, departments and research groups can guarantee that certain needs they have explicitly recognized are met. The need to articulate and explain ethical standards must be among them.

Graduate students reasonably expect departments and research groups to take responsibility in this way. In her investigation of graduate study in science, Judith Swazey asked graduate students to compare the role that a department should take in transmitting ethical standards in research to the role actually taken by the department. Eighty-two percent of students felt the department should take an "active" or "very active" role in transmitting ethical standards, while only 22% felt the department actually took an "active" or "very active" role.

Fortunately, the perceptions of faculty who were surveyed in Swazey's study were much like those of the students. Ninety nine percent of 2000 faculty members canvassed believed that "academics should exercise collective responsibility for the professional conduct of their graduate students". Only 27% of these faculty believed that they actually exercised this responsibility. ... This finding suggests that the situation is ripe for the collective action suggested here.

These considerations offer compelling reasons for assuming collective responsibility for providing for the needs of graduate students. Members of departments and research groups can devise plans to share equitably in a collective effort to train graduate students. One can argue that research groups and departments have an ethical duty to develop collective action strategies. Alan Buchanan urges that there is a fundamental ethical principle of common sense that acting responsibly requires doing what we can to improve the chances of acting responsibly. ... This principle, together with clear evidence of laxity in current circumstances, provides a strong basis for departments and research groups to assume collective responsibility for defining and furnishing an adequate structure of guidance and protection for graduate students.

What should such structures encompass? First to be addressed is the responsibility to provide adequate information about the terms of graduate study in a written statement. Second is the creation of a system for advising, with prescribed duties for advisors and provision for evaluation of performance in the role of advisor. For example, a student's advisor would be required to keep the student informed about milestones in the program and the student's progress in meeting them. Third, training for advisors will be needed to help assure adequate performance in the role.

To prepare students for effectively and responsibly engaging in such activities as writing research reports, submitting abstracts for conferences and meetings, writing proposals, approaching program officers of funding agencies, and participating in peer review, departments and research groups can take collective responsibility, assigning specific duties to specific individuals. Making students aware of ethical aspects of all these activities and of the assigning of credit and authorship should be a collective responsibility as well. To deal with the disparity of power that is one glaring source of problems for graduate students and postdocs, departments and research groups must build protections for the vulnerable into the advising and teaching structures. This would include policies for preventing or responding to problems of conflict of interest.

Guided Reading Questions

1. How does Weil understand the term "mentor"? What are the distinctive features of "ethical mentoring" in Weil's sense? Have you ever had a mentor that fits Weil's conception of a mentor? Have you ever been a mentor in this sense for someone else?

2. Weil stresses that ethical mentorship shouldn't be left to chance in an engineering program. Why do you think this feature of mentioning is so important?

3. Why does Weil think graduate departments have a "collective responsibility" to provide structures for mentorship for graduate students?

4. If you are currently an undergraduate or a graduate student, what sorts of structures, if any, were in place in your program for ethical mentorship? How could these structures have been improved? If you are a professional, answer these questions by thinking back to the time when you were earning your degree(s).

5. At the end of the excerpt, Weil notes that the mentor–mentee relationship has a built in power dynamic. She claims that departments and research groups must protect mentees against the vulnerabilities produces by these dynamics. What sorts of vulnerabilities does Weil have in mind? What could departments and research groups do to offer protection against such vulnerabilities?

Read the Full Article (optional)

You can read the full article online by scanning the QR code or following the link below. Your college library will need to subscribe to the journal, and you may need to login via your library's website or use campus wifi to get access.

https://link.springer.com/article/10.1007/s11948-001-0004-z

Core Reading 2.2: 'Changing the paradigm for engineering ethics' by Jon Alan Schmidt (excerpts)

Preparing to Read

In this article, contemporary philosopher and engineer Jon Alan Schmidt argues that the current approach to engineering ethics—an approach focused on rule following—is ill-suited to handle the complex moral questions that arise in actual engineering practice. As an alternative, Schmidt articulates and defends an approach to engineering ethics that is grounded in Aristotle's account of virtue. In the style of Aristotle, Schmidt offers an explanation of virtuousness in engineering along with insights on how one becomes a "virtuous engineer."

Excerpted from: Schmidt, J. A. (2014). Changing the paradigm for engineering ethics. *Science and Engineering Ethics*, 20, 985–1010. doi.org/10.1007/s11948-013-9491-y. © Springer Nature 2014, reprinted by permission. Internal references omitted.

PARADIGMS IN PHILOSOPHY

The notion of a paradigm should be at least somewhat familiar to most people; in particular, the concept of a "paradigm shift." Kuhn … gave the term its modern sense, defining a paradigm as a specific way of viewing reality—a set of assumptions shared by all practitioners within a particular discipline that effectively dictates what will be observed, what questions will be asked and answered, how such investigations will be carried out, and how their results will be interpreted.

…

So what is the currently dominant paradigm in philosophy? Some helpful context is provided by going all the way back to the ancient Greeks. They identified three different kinds of knowledge:

- *episteme* … designates knowledge-that something is the case;
- *techne* … designates knowledge-how to achieve a predetermined outcome;
- *phronesis* … designates knowledge-how to behave in a manner that is contextually sensitive and appropriate.

[E]pisteme, techne and *phronesis* … for the sake of clarity … will be translated here as theoretical knowledge, technical rationality and practical judgment.

…

Theoretical knowledge is propositional in nature and aims at eternal truth. It consists of conceptual beliefs that count as facts. It is imparted to a student by a process of instructing.

Technical rationality is procedural in nature and aims at external success. It consists of instrumental abilities and decisions on the basis of method grounded in rules. It is imparted to an apprentice by training.

Practical judgment is personal in nature and aims at internal integrity. It consists of ethical dispositions that count as virtues. It is imparted to a disciple by a process of mentoring.

Many scholars have argued that today's culture has largely collapsed theoretical knowledge and practical judgment into technical rationality, with the result that the latter is widely regarded as the *only* legitimate form of reasoning. It might seem natural to associate theoretical knowledge with science and technical rationality with craft. … Likewise, practical judgment has largely been discredited.

…

PARADIGMS IN ETHICS

Perhaps this is what happens when engineers encounter ethics. As mentioned above, it is typically manifested in *codes of ethics* with which engineers are expected to comply. These tend to focus on specific things that engineers should and … should not do.

…

Is there an alternative approach that might be better suited to the unique nature of engineering? … [V]irtue ethics is more heuristic and focuses on developing attitudes. … [E]ngineering is … heuristic … requiring creativity and skill to make choices from among multiple options. If engineering practice cannot be reduced to merely following a set of rules, then surely the same is true of engineering ethics.

…

Recognizing the potential desirability of applying virtue ethics to engineering, how should one go about doing so? Most contemporary proponents hold that virtues can only be properly identified within the context of a particular practice.

VIRTUOUS ENGINEERING

Praxis: The "What" of Engineering

First, the social aspect of engineering is such that engineers engage in a combined human performance in which they play a particular societal role: the assessment, management, and communication of risk. ... Furthermore ... engineers spend the majority of their time at work interacting with others. Engineering is thus always a collaborative endeavor, assembling expertise that is distributed among multiple participants. ... Engineers are the decision-makers in situations where members of the general public are usually the potential harm-bearers, even when they are also supposed to benefit in some way. ... Embracing this responsibility entails not only recognizing these uncertainties and dealing with them appropriately, but also calling attention—preferably beforehand—to any residual risk that is associated with an engineered product or project, including anticipated social and environmental impacts.

Phronesis: The "How" of Engineering

[E]ngineers exercise the intellectual virtue of engineering, which is practical judgment—specifically, engineering judgment—while exhibiting the moral virtues of engineering, which are objectivity, care, and honesty. Engineers routinely confront difficulties and predicaments, rather than well-structured problems that have deterministic solutions. Learning theories, rules, and maxims—also known as heuristics and design procedures—provides a necessary and solid foundation. However, it is only through experience that someone can develop the skill to discern quickly what is important in a specific set of circumstances and then select a suitable way forward. Risk assessment requires objectively evaluating the likelihood and severity of possible threats and identifying alternatives for reducing one or both of these parameters. Risk management requires carefully deliberating over multiple viable options and choosing one that rightly balances caution and ambition on behalf of all those who may be affected. Risk communication requires honestly acknowledging the dangers that cannot reasonably be eliminated and informing everyone who needs to be aware of them.

Eudaimonia: The "Why" of Engineering

[E]ngineers strive to fulfill the proper purpose of engineering, which is to enhance the material well-being of all people, by achieving the internal goods of engineering, which are safety, sustainability, and efficiency. It takes a deliberate decision and ongoing resolve to do this faithfully. Engineers must prioritize it over not only their own immediate interests, but also the external goods that are valued by those who typically make the major decisions and ultimately pay the bills. The prospective reward is the opportunity to escape, at least partially, the "social captivity" that renders engineering largely instrumental, subject to exploitation by managers and clients. As a step in this direction, engineers can pursue their most fundamental aims—protecting people and preserving property, improving environments and conserving resources, and performing functions while minimizing costs—for their own sake, rather than merely as means to another end. When merged, they constitute an overall notion of quality that engineers seek to incorporate into everything that results from their efforts.

Guided Reading Questions

1. What is a "paradigm" and what is a "paradigm shift"? What does Schmidt think is the current paradigm in engineering ethics? Why does he think we need to change this paradigm? What alternative paradigm does he suggest?
2. What role does Schmidt think that professional codes of conduct play in engineering ethics? What are some limitations of professional codes of conduct?
3. Like Marcuse, Schmidt writes about "technical rationality." What does Schmidt mean by technical rationality, and why does he think that technical rationality is an inadequate tool for solving moral problems?
4. What does Schmidt say is the "internal good of engineering"? What are the "moral virtues of engineering," and how does developing these virtues help engineers promote the internal good of engineering?
5. Schmidt describes what he claims is the "what," "how," and "why" of engineering. What does Schmidt mean by each of these terms?

Read the Full Article (optional)

You can read the full article online by scanning the QR code or following the link below. Your college library will need to subscribe to the journal, and you may need to login via your library's website or use campus wifi to get access.

https://link.springer.com/article/10.1007/s11948-013-9491-y

NSPE Board of Ethical Review Cases

Case 18-11: Objectivity and Truthfulness—Use of Drone

Objectivity and Truthfulness—Use of Drone

Case 18-11
Year: 2018
Facts:

Engineer A is a consulting engineer who performs structural inspections using mechanical drones. The scope of Engineer A's services is solely to identify the physical conditions of the bridge and make recommendations regarding bridge repairs. Engineer A deploys a drone to perform a series of bridge inspections as part of Engineer A's contract for inspection services with the state Department of Transportation. During one of Engineer A's drone inspections for the state Department of Transportation, the drone unexpectedly records an encounter between a law enforcement officer and a motorist that results in the exchange of gunfire. Following his review of the drone recording, Engineer A relays it to the state Department of Transportation noting the gunfire event. The state Department of

Transportation advises Engineer A that it does not plan to share the information with state or local law enforcement unless so requested by state or local authorities.

Question from the NSPE:
What are Engineer A's ethical obligations under the circumstances?

Going Beyond—Our Questions for a Deep Dive

1. If Engineer A has an obligation to further act with regard to the incident she witnessed, is this obligation a result of her professional obligation as an engineer or the broader ethical obligations she has as a human being? In other words, does the fact that Engineer A is an engineer play any role in her acquiring the obligation, or would she have been obligated to do something regardless of her professional designation?
2. In this situation Engineer A faces a moral dilemma that requires ethical competence in addition to technical competence. What sort of training could help prepare engineers to face situations such as the one Engineer A faces?
3. Ethical dilemmas are complex and often there is no single "right answer" to them. Because of this, Schmidt argues that it is a mistake to answer questions such as these by appealing to detailed "hard and fast" codes and standards. One very useful resource that the NSPE has provided in addition to its codes of conduct is the repository of case discussions, which includes comparisons and contrasts to ethical issues raised in similar cases. For instance, for the case under discussion see the link below. How might the NSPE's practice of providing this "comparison set" for ethics cases help engineers become "virtuous" in Schmidt's sense of the word?

Read the Board's Discussion and Conclusion

To read the discussion and conclusion of this case by members of the NSPE Board of Ethical Review, go to: www.nspe.org/resources/ethics/ethics-resources/board-ethical-review-cases/objectivity-and-truthfulness-use-drone.

Case 17-3: Public Health, Safety, and Welfare—Discovery of Structural Defect Affecting Subdivision

Public Health, Safety, and Welfare—Discovery of Structural Defect Affecting Subdivision

Case 17-3
Year: 2017
Facts:

Engineer A is a professional engineer and registered architect with extensive design and forensic engineering experience. In performing a forensic engineering investigation for an insurance company, Engineer A is asked to look at a beam that had been burned, as a result of arson, in a residence that was at the time of the arson under construction. Following the initial arson investigation, Engineer A learns that the construction contractor determined that the beam could be reused on the project. Engineer A examines the 15-foot-long beam and determines that it is slightly charred, and it had been located next to a dining room with a two-story ceiling. On the other side, the beam had supported a second-floor bedroom, a wall, and (on both sides of the beam) a significant amount of roof of the residence. Engineer A initially observes that, aside from the slight fire damage, the beam looks too light to provide adequate structural support. Engineer A measures the tributary area of roof, floor, and wall bearing on the beam and runs a series of structural calculations.

Following his review, Engineer A determines that the beam was seriously under-designed. Engineer A observes that since the house was a tract home, there are other identical designs in the subdivision.

Engineer A writes his report and identifies the design defect, and expresses his larger concern regarding the possibility that an inadequate structural member was used in other houses in the subdivision. Engineer A submits his report to the insurance company that retained him. Engineer A, still concerned with his obligation to the public beyond just informing the insurance company, calls the State Board of Professional Engineers, apprises them of the situation, and asks what more could and should be done about the situation. The Board's response is that Engineer A fulfilled his professional obligation by notifying the insurance company, in writing, of the defect.

Question from the NSPE:
Did Engineer A fulfill his ethical obligations under the NSPE Code of Ethics by providing the report to the insurance company that retained him?

Going Beyond—Our Questions for a Deep Dive

1. If Engineer A had been in the role of design engineer in the CTV disaster discussed at the beginning of this chapter, do you think that particular disaster would have taken place?
2. In contrast to the design engineer in the CTV disaster, Engineer A took the responsibility of verifying his initial assessment. What sorts of character traits (or "virtues") might Engineer A have developed that made him "go the extra mile" in this case?
3. Clearly, the first canon of the NSPE Code of Ethics regarding the obligation to hold paramount safety, health, and welfare is highly relevant to this case. How do you think a moral exemplar would interpret the canon in this case? Would she be able to walk away from the situation after filing the report without following up on the matter?
4. Consider Engineer A's behavior up until the point where he received notification from the Board that he had discharged his obligation. What answer do you think he might give to the question posed by the NSPE? What, if anything, might his answer say about his character?

Read the Board's Discussion and Conclusion

To read the discussion and conclusion of this case by members of the NSPE Board of Ethical Review, go to: www.nspe.org/resources/ethics/ethics-resources/board-ethical-review-cases/public-health-safety-and-welfare-1.

Case 08-9: Credit for Engineering Work—Preparation of Grant Application

Credit for Engineering Work—Preparation of Grant Application

Case 08-9
Year: 2008
Facts:

Engineer A is a Ph.D. student working with Professor Smith. Engineer A is near the completion of the research project and has prepared a paper for publication. Professor Smith recently hired another Ph.D. student, Engineer B, who will continue on the same project after Engineer A graduates. Professor Smith would like to renew his funding for that project and prepares a new grant application with the help of Engineer B. Professor Smith has an electronic version of Engineer A's paper and copies most of the figures and about half the text in the grant application from Engineer A's paper. Engineer A has presented some of the work reported in her paper at a conference. That presentation is cited in the grant application, but only in the "background" and "significance" sections. Engineer A is concerned that whoever reads the application may attribute to Engineer B all the work presented in the "progress report" section. Engineer A is also concerned that Engineer B will be submitting exactly the same figures and text when she publishes her paper.

Question from the NSPE:
What is the appropriate ethical course of action for Engineer A, Engineer B, and Professor Smith?

Going Beyond—Our Questions for a Deep Dive

1. What sort of obligations does Professor Smith have, as a mentor, with regard to Engineer A and Engineer B?
2. How might Professor Smith's actions play a role in the moral education of Engineer A and Engineer B?
3. Because of his role as a professor, does Smith have any obligation to put the wellbeing of his students above his own professional needs (for instance, the need to obtain funding)?
4. If Engineer A is not able to receive proper recognition for her work as a result of Engineer B's later work on the project, who, if anyone, is morally responsible for this outcome—Engineer A, Engineer B, or Professor Smith?

Read the Board's Discussion and Conclusion

To read the discussion and conclusion of this case by members of the NSPE Board of Ethical Review, go to: www.nspe.org/resources/ethics/ethics-resources/board-ethical-review-cases/credit-engineering-work-preparation.

Guided Further Reading

Further Reading 2.1: 'The good engineer: Giving virtue its due in engineering ethics' by Charles E. Harris Jr.

Find the Article

Harris, C. E. (2008). The good engineer: Giving virtue its due in engineering ethics. *Science and Engineering Ethics*, 14, 153. doi.org/10.1007/s11948-008-9068-3.

Read the article online by scanning the QR code or following the link below. Your college library will need to subscribe to the journal, and you may need to login via your library's website or use campus wifi to get access.

https://link.springer.com/article/10.1007%2Fs11948-008-9068-3

Preparing to Read

In the introduction to this chapter, we discussed the potential role that virtue ethics might play in helping engineers develop the sort of practical wisdom connected with moral expertise. In this article, Charles Harris compares a virtue-based approach to engineering ethics with more "standard" approaches to engineering ethics, such as those (Harris claims) taken by the NSPE. Standard approaches, Harris argues, often focus on "rule-based" strategies to encourage engineers to "avoid wrongdoing"—what he calls "preventive ethics." Harris claims that virtue-based approaches to ethics are better suited to capture some aspects of engineering ethics. As authors, it is our opinion that virtue-based approaches are not necessarily incompatible with other approaches to ethics, and strategies like Harris's are most useful when combined with the resources from various approaches to ethics.

Guided Reading Questions

1. Harris claims that many of the provisions of professional codes of ethics in engineering focus on "preventive ethics"—for instance preventing disaster or wrongdoing. Prior to reading this book, what was your understanding of your professional ethical responsibilities as an engineer: was it focused on avoiding wrongdoing?
2. Harris claims that there are several limitations to "rule-based" approaches to engineering ethics. Do you agree that rule-based approaches to engineering ethics are limiting in the way he suggests?
3. Could rule-based approaches be beneficial despite their limitations? If so, when and how? Might Harris's approach be combined with rule-based approaches to ethics? If so, when might this combination be useful in engineering practice?
4. Harris introduces the idea of a "virtue portrait"—a "relatively extended description of a virtuous person." What would a virtue portrait look like for an engineer in your specific area of engineering?
5. Following Sarah Kuhn, Harris suggests that developing techno-social sensitivity can be overwhelming for engineers. Harris offers some suggestions for helping engineering students develop

techno-social sensitivity. What do you think of Harris's suggestions? Do you think they would help address Kuhn's concern? Can you think of other methods of helping engineers develop techno-social sensitivity that might make it less overwhelming?

Further Reading 2.2: 'Regulation or responsibility? Autonomy, moral imagination, and engineering' by Mark Coeckelbergh

Find the Article

Coeckelbergh, M. (2006). Regulation or responsibility? Autonomy, moral imagination, and engineering. *Science, Technology, & Human Values,* 31(3), 237–260. doi.org/10.1177/0162243905285839.

Read the article online by scanning the QR code or following the link below. Your college library will need to subscribe to the journal, and you may need to login via your library's website or use campus wifi to get access.

https://journals.sagepub.com/doi/10.1177/0162243905285839

Preparing to Read

We began this chapter by pointing to the difficulty in applying a seemingly straightforward injunction: "perform services only in your area of competence." We, the authors, argued that, in order to understand how to apply this particular code or any code of ethics, engineers needed to develop moral competence in addition to technical competence. In this article, Mark Coeckelbergh explains the relationship between regulatory frameworks such as codes of ethics and two aspects of moral competence: autonomy and imagination.

Guided Reading Questions

1. Coeckelbergh examines the advantages and disadvantages of various "external" methods of risk management. In your experience, how often do engineers (including yourself) rely solely on "external controls" such as legal regulation, managerial oversite, etc. to deal with risk or other ethical issues?

2. Coeckelbergh points out that "prescriptive forms of regulation" such as regulatory codes are often based on historical knowledge. He argues that one drawback to relying on prescriptive forms of regulation is that, especially in the case of new technology, the future does not always resemble the past. Thus, the ethical issues surrounding new and emerging technologies often "outpace" regulatory codes. Can you think of any current or past examples of technologies that fit this description?

3. Coeckelbergh claims that a culture of "blame and punishment," which is built into certain bureaucratic, economic, and political structures, serves to prevent feelings of responsibility in engineers. Does this claim match your experience in engineering? What sort of cultural shifts in bureaucratic, economic, or political structures related to engineering might foster positive feelings in engineers towards moral responsibility?

4. Coeckelbergh argues that the real moral problems in engineering are too complex to be solved by simply applying various codes of ethics, principles, etc. In order to solve moral problems, engineers must employ "moral imagination." According to Coeckelbergh, moral imagination includes "being able to imagine how your actions influence others, being able to empathetically understand others, and being able to envision alternative courses of action if necessary." Recall the NSPE case studies presented in this chapter. How might moral imagination in this sense help us develop solutions to the moral problems raised in any of these cases?

5. Coeckelbergh writes that autonomy is a key factor in helping engineers internalize moral responsibility. He notes that the kinds of external control that are imposed by regulators can impede autonomy. However, he argues that external control could also be used to foster a sense of autonomy in engineers with regard to moral matters. What sorts of regulations, codes, etc. might support engineers in developing a sense of moral autonomy?

Further Reading 2.3: 'Engineering and the problem of moral overload' by Jeroen Van den Hoven, Gert-Jan Lokhorst, and Ibo van de Poel

Find the Article

Van den Hoven, J., Lokhorst, G.-J., & van de Poel, I. (2012). Engineering and the problem of moral overload. *Science and Engineering Ethics*, 18(1), 143–155. doi.org/10.1007/s11948-011-9277-z.

You can read the article online by scanning the QR code or following the link below. The article is available **Open Access** and no subscription or login is required.

www.ncbi.nlm.nih.gov/pmc/articles/PMC3275721

Preparing to Read

As we have discussed in the introduction to this chapter, part of what makes ethical decisions difficult in engineering is that such decisions often involve a tradeoff between conflicting values. We suggested that one way of becoming more proficient at handling ethical dilemmas was to develop "moral expertise" in the way Aristotle recommends. In this article, Jeroen Van den Hoven, Gert-Jan Lokhorst, and Ibo van de Poel suggest an additional tool for addressing moral dilemmas: employ technical solutions to help avoid moral dilemmas arising in the first place.

Guided Reading Questions

1. Recalling the NSPE BER cases presented in this chapter, can you think of any technical solutions that might have helped prevent moral dilemmas arising in each situation?

2. Have you ever found yourself in the kind of "moral overload" situation that Van den Hoven et al. describe—a situation in which there is no way to satisfy all of our moral requirements simultaneously? How did you handle this situation: what values did you have to "compromise" in order to address the situation?
3. Have you ever found yourself with what Van den Hoven et al. describe as "moral residue"—the moral emotions and tensions that result from the moral compromises that necessarily result from moral overload situations?
4. Van den Hoven et al. describe several strategies for dealing with moral overload. They also discuss the benefits and drawbacks to each strategy. Which strategy seems best to you and why?
5. Van den Hoven et al. argue that technical innovation can lead to moral progress because it "enlarges the opportunity set." What is their argument for this claim? Do you agree with it?

Bibliography

Aristotle. (350 BCE). *Nicomachean Ethics* (W. D. Ross, Trans.). MIT Internet Classics Archive. http://classics.mit.edu//Aristotle/nicomachaen.html.

Berti, E. (2003). Practical rationality and technical rationality. *Poznan Studies in the Philosophy of the Sciences and the Humanities*, 81(1), 249–254.

Charette, R. N. (2009, December 15). Automated to death. *IEEE Spectrum*. https://spectrum.ieee.org/computing/software/automated-to-death.

Coeckelbergh, M. (2006). Regulation or responsibility? Autonomy, moral imagination, and engineering. *Science, Technology, & Human Values*, 31(3), 237–260.

Fingas, J. (2016, February 29). Google self-driving car crashes into a bus (update: statement). *Engadget*. www.engadget.com/2016/02/29/google-self-driving-car-accident.

Gomes, L. (2017, December 21). Silicon Valley-driven hype for self-driving cars. *New York Times*. www.nytimes.com/2016/07/10/opinion/sunday/silicon-valley-driven-hype-for-self-driving-cars.html.

Han, H. (2015). Virtue ethics, positive psychology, and a new model of science and engineering ethics education. *Science and Engineering Ethics*, 21(2), 441–460.

Harris, C. E. (2008). The good engineer: Giving virtue its due in engineering ethics. *Science and Engineering Ethics*, 14, 153. doi.org/10.1007/s11948-008-9068-3.

Hoke, Tara (2018). Practicing outside of competence leads to tragic consequences. www.asce.org/question-of-ethics-articles/mar-2018.

Hursthouse, R., & Pettigrove, G. (2018). Virtue ethics. In E. N. Zalta (Ed.), *The Stanford Encyclopedia of Philosophy* (Winter). https://plato.stanford.edu/archives/win2018/entries/ethics-virtue.

Kelly-Detwiler, P. (2012, November 28). BP Deepwater Horizon arraignments: A culture that 'forgot to be afraid.' *Forbes.* www.forbes.com/sites/peterdetwiler/2012/11/28/bp-deepwater-horizon-arraignments-a-culture-that-forgot-to-be-afraid.

Kraut, R. (2018). Aristotle's ethics. In E. N. Zalta (Ed.), *The Stanford Encyclopedia of Philosophy* (Summer). https://plato.stanford.edu/archives/sum2018/entries/aristotle-ethics.

Krulwich, R. (2014, September 4). Glenn Gould in rapture. *NPR.* www.npr.org/sections/krulwich/2014/09/04/345576795/glenn-gould-in-rapture.

Kuhn, S. (1998). When worlds collide: Engineering students encounter social aspects of production. *Science and Engineering Ethics,* 1, 457–472.

Marcuse, H. (1941). *Reason and Revolution: Preface.* www.marxists.org/reference/archive/marcuse/works/reason/preface.htm.

Marcuse, H. (1998). *Technology, War and Fascism* (D. Kellner, Ed.). Routledge.

Marcuse, H. (2013). *Reason and Revolution.* Routledge.

Martin, M. W. (2000). *Meaningful Work: Rethinking Professional Ethics.* Oxford University Press.

Plato. (2004). *Apology, Crito, and Phaedo of Socrates* (The Project Gutenberg EBook of Apology, Crito, and Phaedo of Socrates). www.gutenberg.org/files/13726/13726-h/13726-h.htm.

Schmidt, J. A. (2014). Changing the paradigm for engineering ethics. *Science and Engineering Ethics,* 20(4), 985–1010.

Thielman, S. (2016, July 13). Fatal crash prompts federal investigation of Tesla self-driving cars. *The Guardian.* www.theguardian.com/technology/2016/jul/13/tesla-autopilot-investigation-fatal-crash.

Van den Hoven, J., Lokhorst, G.-J., & van de Poel, I. (2012). Engineering and the problem of moral overload. *Science and Engineering Ethics,* 18(1), 143–155. doi.org/10.1007/s11948-011-9277-z.

Weil, V. (2001). Mentoring: Some ethical considerations. *Science and Engineering Ethics,* 7(4), 471–482.

Zachary, G. P. (2014, June 30). Where are today's engineering heroes? *IEEE Spectrum.* https://spectrum.ieee.org/geek-life/profiles/where-are-todays-engineering-heroes.

Chapter 3

Objectivity

"Issue statements only in an objective and truthful manner."

In this chapter, we will explore the meaning of objectivity, the ways in which engineers can achieve objective beliefs, and the connection between scientific objectivity and public trust.

Descartes, Objectivity, and Science

It is typical to think of scientific research as the very standard of objectivity. When we think of "facts" we almost always have in mind the products of scientific theorizing. And it is no accident that we regard science in this way. Other sources of belief—peers, religion, or government—seem more obviously **fallible** (subject to error). We are more skeptical of these institutions because it is easy to see how each could be driven by the agendas of the individuals who constitute them. Science, however, seems immune such bias. And in this way it seems to be **objective**.

Our faith in scientific practice is not unfounded. Science has proven to be extremely reliable in many respects. However, like any other type of human endeavor, science is an imperfect discipline. Human reasoning is subject to a whole host of errors. The vulnerability of human reasoning to error was a problem that obsessed seventeenth-century philosopher **René Descartes**.

Descartes is perhaps most famous for his work in the philosophical area of **epistemology**—the study of knowledge. Descartes was compelled to understand the very nature of knowledge itself and to develop a theory for how to differentiate between **justified beliefs**—beliefs held on the basis of good reasons—and mere opinions. And once we understand more about the context of Descartes' work, it's easy to see why this sort of project was compelling. In Descartes' time, it was widely believed that the sun revolved around the earth. This was the dominant position of the Roman Catholic Church. And the Roman Church was generally accepted as the fundamental authority on all things natural and supernatural. It was also a political force to be reckoned with. For instance, during Descartes' time **Galileo Galilei** was put on trial by the Church for publicly endorsing the heliocentric picture of the universe championed by **Nicolaus Copernicus**. The view that the sun, and not the earth, was the center of the universe posed a challenge to how many leaders interpreted Church Doctrine, and in doing so seemed to threaten the Roman Church's legitimacy and political power. It is no wonder, then, that the Roman Church was often unfriendly to scientific inquiry that conflicted with what many believed were doctrines found in Scripture and Tradition.

And one can hardly blame the common person for believing the pronouncements of the Roman Church over those of scientists. At that point in history, science had yet to establish a track record of success. Even the instruments scientists used to confirm their hypotheses were subject to suspicion. Consider one of Galileo's instruments of choice—the telescope. With the science of optics still in development, the telescope must have seemed like a darkly magical instrument to the common folk—one that made distant invisible objects suddenly appear. A central part of the scientific revolution was the shift in authority from observations made directly with the senses to those made using instruments. It's no wonder that people might have been hesitant to jump on the scientific bandwagon. Those who did may have seemed foolish or irresponsible.

It is at this point that we begin to understand Descartes' interest in objectivity. Although history remembers Descartes as the father of modern philosophy, he was also a mathematician and a scientist—and at a time when the very shape of the earth was up for debate. If we, including our most trusted authorities, could be mistaken about one of the most fundamental "truths" about our world, one might reasonably wonder what else we could be wrong about. It is in this intellectual background that Descartes began the project of tearing apart all of human knowledge and rebuilding it from the ground up.

The Method of Doubt

Descartes' method for establishing this foundation was to remove from it any belief that was subject to even the slightest possibility of error. This includes not only the possibility that we could be wrong about the shape of the world, but even that we could be wrong about the very existence of the world. Descartes' **Method of Doubt** may seem extreme. However, it becomes more reasonable when we remember that he had just come to accept that one of the most plainly true observations, that the earth was flat as it appeared to the naked eye, was false.

Descartes' method targeted even the most basic of beliefs: the existence of the external world, the existence of other people, the existence of our own bodies, even mathematical proofs. This skepticism stopped, Descartes thought, only when it hit upon the one thing he found utterly immune to doubt: his own existence as a thinking thing. For, if Descartes attempted to doubt that he existed as a thinking thing, he found that this proved his existence. After all, *something* must exist in order to doubt that it exists. As Descartes said, *cogito ergo sum*—"I think therefore I am." Or, more accurately, "I am thinking therefore I am existing." In the **cogito**, as it is called, Descartes believed he had found a belief that is absolutely certain and free from the possibility of error. And this would be solid enough to bear the weight of a completely objective worldview.

Fallacies and Objectivity

Descartes believed he could, using reason and the *cogito* alone, prove the existence of the external world and God. His arguments have been shown to be flawed. But here it is important to keep in mind that skepticism was not the final aim of Descartes' project. Descartes took for granted that objective knowledge was possible. His goal was to show us *how* it is possible. What examining Descartes' work does teaches us is that even our most dearly held beliefs can be wrong, and that this is something we should keep in mind when we make claims to knowledge. It teaches us that we ought to be on guard against errors in judgment—vigilant at all times in our intellectual pursuits.

Here we will consider one class of errors in reasoning that is particularly relevant to engineering—**fallacies of risk**. Such fallacies are errors about probability. For instance, humans are likely to overestimate the risk of an event if it is particularly emotionally salient. For example, far more people report having a fear of flying than a fear of driving even though, statistically, flying is much less dangerous than driving. The thought of plummeting to one's death in a fiery plane crash is especially terrifying and can lead a person to magnify the likelihood of it happening. People also systematically underestimate risk. For example, even though it has been proven that smoking causes lung cancer, many smokers believe that they are the exception to the rule.

Fallacies of risk are especially prevalent in automotive engineering, where the public perception of risk can be at odds with engineering data. Consider the Toyota safety crisis of 2009 and 2010. Consumers believed that "sticky" accelerator pedals were the cause of several fatal accidents. Drivers concluded that Toyota vehicles were prone to uncontrollable acceleration and crashes. However, Toyota engineers investigated the issue and found that sticky pedals made no difference in the time required to stop a car; the brakes were sufficiently powerful to override a sticky accelerator. Federal regulators, who investigated the fatal accidents, further found that the continued acceleration of Toyota vehicles was caused by nonstandard floor mats or driver error; drivers pressed the accelerator thinking it was the brake pedal. This illustrates the fallacies of risk; public misperceptions resulted in deaths that were preventable. It also illustrates the responsibility of engineers to communicate effectively with the public. In his article "Fallacies of Risk" (included in this chapter) Sven Ove Hansson identifies ten important fallacies of risk that are essential for engineers to guard against in their own reasoning and to be aware of when issuing public statements.

Social Engineering

Social engineering makes use of the vulnerability in human reasoning to achieve a variety of ends. It is easy to see cases in which social engineering could be used for morally questionable purposes. The internet, for instance, provides fertile ground for social engineering. In a highly controversial experiment conducted in 2012, Facebook altered the news feeds of users to determine whether "positive" or "negative" content affects the emotional state of the user. The news feeds of close to 700,000 Facebook users were altered, without the knowledge or consent of these users. When positive content was reduced in the news feed, the user's own posts became less positive. When negative content was reduced, the user's own posts became more positive. The authors noted that the experiment provided "the first experimental evidence for massive-scale emotional contagion via social networks" (Kramer et al., 2014, p. 8789). This is problematic. First, the experiment intentionally altered the social community to affect users' moods without notifying the users; such an experiment could be dangerous for users with mental health issues. Second, the results of the experiment could be used in harmful ways; one could easily imagine a situation in which a nefarious actor alters the emotional states of users to introduce harm, induce humans to behave in certain ways, or achieve a political outcome.

Objectivity is essential for the continuation of the scientific enterprise. Clinical trials depend on the voluntary participation of subjects. If individuals do not trust the integrity of the scientific process, they will be unlikely to participate. Furthermore, those who oppose climate change research have been able to cast doubt on the research by implying that the studies are not objective; allegations of bias can destroy an entire scientific or engineering field. Finally, public funding depends on public trust. If citizens have no confidence in the results of science and engineering, they are unlikely to support government funding for these efforts. When lack of objectivity compromises public trust, this threatens the survival of the scientific and engineering professions.

Engineering and Scientific Objectivity

While the goal of the scientist is to find truth, the goal of the engineer is to create and invent. Engineers are less concerned with absolute truths, and more concerned with usefulness and applicability. Engineers are concerned about both internal validity and external validity. A scientific study has internal validity when it has been conducted without systematic bias and the results of the study have been appropriately analyzed and accurately reported. A scientific study has external validity when the results of that study can be generalized more broadly to a real-world situation.

With respect to external validity in biomedical engineering, studies of pharmaceuticals and medical devices have historically excluded women of childbearing age, so the results of these studies have limited applicability to women. Likewise, scientific studies of drugs and devices that are conducted in adults have limited generalizability to children. An analogous situation occurs in civil engineering: a bridge or building tested under ideal weather and use conditions may not hold up under extreme weather or overuse, as demonstrated by the levees breaking during Hurricane Katrina in 2005. With respect to internal validity, engineering has been plagued by biased scientific studies that lack objectivity. The orthopedic spinal fusion device Infuse™ is a prime example. The device, manufactured by Medtronic, was studied by orthopedic surgeons with financial ties to the company. The studies overstated Infuse's benefits and understated the device's risks.

Scientific Integrity

In "The Integrity of Science: What It Means, Why It Matters" (included in this chapter), Susan Haack argues that integrity is relative to the institution one is a part of. If we want to assess the integrity of a politician, we might, for instance, examine their financial dealings. Suppose a politician takes a bribe and, as a result, passes legislation that benefits the source of his bribe. Such a person would fail to have integrity. He might otherwise be a very nice person. But, as a politician he lacks integrity. We might harshly judge a band that once produced beautiful music but now, in order to make money, produces bland music. The members of the band may all be very moral people. Nevertheless, as musicians they lack integrity.

What about engineers? They are part of the institution of science. To assess an engineer, then, we must measure their behavior against the goals and standards of the scientific enterprise. Such goals will include what it takes for the promotion of investigation and dissemination of the truth. We will go into that shortly. But first note that, as in the examples discussed above, an engineer could be criticized on moral grounds for his work but still possess great integrity as an engineer. For example, an engineer that worked on a torture device she knew would be used to harm innocents might conduct her work with the upmost scientific integrity. Yet she would be a despicable person. On the other hand, an engineer could be a moral exemplar in many respects but completely lack integrity as an engineer. Such an engineer might be kind to the office administrator. He might refuse to work on morally objectionable projects. But he might also falsify data or steal ideas from colleagues.

Lack of Integrity in Science and Engineering

In 1999 the US Food and Drug Administration (FDA) approved **Vioxx**. This drug was supposed to have the benefits of traditional pain management drugs without any of the problems. Traditional drugs caused some people to have bleeding ulcers. Studies in the *New England Journal of Medicine* (*NEJM*) claimed to show that Vioxx did not have the relevant problem. As a result, it became very popular. But eventually it was taken off the market. The company behind Vioxx (Merck) was subject to numerous lawsuits. Three subjects of one of Merck's studies died from cardiovascular disease. But the published version of the study omitted these deaths. It turned out that Merck gave the role of first author to an academic scientist who merely did some editing and who was unaware of the deaths. It also turned out that *NEJM*, which had been made aware of problems with Vioxx, only expressed concern about the drug after a public relations specialist advised *NEJM* that Vioxx was going to be exposed and the journal needed to push blame onto Merck and the individual scientists conducting the studies.

This example illustrates Susan Haack's account of **scientific integrity**. In her view, the values of the scientific enterprise center on what it takes to find things out. A purpose of the scientific enterprise is to learn what explains natural and social phenomena. For engineers, that purpose includes how to apply what we know about such phenomena to build helpful things for society. Respect for evidence in the form of honesty and sharing are primary goals of the scientific enterprise, and essential to the integrity of engineers.

What went wrong in the Vioxx case? Contemporary science is expensive. Interesting studies that can be conducted cheaply have already been conducted. Financial support from the government and from industry are now required. However, the aims of these sponsors of scientific work often conflict with the aims of honesty and sharing and general respect for evidence. So there is a temptation for scientists and scientific institutions to give too much weight to the goals of their sponsors and too little weight to the goal of finding things out; and, in the case of engineers, finding things out and applying them in ways that help people.

De Winter and Kosolosky suggest three strategies for pre-empting the temptations to abandon integrity that stem from economic pressure. First, remove some of the pressure to achieve cost-effectiveness. Second, insofar as one funds such agencies on the basis of results and cost-effectiveness, ensure that all relevant data is evaluated independently by independent engineers with no pressure to get particular results. And do not rely solely on contractors with an interest in getting results so that they can get future contracts. Third, define cost-effectiveness partly in terms of safety and not entirely in terms of output.

Academic Pressure

Another obstacle to scientific integrity is that there is enormous pressure on individual scientists to publish and get grants and be deemed by their college or university as productive. Pharmaceutical companies, as in the example above, will often offer an academic scientist the role of first author merely for editing a paper produced by the companies themselves. This looks great for the academic and great for the company. But it shows that the scientist lacks integrity. This pressure to publish and to get grants sometimes leads to supplanting the aims of science in favor of the aims of government or industry. But it can also lead an individual scientist to falsify data, as in the case below.

Marc Hauser was an evolutionary biologist at Harvard University from 1998 until 2011. He studied primates and human infants. One goal of his research was to show that monkeys have cognitive abilities, such as the ability to recognize oneself in a mirror, thought to only be present in humans and a handful of apes. Among other things, Hauser was famous for having conducted experiments demonstrating that cotton-top tamarins could recognize themselves in mirrors. However, his data was later deemed to be fabricated. All of this started to unravel after a suspicious graduate student and research assistant decided to look at recordings of Hauser's experiments without notifying him. They noticed that the tapes were inconsistent with what Hauser reported. This led to a long investigation which resulted in the judgment that Hauser had fabricated data. By all accounts Hauser was an incredibly nice person. He was beloved by his colleagues and students. But, whatever his virtues might have been, he displayed a lack of scientific integrity by violating norms of honesty and evidence sharing. He failed to respect evidence.

The Hauser example also illustrates Haack's account of scientific integrity. By all accounts Hauser was an incredibly nice, friendly person. But he outright fabricated data. He failed to be honest with others, and perhaps even to himself, about what data existed and what the data supported. Under enormous pressure to produce interesting results, Hauser displayed a lack of integrity. At the same time, his grad student and research assistant chose to expose the fabrication—and even to take the first steps to scrutinize Hauser's work to make sure the data said what he claimed it said. For this reason, it is essential to public trust that engineers, along with the wider scientific community, work to maintain an atmosphere of accountability. This includes submitting their own work and the work of their colleagues to the most rigorous standards of verification. Furthermore, it involves rejecting work that falls short of those standards, just as Hauser's assistants did.

The Obligation to Explain Well

As we have seen, a central part of the practice of science is explanation giving. And so norms concerning truth and concerning evidence sharing must be observed if a scientist is to possess integrity. As Brindell (2000) points out, however, explanation giving often occurs in the context of differences in power. The person or group seeking an explanation renders itself vulnerable to the person or group providing the explanation. Often the vulnerable party won't be in a position to assess the quality of the explanation provided in a way that is independent of the one who provided the explanation. Think about your professional life as an engineer. Clients, the public, and members of your engineering team will all rely on you for explanations. They will need to trust you to not just give them the truth but to **explain well**.

But what does it take to explain well? How is it different than just giving the truth? These questions will be addressed in Chapter 5. But what concerns us in the present chapter is that good explanations need to be **relevant**. Brindell holds that there are three requirements that must be met in order for a speaker to give a relevant answer to an inquirer. First, the speaker must understand and cooperate with the inquirer's goals. A student's goal might be to learn the consensus of one's field. A journalist's goal might be to learn the quirky intricacies of a particular scientist's unique perspective. A scientist teaching a student would give a poor explanation if she only told the student about her particular views. But that very same scientist would be giving an excellent explanation if she were to share her take on some particularly controversial topic with a journalist. So part of being objective and having integrity requires correctly identifying and cooperating with the goals of one's audience.

Second, the speaker must be reflective about the content of and the support for her beliefs. An engineer working for a client might think a project is likely to succeed. But he might also recognize that there is a legitimate possibility that it won't. Such an engineer must be aware of such possibilities. And he must communicate them to his clients.

Third, the speaker must avoid co-opting the interests of the inquirer. The speaker might have a certain agenda or goal. She might have an axe to grind. It will be easy for the speaker to give her explanation in such a way that the vulnerable inquirer is sold the speaker's agenda without the inquirer being made aware of exactly what is going on. An engineer, for example, might wish to proceed with a project in a certain way because it will net her more money. The inquirer, on the other hand, just wants to know about the best way to get the project done. By explaining things in a way that might lead the inquirer to accept the speaker's favored project, she is in danger of surreptitiously co-opting the client's agenda.

Conclusion

Among the many dimensions of objectivity and truthfulness, three stand out from our discussion in this chapter. First, the public uses and interprets language about risk in ways that are different than the expert engineer. And both the public and experts are prone to a series of fallacies regarding thinking about risk. Second, experts, like everyone else, can be tempted to stray from the ideals of their discipline. Legitimate science journals and legitimate researches can tinker with data, ignore problems, or fail to show due diligence in investigated things they sign off on because funding is at stake. Third, whether an expert answers the question of an inquirer well depends on the interests and background of the inquirer. The expert should offer relevant information. And the expert has tremendous power to manipulate the inquirer based on the way the expert answers. Being an objective and honest engineer requires being mindful of these issues.

Chapter 3 Key Terms and Concepts

Fallible
Objective
René Descartes
Epistemology
Justified Beliefs
Galileo Galilei
Nicolaus Copernicus
Method of Doubt

Cogito
Fallacies of Risk
Social Engineering
Vioxx
Scientific Integrity
Marc Hauser
Explaining Well
Relevant Explanations

Chapter 3: End of Chapter Reading and NSPE Board of Ethical Review Cases

Guided Core Reading   119

Core Reading 3.1: 'Fallacies of risk' by Sven Ove Hansson (excerpts)
Core Reading 3.2: 'The integrity of science: What it means, why it matters' by Susan Haack (excerpts)

NSPE Board of Ethical Review Cases   129

Case 65-1: Endorsement of Competitive Products or Service (1965)
Case 85-5: Engineer's Duty to Report Data Relating to Research (1985)
Case 60-9: Gifts (1960)

Guided Further Reading   134

Further Reading 3.1: 'The epistemic integrity of scientific research' by Jan De Winter and Laszlo Kosolosky
Further Reading 3.2: 'Trustworthiness in explanation: The obligation to explain well' by Sheralee Brindell
Further Reading 3.3: 'Epistemic trust and the ethics of science communication: Against transparency, openness, sincerity and honesty' by Stephen John

Tip: If you can't use the QR codes, use the hyperlinks found on the book's webpage instead: www.routledge.com/9781138183865.

Guided Core Reading

Core Reading 3.1: 'Fallacies of risk' by Sven Ove Hansson (excerpts)

Preparing to Read

Hansson discusses ten fallacies of risk—errors in reasoning scientists and the public make. These are fallacies about reasoning about whether to take action on a risk. Hansson gives examples to illustrate why these are fallacies and where they occur in scientific and public discussion.

Excerpted from: Hansson, S. O. (2004). Fallacies of risk. *Journal of Risk Research*, 7(3), 353-360. doi.org/10.1080/1366987042000176262. © Taylor & Francis 2010. Internal references omitted.

1. The sheer size fallacy

X is accepted.
　　Y IS A SMALLER RISK THAN X.
　　Y should be accepted.

The problem with these arguments is, of course, that we do not have a choice between the defended technology and the atmospheric phenomena referred to. Comparisons between risks can only be directly decision-guiding if they refer to objects that are alternatives in one and the same decision. When deciding whether or not to accept a certain pesticide, we need to compare it to other pesticides (or non-pesticide solutions) that can replace it....

[T]he sheer size fallacy involves the treatment of risks as "free-floating" objects, dissected out of their social context – in this case, out of the context of associated benefits. Strictly speaking, it is on most occasions wrong to speak of acceptance of a risk *per se*. Instead, the accepted object is a package or social alternative that contains the risk, its associated benefits, and possibly other factors that may influence a decision.

2. The converse sheer size fallacy

X is not accepted.
　　Y IS A LARGER RISK THAN X.
　　Y should not be accepted.

This line of argument may be described as the converse of the sheer size fallacy, and it is equally fallacious. For an example, consider two pesticides X and Y, such that X can easily be replaced by some less harmful alternative, whereas Y can at present be dispensed with only at high economic costs. It may then be reasonable to accept Y but not X, even if Y gives rise to more serious risks to health and the environment....

...

3. The fallacy of naturalness

X is natural.

X should be accepted.

...

The terms "natural" and "unnatural", as used in this and many other contexts, have a strong normative component. By saying that a child's behaviour is natural you call for acceptance or at least tolerance. By saying that it is unnatural you condemn it. More generally, we tend to call those, and only those, fruits of human civilization unnatural that we dislike. What is commonly accepted is not considered unnatural....

...

It is often more correct to say that we call something natural because we accept it than to say that we accept it because it is natural.... [A] discussant who is not already convinced that a risk is acceptable cannot either be expected to regard it as natural....

...

4. The ostrich's fallacy

X does not give rise to any detectable risk.

X does not give rise to any unacceptable risk.

The standpoint that indetectable effects are no matter of concern is a common implicit assumption in both scientific and more popular discussions of risk. On occasions we also find it stated explicitly. An unusually clear example is a statement by a former chairman of the American Conference of Governmental Industrial Hygienists (ACGIH), a private standard-setting body with a strong influence on occupational exposure limits throughout the world. He conceded that the organization's exposure limits "can never be used to guarantee absolute safety", but found it sufficient that "they can be used to control adverse health effects of all types below the point at which they cannot be distinguished from their background occurrence"....

...

5. The proof-seeking fallacy

<u>There is no scientific proof that X is dangerous.</u>
   No action should be taken against X.
   Science has fairly strict standards of proof....

. . .

In many risk-related issues, standards and burdens of proof have to be different from those used for intrascientific purposes. Consider a case when there are fairly strong indications that a chemical substance may be highly toxic, although the evidence is not (yet) sufficient from a scientific point of view. It would not be wise to continue unprotected exposure to the substance until full scientific proof has been obtained. According to the precautionary principle, we must be prepared to take action in the absence of full scientific proof....

. . .

6. The delay fallacy

<u>If we wait we will know more about X.</u>
   No decision about X should be made now.
   In many if not most decisions about risk we lack some of the information that we would like to have. A common reaction to this predicament is to postpone the decision. It does not take much reflection to realize the problematic nature of this reaction. In the period when nothing is done, the problem may get worse. Therefore, it may very well be better to make an early decision on fairly incomplete information than to make a more well-informed decision at a later stage....

. . .

7. The technocratic fallacy

<u>It is a scientific issue how dangerous X is.</u>
   Scientists should decide whether or not X is acceptable.
   It should be a trivial insight, but it needs to be repeated again and again: Competence to determine the nature and the magnitude of risks is not competence in deciding whether or not risks should be accepted. Decisions on risk must be based both on scientific information and on value judgments that cannot be derived from science....
   A clear case is that of the official German committee for occupational exposure limits. In statements by that committee, it is claimed that its exposure limits are based exclusively on scientific information on health effects, and thus unaffected by economic, political, or technological considerations. In

spite of these declarations, the committee's decisions can be shown to have been influenced by techno-economical factors....

...

8. The consensus fallacy

We must ask the experts about X.

We must ask the experts for a consensus opinion about X.

...

The search for consensus has many virtues, but in advisory expert committees it has the unfortunate effect of underplaying uncertainties and hiding away alternative scenarios that may otherwise have come up as minority opinions. If there is uncertainty in the interpretation of scientific data, then this uncertainty can often be reflected in a useful way in minority opinions....

...

9. The fallacy of pricing

We have to weigh the risks of X against its benefits.

We must put a price on the risks of X.

There are many things that we cannot easily value in terms of money. I do not know which I prefer, $8000 or that my child gets a better mark in math. If I am actually placed in a situation when I can choose between the two, the circumstances will be crucial for my choice. (Is the offer an opportunity to bribe the teacher, or is it an efficient extra course that I only have to pay for if he achieves a better mark?) There is no general-purpose price that can meaningfully be assigned to my son's receiving the better grade, simply because my willingness to pay will depend on the circumstances....

...

10. The infallibility fallacy

Experts and the public do not have the same attitude to X.

The public is wrong about X.

....

Experts have been wrong on many occasions. A rational decision-maker will have to take into account the possibility that this may happen again. ... In fact, when the output of a risk analysis of a complex technology indicates a low level of risk, the possibility that this analysis was wrong may very well be a dominant part of the legitimate concerns that a rational decision-maker can and should have with respect to the technology in question.

When there is a wide divergence between the views of experts and those of the public, this is certainly a sign of failure in the social system for division of intellectual labour. However, it does not necessarily follow that this failure is located within the minds of the non-experts who distrust the experts. It cannot be a criterion of rationality that one takes experts for infallible.

Avoiding the fallacies

Discussions on risk are much influenced by their political context. Proponents of technologies that are associated with risks tend to use a rhethoric [sic] of rationality; they maintain that the acceptance of certain risks is required by rationality. Their adversaries are prone to employ a rhethoric [sic] of morality, claiming that it is morally reprehensible to make use of these same technologies. In such a polarized situation it is no surprise to find arguments being used that are less impressive from an inferential than a rhethorical [sic] point of view.

Arguably, this is how it has to be. A fallacy-free public discussion in a contested social issue is probably an idle dream. Therefore, the task of exposing fallacious reasoning is much like garbage collecting: Neither task can ever be completed, since new material to be treated arrives all the time. However, in neither case does the perpetuity of the task make it less urgent. In order to improve the intellectual quality of public discussions on risks it is essential that more academics take part in these discussions, acting as independent intellectuals whose mission is not to advocate a standpoint but to promote science and sound reasoning.

Guided Reading Questions

1. What are the sheer size and converse sheer size fallacies? Highlight why Hansson thinks these are fallacies?
2. What is the fallacy of naturalness? What are the different ways to understand "natural"? How is each way problematic?
3. What is the proof-seeking fallacy? How, according to Hansson, is the burden of proof different in scientific and risk-related contexts? How does this difference serve to explain the proof-seeking fallacy?
4. What is the delay fallacy? How does the fact that problems may get worse without action and scientific uncertainty is sometimes recalcitrant illustrate that this is a fallacy?
5. What is the technocratic fallacy? How do statements by the German committee for occupational exposure limits illustrate this fallacy?

Read the Full Article (optional)

You can read the full article online by scanning the QR code or following the link below. Your college library will need to subscribe to the journal, and you may need to login via your library's website or use campus wifi to get access.

www.tandfonline.com/doi/abs/10.1080/1366987042000176262

Core Reading 3.2: 'The integrity of science: What it means, why it matters' by Susan Haack (excerpts)

Preparing to Read

In this reading, Haack presents an account of the nature of integrity. She then focuses on scientific integrity. For her, integrity for the institution of science is connected to norms of evidence sharing and respect for evidence. Haack then highlights some ways in which scientific integrity may be compromised. She illustrates this with examples about problematic practices and links between medical journals and pharmaceutical companies.

Excerpted from: Haack, S. (2007). The integrity of science: What it means, why it matters. *Contrastes: Revista International de Filosofía*, 12, 5–26. Available at SSRN: https://ssrn.com/abstract=1105831. © 2006 Susan Haack, reprinted with permission of the publisher. Internal notes and references omitted; punctuation slightly amended.

2. The Integrity of Science: Core Values

...

The core epistemological values of science are rooted in the central, defining concern of inquiry generally: finding things out. A scientific inquirer starts with a question about what might explain this or that natural or social phenomenon; makes an informed guess; and assesses how well his conjecture stands up to whatever evidence is already available, or can be obtained: i.e., how firmly it is anchored in experimental results and experiential evidence generally; how well it interlocks with the whole explanatory mesh of the body of thus-far well-warranted claims and theories; whether relevant evidence might have been overlooked; and what else could be done to get hold of evidence not presently available. So a scientist needs to take into account not only whatever evidence he can discover for himself, but also whatever evidence others have that may be relevant to the question(s) at issue; and to keep track not only of how well each new conjecture would explain the phenomenon in question, but also of how well it fits in with already well-established claims and theories in the field....

...

However, potentially highly profitable scientific work is in some ways especially vulnerable; and some of the most important threats to the integrity of science do come from the intrusion of the competing values of the larger society in which scientific work takes place. Some social and cultural environments are hospitable to good, honest scientific work; others are in varying degrees inhospitable, or even hostile. And while good, honest scientific work may continue even in a surrounding culture which is less than perfectly hospitable, to the extent that the surrounding culture tends to undermine the norms of evidence-sharing and respect for evidence, or seriously to erode or compromise them, the integrity of science comes under threat....

...

4. Erosion of Integrity in Biomedical Research

...

Mechanisms for evidence-sharing that once worked, if not perfectly, well enough, are falling into disrepair as the burdens placed on them has grown. One factor is the increased pressure on scientists to publish.... Another factor contributing to the erosion both of sharing and of honesty is the role of industrial sponsors, especially the pharmaceutical companies.... Many medical journals publish symposia organized by pharmaceutical companies, a privilege for which they often charge significant fees; some suspend the peer-review process for such publications…. Moreover, the evidence is that company sponsorship has a significant effect on the results reported….

5. Trials and Tribulations: Troubling Tales of Vioxx and Celebrex

…

For more than forty years, conventional NSAIDS were used for the control of chronic pain; but these drugs carry increased risk of bleeding ulcers in susceptible patients. So it seemed a big advance when new NSAIDS were developed…. These included Vioxx [rofecoxib] and Celebrex [celecoxib], approved for sale by the U.S. Food and Drug Administration in 1999….

Merck's first large clinical trial, the vigor study, showed that Vioxx carried a lower risk of adverse gastro-intestinal effects than the rival drug naproxen (Aleve); as did the company's subsequent, smaller advantage study. The FDA approved Vioxx in less than a year, before the vigor trial was completed; after FDA approval a report of the vigor study was submitted to the NEJM, where it appeared in November 2000. This study indicated the gastro-intestinal benefits; but it also suggested a significantly higher rate of myocardial infarction, among patients given one or the other drug for more than 18 months, in those taking Vioxx than in those taking naproxen….

…

In April 2005 the *New York Times* reported that the published account of the ADVANTAGE trial had omitted three cardiac deaths among the patients given Vioxx. The purported lead author explained that Merck scientists had designed, paid for, and run the study, and written the report; his role was only to give editorial help after the paper was written, and he hadn't known about the additional deaths….

…

But there is more to the story. We now know that in June 2001 the editors of the NEJM had received a letter from pharmacist Jennifer Hrachovec asking that the article be corrected in light of the information on the FDA website, but had declined to publish it on the grounds that "the journal can't be in the business of policing every bit of data we put out…." What changed the minds of the editors of the NEJM and prompted them to post that "expression of concern"—four and a half years after they were made aware of the problem—was an urgent e-mail from public-relations specialist Edward Cafasso…. We also now know that the NEJM—which listed $88 million in total publishing revenue for the year ending May 31st, 2005—had sold 929,000 offprints of the article, most of them to Merck, for revenue estimated to be between $679,000 and $836,000.

6. And Why the Erosion of Integrity Matters

In the words of H. L. Mencken, "there is always a well-known solution to every human problem—neat, plausible, and wrong." Even if I had one, a neat, plausible solution to the thicket of problems explored here surely would be wrong. But anyway, having no such solution to offer, I will end instead by trying to articulate briefly why, as my subtitle says, the integrity of science matters, why the creeping corruption I have described should concern us.

For some people, the commitment to finding out—the "scientific attitude," as C. S. Peirce called it, "the Will to Learn"—is both firm and deep; as Percy Bridgman puts it, some feel the emotional pull of the ideal of intellectual honesty almost as the religious man feels the call to serve Something much more significant than himself. But for many people intellectual honesty flourishes only with the right kind of encouragement and incentives, and with good example; in an inhospitable environment it wilts and withers.

...

The erosion of commitment to these norms matters, first, because it is apt to impede the progress of science; as a result of which we don't know things we could have known by now, and we lose out on the benefits that knowledge would have provided had we had it. Once again, the saga of Vioxx and Celebrex makes the point vivid. Between 1999 (when Vioxx was approved by the FDA) and 2004 (when it was taken off the market) it is estimated that there were between 88,000 and 140,000 excess cases of serious coronary heart disease in the U.S. In late 2004 we learned that Celebrex may protect against colon cancer; and in late 2005 the Cleveland Clinic announced that it will direct a world-wide clinical trial of around 20,000 patients to assess the relative safety of ibuprofen, naproxen, and celecoxib. Think about it: if sponsors' interests hadn't got in the way, mightn't we have known much more, years ago, about which patients which NSAIDs could most benefit, and which patients which NSAIDs were likely to do more harm than good?

Second, and almost as obviously, the erosion of the integrity of science matters because when the public reads, day after day, week after week, one story after another of scientific dishonesty and corruption—Dr. Hwang Woo Suk's fraudulent work on stem-cell cloning; that laughable Columbia "Prayer Study"; the amateurishly fabricated data in Jon Sudbø's oral-cancer study—its confidence in the sciences will inevitably be damaged. Indeed, public trust in science may well be damaged more than the erosion of integrity, thus far, really warrants; especially when, as now, the press takes a particularly keen interest in stories of scientific fraud and misconduct. As a result, the public is likely to become more reluctant to support government funding of an institution they come to perceive as corrupt and untrustworthy; and again we lose out on knowledge we might otherwise have had, and on the benefits such knowledge might have brought.

And third, less obviously but perhaps most consequentially, the erosion of the integrity of science matters because it feeds the anti-intellectualism, the cynicism about the very possibility of discovering how things are, even about the very idea of truth, that lies not far beneath the surface even of supposedly "civilized" societies. Our capacity to figure things out is one of the best talents human beings have: we aren't especially fast; we aren't especially strong; but if we really want to, if we are willing to work and think hard, if we have enough patience, enough persistence, if we are ready to fail and try again, perhaps over and over, we can find out something of how the world is. But this is hard work, often painful and frustrating; and there is another, less admirable, side of human nature, a side that really doesn't want to go to all the trouble of finding out, that prefers to believe things are as we would like them to be, and that loves the mysterious and the impressively incomprehensible....

Guided Reading Questions

1. What is scientific integrity? How can such integrity be eroded?
2. What are the Vioxx and Celebrex scandals?
3. What problems with scientific journal practices and the pharmaceutical industry do the Vioxx and Celebrex scandals reveal?
4. Why does Haack think these problems about scientific integrity matter?

Read the Full Article (optional)

You can read the full article online by scanning the QR code or following the link below. *No subscription is required*, although you do need to register for a free SSRN account.

https://ssrn.com/abstract=1105831

NSPE Board of Ethical Review Cases

Case 65-1: Endorsement of Competitive Products or Service

Endorsement of Competitive Products or Service

Case 65-1
Year: 1965
Facts:

Two full-page advertisements of manufacturers and one of an association of companies which sell energy services contain the names of engineers in private practice, their pictures (in two examples) and pictures of the projects designed by the engineers (in two examples). The advertisements all deal generally with the virtues of the products or services advertised and associate the engineers' favorable experience with the products or services.

Example 1 quotes the named engineer as having used the particular type of energy source to the benefit of his clients. The advertisement is carried under the name of an association of companies which provide the particular type of energy source involved. It does not mention competitive energy sources.

Example 2 is an advertisement of a manufacturing company, featuring pictures of a consulting engineer (in four poses) and quotes the engineer in terms of the advantages to a client in retaining a consulting engineer for his engineering requirements. The statements of the engineer do not refer to the, [*sic*] products of the advertiser, but refer generally to the type of environment in which such products would be used. The statements of the manufacturer in the same advertisement recommend talking to a consulting engineer early in the planning stages of a project and emphasize that it will be to the client's advantage to utilize the specialized knowledge, experience, and independent judgment of a consulting engineer. It then states that the manufacturer has led in the design and development of the finest products related to the indicated equipment requirements for buildings.

Example 3 is an advertisement of a manufacturer stating that a named consulting engineering firm has used its products successfully in connection with a particular project to solve difficult engineering problems. The balance of the text states the various advantages and quality of the particular product. The advertisement contains four pictures illustrating use of the product.

Question from the NSPE:

Is it ethical for an engineer to authorize the use of his name in such commercial advertisements?

Going Beyond—Our Questions for a Deep Dive

1. How, if at all, could the involvement of engineers in advertising campaigns compromise their professional objectivity?
2. How, if at all, could the association of engineers with particular products or specific companies lead to the erosion of public trust in the objectivity of the engineering profession?
3. Do these three examples vary with regard to any of the relevant moral details? For instance, does the level of involvement of the engineers with the advertisements make a difference to whether the example is ethically permissible? Does that content of the advertisers' claims make a difference?
4. Assume the engineers involved in the advertisements were not paid for their involvement. Could their involvement potentially still compromise either their objectivity or the public's opinion of their objectivity?

Read the Board's Discussion and Conclusion

To read the discussion and conclusion of this case by members of the NSPE Board of Ethical Review, go to: www.nspe.org/resources/ethics/ethics-resources/board-ethical-review-cases/endorsement-competitive-products-or.

Case 85-5: Engineer's Duty to Report Data Relating to Research

Engineer's Duty to Report Data Relating to Research

Case 85-5
Year: 1985
Facts:

Engineer A is performing graduate research at a major university. As part of the requirement for Engineer A to complete his graduate research and obtain his advanced degree, Engineer A is required to develop a research report. In line with developing the report, Engineer A compiles a vast amount of data pertaining to the subject of his report. The vast majority of the data strongly supports Engineer A's conclusion as well as prior conclusions developed by others. However, a few aspects of the data are at variance and not fully consistent with the conclusions contained in Engineer A's report. Convinced of the soundness of his report and concerned that inclusion of the ambiguous data will detract from and distort the essential thrust of the report, Engineer A decides to omit references to the ambiguous data in the report.

Question from the NSPE:
Was it unethical for Engineer A to fail to include reference to the unsubstantiative data in his report?

Going Beyond—Our Questions for a Deep Dive

1. Compare Engineer A's case to that of Mark Hauser's discussed earlier in this chapter. In Hauser's case, the extent of his data fabrication and the notoriety of his research contributed to the damage to the public's perception of scientific objectify. Assuming Engineer A's research does not receive the kind of attention that Hauser's does, and that the inconstancies in the data were truly "relatively minor," is Engineer A's situation morally different than Hauser's?

2. Assume Engineer A is correct in thinking that including the entirety of the data would lead readers to distort the essential thrust of his report. Does that justify any potential loss of public trust in scientific/academic objectivity?

3. Imagine Engineer A has reason to think that it would be potentially dangerous for readers to "misinterpret" his report when presented with the full data set. Would this justify him excluding the inconsistent data from the report? How does this question relate to the issue of paternalism discussed in Chapter 1?

4. To what extent, if at all, does Engineer A have the moral authority to influence the conclusions that readers draw from his report?
5. In general, does the public have the right to be presented with all of the data relevant to an academic study, even in cases where the public may not have the expertise required to "properly" interpret those data?

Read the Board's Discussion and Conclusion

To read the discussion and conclusion of this case by members of the NSPE Board of Ethical Review, go to: www.nspe.org/resources/ethics/ethics-resources/board-ethical-review-cases/engineers-duty-report-data-relating.

Case 60-9: Gifts

Gifts

Case 60-9
Year: 1960
Facts:

The following situations are consolidated into one case because they involve the same ethical principles:

Situation "A"-A consulting engineer who has done considerable work for a public body makes it a practice to take certain staff engineering employees of the agency to lunch or dinner three or four times a year, at an average cost of $5 per person. He also makes it a practice to give certain members of the engineering staff Christmas presents at an average cost of $10 each.

Situation "B"-Certain engineering employees of an industrial firm, who are in a position to recommend for or against the purchase of products used by the company, regularly receive cash gifts ranging from $25 to $100 from salesmen for particular products.

Situation "C"-Upon completion of a major engineering contract held by a consulting engineer, the chief engineer of the client who worked directly and intimately with the consultant receives a new automobile of the value of approximately $4,000 from the consultant with a letter stating that the gift is in appreciation of his close and friendly cooperation and assistance in the successful performance of the work.

Questions from the NSPE:

1. Was it ethical for the engineers in the above instances to offer any of the gifts to the employees?
2. Was it ethical for the engineers in the above instances to accept any of the gifts tendered them?

Going Beyond—Our Questions for a Deep Dive

1. How might a gift from a third party, even a small one, potentially compromise an engineer's impartiality?
2. Even if an engineer's judgment was not compromised by receiving a gift, how might the appearance of compromise affect public trust in the objectivity of the profession?
3. In the medical profession, there has been much discussion of the potential ethical issues involved with the relationship between doctors and pharmaceutical companies. Can doctors remain medically "objective" regarding a particular drug if, for instance, they have received gifts from the manufacturers of that drug?
4. Are there any situations in engineering that are analogous to the pharmaceutical situation in medicine? If so, then what do you think has led to the development of this kind of situation in engineering (and what can be done about it)? If not, then why is engineering immune to a problem that medicine is not?

Read the Board's Discussion and Conclusion

To read the discussion and conclusion of this case by members of the NSPE Board of Ethical Review, go to: www.nspe.org/resources/ethics/ethics-resources/board-ethical-review-cases/gifts.

Guided Further Reading

Further Reading 3.1: 'The epistemic integrity of scientific research' by Jan De Winter and Laszlo Kosolosky

Find the Article

De Winter, J., & Kosolosky, L. (2013). The epistemic integrity of scientific research. *Science and Engineering Ethics*, 19, 757–774. doi.org/10.1007/s11948-012-9394-3.

Read the article online by scanning the QR code or following the link below. Your college library will need to subscribe to the journal, and you may need to login via your library's website or use campus wifi to get access.

https://link.springer.com/article/10.1007/s11948-012-9394-3

Preparing to Read

In this chapter, we have emphasized the moral importance of scientific integrity. We've discussed the dangers of engineers failing in their obligation towards scientific integrity—especially when it comes to scientific/engineering research. But what does "research integrity" really amount to? In this article, Jan De Winter and Laszlo Kosolosky offer an account of research integrity based on the work of twentieth-century philosopher Rudolf Carnap.

Guided Reading Questions

1. What is Carnap's characterization of explication? Do you think that it is a useful model for analyzing the concept of scientific integrity? What are some strengths of this approach? What are the weaknesses?
2. What is a deceptive statement according to De Winter and Kosolosky? How does whether a statement is deceptive depend on an audience's background assumptions? What are other examples of deceptive statements that fit this model?
3. How can the degree of a statement's deceptiveness change? How do the examples about Dr. Smith and climate change illustrate this? Can you think of any examples that are particularly relevant to engineering in which the degree of a statement's deceptiveness changes?
4. What does it mean for epistemic integrity to be "a property of practices resulting in certain statements"? How is this a difference between epistemic integrity and deceptiveness?
5. Why do De Winter and Kosolosky think their explication of epistemic integrity satisfies Carnap's four requirements for explication? Do you agree with them, or do you think they are mistaken?

Further Reading 3.2: 'Trustworthiness in explanation: The obligation to explain well' by Sheralee Brindell

Find the Article

Brindell, S. (2000). Trustworthiness in explanation: The obligation to explain well. *Science and Engineering Ethics*, 6, 351–364. doi.org/10.1007/s11948-000-0037-8.

Read the article online by scanning the QR code or following the link below. Your college library will need to subscribe to the journal, and you may need to login via your library's website or use campus wifi to get access.

https://link.springer.com/article/10.1007/s11948-000-0037-8

Preparing to Read

Because of the technical nature of scientific information, some individuals are in a better position than others to access that information. This means that scientific and technical experts have an "epistemic advantage"—an advantage with regard to knowledge—over non-experts (e.g., members of the general public). In order to lessen this disparity, it is not enough for experts to offer scientific explanations to non-experts that are true. The truth is hardly of use to someone who can't understand it. Instead, experts must offer explanations that are accessible and, arguably, relevant to non-experts. Sheralee Brindell understands scientific explanations as requests from epistemically disengaged agents. She argues that a good scientific explanation must be relevant as well as true. And that relevance is not formally defined but, instead, attached to the moral character of the explainer. She then draws lessons about the nature of scientific integrity, and shows that such integrity requires much more than merely refraining from the falsification of data or references.

Guided Reading Questions

1. What is epistemic vulnerability? What examples does Brindell give to illustrate this phenomenon? Think of some additional examples.

2. Brindell holds that when thinking about what a good explainer is, we should "approach the [topic] from the point of view of a sub-stantially 'disadvantaged' inquirer." What is a disadvantaged inquirer? Do you agree with Brindell or disagree? What reasons can be given for this approach? What reasons can be given against it?

3. Brindell points out that a disadvantaged inquirer needs to be able to trust that her interlocutor won't intentionally give a false or irrelevant answer. But she also argues that the inquirer must be able to trust that her interlocutor won't unintentionally do so. How could one unintentionally give a false or irrelevant answer? What examples does Brindell give? What examples can you come up with on your own?

4. What is the difference between trust and mere reliance? What are examples that illustrate the difference?

5. What is the relevance problem? How could thinking about things from the point of view of the disadvantaged inquirer help solve this problem in the context of engineering communication?

Further Reading 3.3: 'Epistemic trust and the ethics of science communication: Against transparency, openness, sincerity and honesty' by Stephen John

Find the Article

John, S. (2018). Epistemic trust and the ethics of science communication: Against transparency, openness, sincerity and honesty. *Social Epistemology*, 32(2), 75–87. doi.org/10.1080/02691728.2017.1410864.

Read the article online by scanning the QR code or following the link below. Your college library will need to subscribe to the journal, and you may need to login via your library's website or use campus wifi to get access.

www.tandfonline.com/doi/abs/10.1080/02691728.2017.1410864

Preparing to Read

In order to help fulfill their obligation to convey objective information to the public, technical experts are often encouraged to develop various "communicative virtues"—such as transparency, openness, sincerity, and honesty. However, Stephen John argues that, in practice, such "virtues" might do more epistemic and even political harm than good. In this article, John offers an alternative method for experts to fulfill their moral obligation to communicate information to non-experts.

Guided Reading Questions

1. What is John's model of how non-experts learn from scientific experts? Do you agree with this model? Do you think the model extends to communication in the context of engineering? What are some engineering-related examples that conform to the model? Are there any examples that the model has trouble handling?

2. John holds that, given his model, there is no significant difference between learning something about the world yourself and learning from the testimony of experts. Do you agree with this implication of the model? If so, why? If not, why not?

3. John identifies a number of cases that he thinks pose a problem for the idea that sincerity should be a virtue in scientific communication. Most of these cases are ones in which the science supports some conclusion but for various reasons the individual scientists or group of scientists doing the reporting cannot themselves believe the relevant data. Do you think John is right that these cases pose a problem for the notion that sincerity is a virtue? If so, why? If not, why not?

4. John uses the climategate email leaks to argue that openness and transparency are not virtues in scientific communication. One key dimension to John's argument is that what a member of the public may think is an appropriate means to reaching a scientific conclusion might depart from what the experts know is an appropriate means. So when members of the public see how scientists arrive at a conclusion, they might then disregard expert testimony when they otherwise would have accepted it. Do you agree with John

about this? How might this issue arise in the context of testimony from engineers?

5. A number of John's examples involve scientific communication about climate change. What are some examples from engineering that can be used to make similar points?

Bibliography

Berenson, A., Harris, G. & Meier, B. (2004, November 14). Despite warnings, drug giant took long path to Vioxx recall. *New York Times*. www.nytimes.com/2004/11/14/business/despite-warnings-drug-giant-took-long-path-to-vioxx-recall.html.

Brindell, S. (2000). Trustworthiness in explanation: The obligation to explain well. *Science and Engineering Ethics*, 6(3), 351–364.

De Winter, J., & Kosolosky, L. (2013). The epistemic integrity of scientific research. *Science and Engineering Ethics*, 19(3), 757–774.

Descartes, R. (1881). *The Method, Meditations, and Selections from the Principles of Descartes*, Vol. 5 (J. Veitch, Trans. and Ed.). Blackwood.

Evans, S., & MacKenzie, A. (2010, January 27). The Toyota recall crisis. *MotorTrend*. www.motortrend.com/news/toyota-recall-crisis.

Garber, D. (2001). Descartes and the scientific revolution: Some Kuhnian reflections. *Perspectives on Science*, 9(4), 405–422. doi.org/10.1162/106361401760375802.

Haack, S. (2007). The integrity of science: What it means, why it matters. *Contrastes: Revista Interdisciplinar de Filosofía*, 12, 5–26.

Hansson, S. O. (2004). Fallacies of risk. *Journal of Risk Research*, 7(3), 353–360. doi:10.1080/1366987042000176262.

Fauber, J. (2011, June 22). Senate launches investigation of Medtronic spine fusion device *ABC News*. https://abcnews.go.com/Health/medtronic-spine-fusion-device-subject-senate-investigation/story?id=13897739.

Jenkins, A. (2018, April 6). We're keeping track of all of Facebook's scandals so you don't have to. *Fortune*. http://fortune.com/2018/04/06/facebook-scandals-mark-zuckerberg.

John, S. (2018) Epistemic trust and the ethics of science communication: Against transparency, openness, sincerity and honesty. *Social Epistemology*, 32(2), 75–87.

Johnson, C. Y. (2012), September 5). Harvard professor who resigned fabricated, manipulated data, US says. *Boston Globe*. www.bostonglobe.com/news/science/2012/09/05/harvard-professor-who-resigned-fabricated-manipulated-data-says/6gDVkzPNxv1ZDkh4wVnKhO/story.html.

Kramer, A. D. I., Guillory, J. E., & Hancock, J. T. (2014). Experimental evidence of massive-scale emotional contagion through social networks. *Proceedings of the National Academy of Sciences*, 111(24), 8788–8790. doi:10.1073/pnas.1320040111.

Krumholz, H. M., Ross, J. S., Presler, A. H., & Egilman, D. S. (2007). What have we learnt from Vioxx? *BMJ*, 334(7585), 120–123. doi.org/10.1136/bmj.39024.487720.68.

Kumar, G. S., & Ryan, J. L. (2011, July 19). Embattled professor Marc Hauser will resign from Harvard. *Harvard Crimson*. www.thecrimson.com/article/2011/7/19/marc-hauser-resigns-psychology-harvard.

Liker, J. (2011, February 11). Toyota's recall crisis: What have we learned? *Harvard Business Review*. https://hbr.org/2011/02/toyotas-recall-crisis-full-of.

Macalister, T. (2010, January 28). Toyota fights for reputation as safety recall crisis widens. *Guardian*. www.theguardian.com/business/2010/jan/28/toyota-recall-widens-europe-china.

MassDevice Staff (2011, July 1). Medtronic Infuse controversy raises lingering ethical questions. *MedCityNews*.https://medcitynews.com/2011/07/medtronic-stocks-recover-amid-infuse-controversy.

Patel, A. H. (2013, September 27). Marc Hauser, former professor found guilty of academic misconduct, publishes first book since resignation. *Harvard Crimson*. www.thecrimson.com/article/2013/9/27/mark-hauser-publishes-book.

Prakash, S., & Valentine, V. (2007, November 10). Timeline: The rise and fall of Vioxx. *NPR*. www.npr.org/templates/story/story.php?storyId=5470430.

Resnik, D. (2011). Scientific research and the public trust. *Science and Engineering Ethics*, 17(3), 399–409.

Shapin, S. (1995). Trust, honesty, and the authority of science. In R. E. Bulger, E. M. Bobby, & H.V. Fineberg (Eds.), *Society's Choices: Social and Ethical Decision Making in Biomedicine* (pp. 388–408). National Academy Press.

Thompson, N., & Vogelstein, F. (2018, February 12). Inside Facebook's hellish two years—and Mark Zuckerberg's struggle to fix it all. *Wired*. www.wired.com/story/inside-facebook-mark-zuckerberg-2-years-of-hell.

Van de Poel, I. (2011). *Ethics, Technology, and Engineering: An Introduction*. Wiley-Blackwell.

Wilson, F. (n.d.). René Descartes: Scientific Method. *Internet Encyclopedia of Philosophy*. https://iep.utm.edu/desc-sci.

Chapter 4

Loyalty

"Act for each employer as faithful agents or trustees."

The fourth canon is contentious and widely discussed: "Act for each employer or client as faithful agents or trustees." Most discussions of this canon focus on legal cases. Our discussion, however, will focus on treatments of the morality of loyalty. We will find lessons about loyalty from the history of philosophy and contemporary debates in engineering concerning whistleblowing and professional faithfulness.

Fiduciary Obligations

Faithfulness or, as philosophers sometimes call it, "loyalty" is distinct from **fiduciary obligation**. These are the obligations we have because we receive a paycheck from an employer. Such commitments are much weaker than the sort of loyalty we are interested in. Consider the DuPont titanium dioxide espionage case. Disgruntled former DuPont employees Tim Spitler and Robert Maegerle sold trade secrets related to the production of titanium dioxide, including blueprints for chemical plants, to Chinese technology consultant Walter Liew. The theft of trade secrets took place from 1997 to 2011; at the time, titanium dioxide was a $2.6 billion business for DuPont.

Divided Loyalties in Engineering

Engineers bear simultaneous and sometimes divided loyalties to their employers, their country, their colleagues, the engineering profession, their families, their communities, and their principles. Situations of divided loyalty require engineers to make decisions that will compromise their loyalties to at least one of these constituents; such decisions can involve very high stakes. Decisions involving divided loyalty can also be deeply unpopular and can have serious consequences.

The case of computer engineer **Edward Snowden** illustrates the complexity and societal significance of divided loyalty in engineering. Snowden enlisted in the United States Army Reserves in 2004 because he believed he "had an obligation as a human being to help free people from oppression." He was discharged from the military after breaking both legs in a training accident, but continued his career as a public servant in the Central Intelligence Agency (CIA). By 2009, he became a sub-contractor for the National Security Agency (NSA) as an employee of computer company Dell, followed by consulting firm Booz Allen Hamilton. During this time, Snowden became aware that the United States government was conducting a top-secret global electronic spying program, including surveillance of its own citizens. Specifically, beginning in 2007, an NSA program called PRISM collected internet communications of US citizens from at least nine major US internet companies, including Microsoft, Yahoo, Google, Facebook, Skype, AOL, and Apple. Collected content included email, instant messages, photos, videos, and voice calls.

Snowden became deeply concerned about the impacts of massive government surveillance on the rights of citizens, and believed that the public had a right to know of the scope of these programs. In 2013 the 29-year-old Snowden leaked classified NSA documents to journalists at *The Guardian* and *The Washington Post*. The US Department of Justice charged Snowden with two counts of violating the 1917 Espionage Act, and theft of government property. He fled to Russia to seek asylum. Snowden has been called a hero, a patriot, a dissident, and a whistleblower. He has alternatively been called a criminal and a traitor.

Consider Snowden's **conflicting loyalties**. One loyalty was to his employers (Booz Allen Hamilton, Dell, and the NSA) and included a duty to act as a faithful employee. He also bore a loyalty to the laws of the nation in terms of protecting national security and classified information. He had loyalties to members of the US military with regard to safeguarding information on military operations. He additionally had loyalties to his friends and family in terms of protecting himself, his ability to earn a salary, and his ability to work and live in the US. Had Snowden given the above loyalties the greatest weight, he might have decided not to disclose the top-secret documents.

However, Snowden's loyalties to his employers, the laws of the nation, the US military, and even his friends and family were outweighed by his loyalty to the public good in terms of protecting citizens' privacy and civil liberties. Snowden passionately believed that the NSA surveillance activities represented an abuse of government power. He characterized the NSA spying programs as an "existential threat to democracy." Ultimately, Snowden decided that it was more important to guarantee privacy than to guarantee national security. He concluded that it was vital to expose potential government abuses, even if this exposure violated the laws of the country. He also decided that his duty to protect civil liberties was more important than his duty to his employers, and he was willing to sacrifice his employment, his relationships with friends and family, and his own personal freedom.

It is interesting to reflect on the loyalties of the many employees at NSA, Dell, Booz Allen Hamilton, Microsoft, Yahoo, Google, Facebook, Skype, AOL, and Apple who supported the PRISM program and other surveillance activities. These individuals may well have considered their beliefs in privacy and civil liberties, and they possibly experienced internal conflict over their work. However, they likely valued their loyalties to employers, friends, family, and national laws even more. Snowden's case shows that individuals who have similar divided loyalties, presented with the same information, may arrive at radically different conclusions. Even the same individual may arrive at different conclusions at various points in his engineering career, depending on perspective, experience, and context. In 2009, just four years before his own disclosure of classified information, Snowden himself publicly expressed outrage in the form of an online comment on a *New York Times* article, that anonymous sources had disclosed classified information on the White House's plans to sabotage Iran's main nuclear facility.

Though one can disagree with Snowden's decisions and actions, one must recognize his loyalty to the cause of civil liberties and human rights. But what about a case when an individual reflects deep loyalty to a cause that is not morally good? Two twentieth-century philosophers, Josiah Royce and Hannah Arendt, provide insight into the nature of **degenerate loyalty**, and therefore shed light on the potential moral hazard of upholding the fourth NSPE canon.

Predatory Loyalty

In *The Philosophy of Loyalty*, Josiah Royce defines loyalty as the willing, practical and thoroughgoing devotion to a cause. The cause is general enough that it unites many individuals in its service, and it gives the life of a devotee, to use the words of a reviewer of Royce's book, a certain "center, fixity and stability." Royce believes that we are in dire need of this fixity and moral centeredness. When he wrote the book, Royce attempted to make two simultaneous moral arguments. First, he wanted to argue against the egoistic hedonism that seems to define our modern age—against the crass selfishness that we are inclined to adopt in our Gyges-like moments. He says, along these lines, that only loyalty can save us from a hedonism that not only makes us bad people, but ultimately unhappy and alienated ones. Second, and more relevant in this chapter, he argued against what he termed

predatory loyalty. This is loyalty to causes that are unjust and causes that exclude other goods.

Narrow Loyalty

Companies like Google, Boeing, and Raytheon have unique professional cultures that foster unique loyalties and beliefs in their employees. This is often a good thing. But it can set the stage for moral shortsightedness. Such intimate professional settings can breed loyalties that unreflectively prioritize the monetary benefit of a company over the moral wellbeing of its employees or the organization as a whole. You can easily form a list of companies that produce devices that might be used for evil ends. The engineers employed by these companies are at least indirectly responsible for the consequences of their inventions. But they can be blinded to such responsibilities when a company culture encourages professionals to keep their loyalties close to home.

In 2015 the US Environmental Protection Agency (EPA) discovered that Volkswagen diesel engines emitted up to 40 times the legally allowed amount of carbon dioxide. The engines had been programmed in such a way that they emitted legally acceptable levels during laboratory testing but not under normal circumstances. The **VW Emissions Scandal** contributed to deaths and various environmental problems. After the EPA's finding, VW suffered a large decline in sales and stock value. By 2018, VW admitted guilt, and former CEO Martin Winterkorn had been charged with fraud and conspiracy. Internal documents showed that in 2006 supervisors in the engine department had realized their engines could not meet emission requirements, and asked their engineers to design engines with emission controls that would activate during testing and deactivate under ordinary circumstances. Perhaps the engineers who followed these orders thought that their actions were permissible. After all, in following orders they were acting as agents of their employers. However, blind obedience to authority is not morally acceptable.

Another company that faced problems due to a culture of blind obedience is **Korean Air**. In the 1980s the airline hired large numbers of pilots to accommodate rapid growth. Many of the new pilots had previously served in the Korean Air Force. Veterans who were higher ranking sometimes had veterans that they had previously commanded as copilots. The higher ranking veterans tended to ignore warnings from the lower ranking veterans. In general, the culture of the airline encouraged junior pilots to keep quiet if they had doubts about decisions made by senior pilots. This led to a number of fatal crashes during the 1980s and 1990s. However, the airline was able to turn things around. By 2009 a number of changes to the company were implemented. Such changes included the introduction of an operational command center in which all planes were monitored before and during flights. Pilots were trained to follow set procedures rather than make decisions based on personality and deference to authority. As a result, Korean Air became a much safer and much more prestigious airline.

Attitude Loyalty

Implicit bias is difficult to identify and counteract; so too are predatory loyalties that become the guiding force of an institution, company, or organization. Martin and Schinzinger note that an engineer is encouraged to foster what they term **attitude-loyalty**, that is, to contribute to the sense of corporate community and to form a personal attachment to their employer's stated and unstated objectives. When attitude loyalty is fulfilled, an engineer will not work begrudgingly or unwilfully, but will do her best to further the ends of her team. In a climate like this, the team will work at maximum efficiency. But this should put our moral sensitivities on high alert. It is in these highly efficient moments that, as Martin and Schinzinger suggest, we are apt to lapse into "the attitude that the corporation is all that matters or is more important than life itself." And this can have dire consequences.

In 1961, Hannah Arendt was a reporter for the *New Yorker* at the trial of Adolf Eichmann, one of the many masterminds of the Holocaust. She went to the trial expecting Eichmann to be a monster, but what she found was just an ordinary man following orders, working in a terribly efficient institution. "The trouble with Eichmann," Arendt wrote in 1963,

> was precisely that so many were like him, and the many were neither perverted or sadistic, that they were, and still are, terribly and terrifyingly normal. From the viewpoint of our legal institutions and our moral standards of judgment, this normality was much more terrifying than all the atrocities put together.

Eichmann's normality is what inspires Arendt to coin the term the **banality of evil**, and to argue that great acts of evil are not committed by a few extraordinary fiends, but by a large number of largely unreflective, normal people. Bringing up the Holocaust as a warning to today's engineers might seem like a stretch, like an unnecessary scare tactic; but we should think carefully about how the banality of evil might work its way into the culture of large engineering corporations. Perhaps when we do we will find nothing to criticize, but maybe we will catch a morally problematic situation before it is too late.

Whistleblowing

Turning our attention to what is the most publicized issue in engineering ethics, it is worth noting that **whistleblowing** stands to counteract the banality of evil and interrupt the normal practices that might lead to disastrous outcomes. The idea that engineers ought to hold paramount the public good is a familiar one. For this reason, we might wonder why it deserves particular mention (much less emphasis). However, before engineers blithely commit themselves to this task, it's worth questioning what it entails. What does it really mean to for an engineer to hold *paramount* the public good? And how is this obligation to be interpreted within the context of whistleblowing?

On one interpretation, holding paramount means an engineer must put public wellbeing before all other considerations—be they professional or personal. If we interpret the obligation in this way, then it would seem that engineers are morally required to blow the whistle in *any* case where public wellbeing is at risk.

This sort of answer to the **problem of whistleblowing** has some appeal. Although every person has a general obligation toward beneficence (doing good) and non-maleficence (refraining from harm), it could be argued that engineers have a much stronger duty in this regard. The combination of their knowledge, skill, and position allows them to either help or harm on an unusually large scale. In that case, although it might be personally or professionally detrimental in some cases for an engineer to blow the whistle, her suffering could hardly compare to the potential suffering of the public as a whole should she choose to remain silent. Furthermore, the thinking goes, who could be in a better position than an engineer to warn the public of possible danger? After all, engineers are intimately familiar with the technical details of a given project, and, as a result, they are in a special position to determine the accompanying risks. And if engineers won't do the job, then who will? Responsibility is all too easy to shift. Unless someone takes up the guardianship of public wellbeing, then perhaps no one will.

As convincing as this line of reasoning may seem, we ought to be careful not to rush to the conclusion that whistleblowing is an obligation that holds for every engineer regardless of their particular circumstances. For instance, one might argue that, although whistleblowing is acceptable, it is not mandatory. In other words, the idea is that blowing the whistle is often a good thing for an engineer to do, but it is not a moral or professional requirement. It is easy to forget that engineers are people with rights and obligations outside of their commitment to promote public wellbeing. For instance, engineers have the right to pursue satisfying and productive careers. And they have the obligation to protect and provide for those that might be dependent on them. The potential fallout from blowing the whistle could interfere with such rights and responsibilities. Because of this, we might argue that whistleblowing is somehow "above and beyond the call of duty" of engineers.

There are also reasons to think that whistleblowing may even be immoral in certain situations. Engineers operate within complex professional and political systems. Often, engineers have limited insight into the larger scope of a project, including its potential financial, political, and ethical ramifications. It's possible that what might look like a serious moral transgression from the point of view of the engineer is actually ethically unproblematic given the larger overall situation. Consider, for instance, the dilemma faced by potential whistleblowers who work in high-level government agencies. In some such cases in order to ensure informational security, engineers will often not be privy to the larger organizational plans and objectives. In such situations the release of classified information—even when necessary to protect some aspect of public wellbeing—may have the unintended effect of jeopardizing national security to some extent. It could be argued, then, that because engineers are sometimes epistemically disadvantaged as compared to managers or policy makers, it would be morally impermissible for them to blow the whistle.

One might also argue that whistleblowing expends a great deal of mental and emotional effort on the part of the engineer—energy that could have been used to forward the progress of potentially beneficial projects. Furthermore, one might worry that requiring engineers consider all of the moral implications of their work itself slows progress. In that case, it could be argued that engineers ought to stick to the technical decisions—leaving moral judgments to managers or policy makers. According to this position whistleblowing is supererogatory at best, but even may be impressible when it comes at the cost of technological progress.

However, the three positions we have catalogued so far—the view that whistleblowing is obligatory, the view that it is supererogatory, and the view that is impermissible—are all extreme. We can feel the pull of each, and yet they are potentially in conflict with one another. Perhaps, then, we should look for a "middle-ground approach"—an approach that argues that whistleblowing is sometimes morally obligatory, but which details the circumstances and the limits of this obligation. There are many middle ground solutions to the problem of whistleblowing. In the chapter resources we have included one example offered by the philosopher Mike W. Martin.

Genuine Loyalty

In most cases, whistleblowing occurs when an individual prioritizes the public good over the more immediate benefit of their coworkers or corporation.

The whistleblower is critical of the current practices of their employer on the basis of their more inclusive loyalties to other stakeholders (like fellow citizens who might be harmed in the production of faulty devices). In this case, we are asked to consider the interests of their employer only to the extent that these interests do not come into conflict with the professional code of ethics to which the corporation should ascribe.

For Royce, the real question of loyalty is not how loyal one should be but, rather, to what causes should one be loyal to. In *The Philosophy of Loyalty* he spends no small amount of time distinguishing between good and bad causes—insisting that genuine loyalty can only be directed toward a good cause which

> is good, not only for me, but for mankind, in so far as it is essentially a *loyalty to loyalty*, that is, an aid and a furtherance of loyalty in my fellows. It is an evil cause in so far as, despite the loyalty that it arouses in me, it is destructive of loyalty in the world of my fellows.
>
> (Royce, 1908, pp. 118–119)

"Loyalty to loyalty" seems highly abstract until we think about how loyalty actually works. Remember that loyalty is the ability to choose a cause and serve it—to be willing and able to devote oneself to a stated objective. The loyalties that we assume are always set in a wider social context in which other individuals are in the process of forming their own commitments. In this case, it is imperative that our devoted actions do not impede on others' ability to be loyal.

In the areas of energy and environment in particular, the actions of engineers have compromised communities and jeopardized individuals' abilities to be loyal to their own children and future generations. Specifically, engineering firms in the oil and gas industry, whose activities contribute to greenhouse gas emissions, interfere with the ability of families to protect their children from climate change and extreme weather. Semiconductor firms—whose manufacturing processes release pollutants and toxins into the air and water, and whose waste products cause accumulation of heavy metals in the ground—interfere with the ability of communities to protect the public health of their constituents. In the area of biomedical engineering and healthcare, pharmaceutical, biotechnology, and medical device firms who set unaffordable prices on their products interfere with the ability of doctors to be loyal to their patients and provide the best possible care. In the area of cybersecurity, when government agencies require private communications firms to provide personal data of consumers, these actions interfere with the ability of companies to be loyal to consumers. These actions took place in the case of the NSA as revealed by Edward Snowden, as well as in the case of Apple vs. the FBI, when the US Federal Bureau of Investigation requested that Apple unlock the iPhone of a terrorist shooter in San Bernardino, California.

In contrast to these examples, Royce suggests that our loyal actions should attempt to maximize the possibilities for others to form loyal commitments. This point can also help adjudicate between two causes when one experiences the dilemma of divided loyalties. One should pursue the cause that fosters, or at least does not prohibit, wider and more inclusive loyalties. In this case, certain engineering projects appear more morally advantageous than others. As an example, a manufacturing effort that lowers the cost of a lifesaving drug, while simultaneously creating manufacturing jobs, would generally be considered as morally advantageous. Similarly, an engineering effort to improve sanitation in a low-income community, while also generating opportunities for community members, would be morally advantageous. Finally, an engineering project to create alternative energy sources for a community, while improving access to energy, is morally advantageous.

Chapter 4 Key Terms and Concepts

Fiduciary Obligations
Edward Snowden
Conflicting Loyalties
Degenerate Loyalty
Predatory Loyalty
VW Emissions Scandal

Korean Air
Attitude Loyalty
The Banality of Evil
Whistleblowing
The Problem of Whistleblowing

Chapter 4: End of Chapter Reading and NSPE Board of Ethical Review Cases

Guided Core Reading   151

Core Reading 4.1: The Philosophy of Loyalty by Josiah Royce (excerpt)

Core Reading 4.2: 'Whistleblowing: Professionalism, personal life, and shared responsibility for safety in engineering' by Mike W. Martin (excerpts)

NSPE Board of Ethical Review Cases   160

Case 85-4: Objectivity of Engineer Retained as Expert (1985)

Case 06-8: Ethical Obligations as a Member of the U.S. Military (2006)

Case 89-7: Duty to Report Safety Violations (1989)

Guided Further Reading   165

Further Reading 4.1: 'Organizational loyalty' by John Fielder

Further Reading 4.2: 'Whistle blowing and rational loyalty' by Wim Vandekerckhove and M. S. Ronald Commers

Further Reading 4.3: 'Is whistle-blowing compatible with employee loyalty?' by Jukka Varelius

Tip: If you can't use the QR codes, use the hyperlinks found on the book's webpage instead: www.routledge.com/9781138183865.

Guided Core Reading

Core Reading 4.1: *The Philosophy of Loyalty* by Josiah Royce (excerpt)

> ### Preparing to Read
>
> In this passage Royce classifies the sorts of people that are capable of being loyal, and describes how to detect sincere loyalty. He also offers an explanation of why loyalty is so rare. Finally, Royce puts forward a test for whether one is loyal to a good cause or an evil cause. His test, roughly, is that a good cause is one that engenders loyalty to loyalty. An evil cause is one that is destructive of loyalty.

Excerpted from: Royce, J. (1908). *The Philosophy of Loyalty.* New York: The Macmillan Company, Chapter 3, Section 3, pp. 111–119.

In order to overcome such difficulties, now that they have arisen in our way, and in order to discover a principle whereby one may be guided in choosing a right object for his loyalty, we must steadfastly bear in mind that, when we declared loyalty to be a supreme good for in the loyal man himself, we were not speaking of a good that can come to a few men only to heroes or to saints of an especially exalted mental type. As we expressly said, the mightiest and the humblest members of any social order can be morally equal in the exemplification of loyalty. Whenever I myself begin to look about my own community to single out those people whom I know to be, in the sense of our definition, especially loyal to their various causes, I always find, amongst the most exemplary cases of loyalty, a few in deed of the most prominent members of the community, whom your minds and mine must at once single out because their public services and their willing sacrifices have made their loyalty to their chosen causes a matter of common report and of easy observation. But my own mind also chooses some of the plainest and obscurest of the people whom I chance to know, the most straightforward and simple-minded of folk, whose loyalty is even all the more sure to me because I can certainly affirm that they, at least, cannot be making any mere display of loyalty in order that they should be seen of men. Nobody knows of their loyalty except those who are in more or less direct touch with them; and these usually appreciate this loyalty too little. You all of you similarly know plain and wholly obscure men and women, of whom the world has never heard, and is not worthy, but who have possessed and who have proved in the presence of you who have chanced to observe them, a loyalty to their chosen causes which was not indeed expressed in martial deeds, but which was quite as genuine a loyalty as that of a Samurai, or as that of Arnold von Winkelried when he rushed upon the Austrian spears. As for the ordinary expressions of loyalty, not at critical moments and in the heroic instants that come to the plainest lives, but in daily business, we are all aware how the letter carrier and the housemaid may live, and often do live, when they choose, as complete a daily life of steadfast loyalty as could any knight or king. Some of us certainly know precisely such truly great personal embodiments of loyalty in those who are, in the world's ill-judging eyes, the little ones of the community.

Now these facts, I insist, show that loyalty is in any case no aristocratic gift of the few. It is, indeed, too rare a possession today in our own American social order; but that defect is due to the state of our present moral education. We as a nation, I fear, have been forgetting loyalty. We have been neglecting to cultivate it in our social order. We have been making light of it. We have not been training ourselves for it. Hence we, indeed, often sadly miss it in our social environment. But all sound human beings are made for it and can learn to possess it and to profit by it. And it is an essentially accessible and practical virtue for everybody.

This being true, let us next note that all the complications which we just reported are obviously due, in the main, to the fact that, as loyal men at present are, their various causes, and so their various loyalties, are viewed by them as standing in mutual, sometimes in deadly conflict. In general, as is plain if somebody's loyalty to a given cause, as for instance to a family, or to a state, so expresses itself as to involve a feud with a neighbor's family, or a warlike assault upon a foreign state, the result is obviously an evil; and at least part of the reason why it is an evil is that, by reason of the feud or the war, a certain good, namely, the enemy's loyalty, together with the enemy's opportunity to be loyal, is assailed, is thwarted, is endangered, is, perhaps, altogether destroyed. If the loyalty of A is a good for him, and if the loyalty of B is a good for him, then a feud between A and B, founded upon a mutual conflict between the causes that they serve, obviously involves this evil, namely, that each of the combatants assails, and perhaps may altogether destroy, precisely what we have seen to be the best spiritual possession of the other, namely, his chance to have a cause and to be loyal to a cause. The militant loyalty, indeed, also assails, in such a case, the enemy's physical comfort and well-being, his property, his life; and herein, of course, militant loyalty does evil to the enemy. But if each man's having and serving a cause is his best good, the worst of the evils of a feud is the resulting attack, not upon the enemy's comfort or his health or his property or his life, but upon the most precious of his possessions, his loyalty itself.

If loyalty is a supreme good, the mutually destructive conflict of loyalties is in general a supreme evil. If loyalty is a good for all sorts and conditions of men, the war of man against man has been especially mischievous, not so much because it has hurt, maimed, impoverished, or slain men, as because it has so often robbed the defeated of their causes, of their opportunities to be loyal, and sometimes of their very spirit of loyalty.

If, then, we look over the field of human life to see where good and evil have most clustered, we see that the best in human life is its loyalty; while the worst is whatever has tended to make loyalty impossible, or to destroy it when present, or to rob it of its own while it still survives. And of all things that thus have warred with loyalty, the bitterest woe of humanity has been that so often it is the loyal themselves who have thus blindly and eagerly gone about to wound and to slay the loyalty of their brethren. The spirit of loyalty has been misused to make men commit sin against this very spirit, holy as it is. For such a sin is precisely what any wanton conflict of loyalties means. Where such a conflict occurs, the best, namely, loyalty, is used as an instrument in order to compass the worst, namely, the destruction of loyalty.

It is true, then, that some causes are good, while some are evil. But the test of good and evil in the causes to which men are loyal is now definable in terms which we can greatly simplify in view of the foregoing considerations.

If, namely, I find a cause, and this cause fascinates me, and I give myself over to its service, I insofar attain what, for me, if my loyalty is complete, is a supreme good. But my cause, by our own definition, is a social cause, which binds many into the unity of one service. My cause, therefore, gives me, of necessity, fellow-servants, who with me share this loyalty, and to whom this loyalty, if complete, is also a supreme good. So far, then, in being loyal myself, I not only get but give good; for I help to sustain, in each of my fellow-servants, his own loyalty, and so I help him to secure his own supreme good. In so far, then, my loyalty to my cause is also a loyalty to my fellows loyalty. But now suppose that my cause, like the family in a feud, or like the pirate ship, or like the aggressively warlike nation, lives by the destruction of the loyalty of other families, or of its own community, or of other communities. Then, indeed, I get a good for myself and for my fellow-servants by our common loyalty; but I war against this very spirit of loyalty as it appears in our opponent s loyalty to his own cause.

And so, a cause is good, not only for me, but for mankind, in so far as it is essentially a loyalty to loyalty, that is, is an aid and a furtherance of loyalty in my fellows. It is an evil cause in so far as, despite the loyalty that it arouses in me, it is destructive of loyalty in the world of my fellows.

Guided Reading Questions

1. Who does Royce think is capable of being loyal? What is the difference between the loyalty of the noble person and the loyalty of the common person? Why does Royce believe that loyalty is rare? Does it have to be rare?
2. Under what circumstances does loyalty generate conflict, between oneself and between persons?
3. How can increasing loyalty be evil when loyalty is good? In what way can loyalty be misused?
4. How does one distinguish between good causes and evil causes to which one might be loyal? How does this provide guidance in deciding which causes to be loyal to?
5. What goods does one receive from being loyal to an evil cause? What is the problem with loyalty to an evil cause?

Read the Full Chapter (or Book)

You can read the full chapter (or even the whole book) online by scanning the QR code or following the link below. No login is required; just click on '1908—The Philosophy of Loyalty'.

https://royce-edition.iupui.edu/online-royce-volumes

Core Reading 4.2: 'Whistleblowing: Professionalism, personal life, and shared responsibility for safety in engineering' by Mike W. Martin (excerpts)

Preparing to Read

In this paper Martin articulates the problem of whistleblowing, and offers a novel solution to the problem. As a precursor to his project, he surveys several alternative approaches to the problem of whistleblowing, and draws out the strengths and shortcomings of each. Martin attempts to strike a balance between an engineer's professional and personal obligations, and emphasizes the role of character and virtue in professional life.

Excerpted from: Martin, M. (1992). Whistleblowing: Professionalism, personal life, and shared responsibility for safety in engineering. *Business and Professional Ethics Journal*, 11(2), 21–40. doi.org/10.5840/bpej19921122. © 1992 Philosophy Documentation Center, reprinted with permission. Internal references omitted.

Engineers work on projects that affect the safety of large numbers of people. … As professionals, they live by … codes … which ascribe to them a paramount obligation to protect the … public, an obligation that sometimes implies whistleblowing. As employees of corporations, however, their obligation is to respect the authority of managers who sometimes give insufficient attention to safety matters.

…

Three Approaches to Whistleblowing Ethics

The literature on whistleblowing is large…. Here I mention three … approaches. The first is to condemn whistleblowers as disloyal troublemakers…. I once dismissed this attitude as callous, as sheer corporate egoism that misconstrues loyalty to a corporation as an absolute moral principle. If, however …, the public accepts this attitude …, then so be it…. [I]t tacitly accepts the added risks from not having available important safety information.

A second approach … is to regard whistleblowing as a tragedy to be avoided. On occasion whistleblowing may be a necessary evil … but it is always bad…. There are many things that can be done to improve organizations to make whistleblowing unnecessary…. Nevertheless, this second approach is not enough. There will always be corporations and managers willing to cut corners on safety in the pursuit of short-term profit, and there will always be a need for justified whistleblowing….

…

A third approach is to affirm unequivocally the obligation of engineers
… to whistleblow … and to treat this obligation … as overriding all other
considerations, whatever the sacrifice….

…

I want to call into question the whole attempt to offer a general rule
that tells us when whistleblowing is mandatory…. Final judgments about
obligations to whistleblow must … take into account the burdens imposed
on whistleblowers….

…

The Moral Relevance of Personal Life to Professional Duty

[T]here is a strong prima facie obligation to whistleblow when one has good
reason to believe there is a serious moral problem, has exhausted normal organizational channels, has available a reasonable amount of documentation, and has
reasonable hope of solving the problem. Nevertheless … the obligation is only
prima facie: It can sometimes have exceptions…. [T]he considerations which
need to be weighed include … considerations about one's personal life….

…

Engineers … have personal obligations … which can be met only if they
have an income. They also have personal rights…. These … legitimately
interact with professional obligations in ways that sometimes make it permissible for engineers not to whistleblow, even when they have a *prima facie*
obligation to do so….

…

Few discussions of whistleblowing take personal considerations seriously.
But responsibilities to family and the right to pursue one's career are moral
considerations. Argument is needed to dismiss them as irrelevant. I will consider three.

(i) The *Prevent-Harm Argument* says that morality requires us to prevent
harm and in doing so to treat others' interests equally and impartially with
our own. This assumption is often associated with utilitarianism…. The idea
is that even though engineers and their families must suffer, their suffering is
outweighed by the lives saved through whistleblowing….

…

I … block any straightforward move from impartiality to … exceptionless
whistleblowing obligations, thereby undermining the Prevent-Harm
Argument…. [A] universal requirement of strict impartiality is …
self-demeaning….

…

Right now, you and I could dramatically lower our lifestyles in order to
help save lives by making greater sacrifices. We could even donate one of
our kidneys to save a life. Yet we have a right not to do that, a right to give

ourselves and our families considerable priority in how we use resources. Similarly, engineers' rights have relevance in understanding the degree of sacrifice required by a prima facie whistleblowing obligation.

(ii) The *Avoid-Harm Argument* proceeds from the obligation not to cause harm to others. It then points out that engineers are in a position to cause or avoid harm on an unusual scale....

...

[T]here is a general obligation not to cause harm.... I have an obligation not to harm others by polluting the environment, but it does not follow that I must stop driving my car at the cost of my job....

...

(iii) The *Professional-Status Argument* asserts that engineers have special responsibilities as professionals.... Most engineering codes hint at a whistleblowing obligation ... [that] implies whistleblowing in some situations, no matter what the personal cost.

I agree that the obligation to protect public safety is an essential professional obligation.... It is not clear, however, that it is paramount in the ... sense of overriding all other obligations in all situations.... I reject the ... assumption that codified professional duties are all that are morally relevant in making whistleblowing decisions. It is quite true that professional considerations require setting aside personal interests in many situations. But it is also true that personal considerations have enormous and legitimate importance....

...

Character, Integrity, and Personal Ideals

Isn't there a danger that denying the existence of absolute, all-things considered, principles for whistleblowers will further discourage whistleblowing in the public interest? ... I think not.

If all-things-considered judgments about whistleblowing are not a matter of general rule, they are still a matter of good moral judgment. Good judgment ... is a product of good character ... defined by virtues. Here are some of the most significant virtues....

(1) *Virtues of self-direction* are those which enable us to guide our lives. They include the intellectual virtues which characterize technical expertise: mastery of one's discipline, ability to communicate, skills in reasoning, imagination, ability to discern dangers, a disposition to minimize risk, and humility.... They also include *integrity virtues* which promote coherence among one's attitudes, commitments, and conduct based on a core of moral concern. They include honesty, courage, conscientiousness, self-respect, and fidelity to promises and commitments.... And *wisdom* is practical good judgment in making responsible decisions....

(2) *Team-work virtues* include (a) loyalty: concern for the good of the organization for which one works; (b) collegiality: respect for one's colleagues and a commitment to work with them in shared projects; and (c) cooperativeness: the willingness to make reasonable compromises....

(3) *Public-spirited virtues* are those aimed at the good of others, both clients and the general public.... *Justice virtues* concern fair play. One is respect for persons: the disposition to respect people's rights and autonomy, in particular, the rights not to be injured in ways one does not consent to....

This helps us understand the sense of responsibility to protect the public that often motivates whistleblowers....

Depth of commitment to the public good is a familiar theme in whistleblowers' accounts of their ordeals. The depth is manifested in how they connect their self-respect and personal integrity to their commitments to the good of others. There is such a thing as voluntarily assuming a responsibility and doing so because of commitments to (valid) ideals, to a degree beyond what is required of everyone....

According to this line of thought, whistleblowing done at enormous personal cost, motivated by moral concern for the public good, and exercising good moral judgment is both (a) beyond the general call of duty incumbent on everyone and (b) motivated by a sense of responsibility....

Earlier I drew attention to the importance of personal rights and responsibilities, and to the unfair personal burdens when others involved in collective enterprises fail to meet their responsibilities. Equally important, we need to appreciate the role of personal integrity grounded in supererogatory commitments to ideals. This appreciation of personal integrity and commitments to ideals is compatible with a primary emphasis on laws that make it possible for professionals to serve the public good without having to make heroic self-sacrifices.

Guided Reading Questions

1. What are the three approaches to whistleblowing Martin describes? What does Martin think about each of these approaches?
2. What does Martin mean by saying that the obligation to whistleblow is prima facie?
3. Martin says that the obligation to blow the whistle can be overridden by other important considerations. What are these considerations, and under what circumstances does Martin think they ought to come into play?

4. What role does "character" and "virtue" play in Martin's approach to whistleblowing? What sorts of virtues or character traits does Martin suggest are relevant to would-be whistleblowers?

Read the Full Article (optional)

If your college library subscribes to the journal, you can read the full article online by scanning the QR code or following the link below. You may need to login via your library's website or use campus wifi to get access.

www.pdcnet.org/bpej/content/bpej_1992_0011_0002_0021_0040
Also available on JSTOR: www.jstor.org/stable/27800878

NSPE Board of Ethical Review Cases

Case 85-4: Objectivity of Engineer Retained as Expert

Objectivity of Engineer Retained as Expert

Case 85-4
Year: 1985
Facts:

Engineer A is a forensic engineer. He is hired as a consultant by Attorney Z to provide an engineering and safety analysis report and courtroom testimony in support of a plaintiff in a personal injury case. Following Engineer A's review and analysis, Engineer A determines that he cannot provide an engineering and safety analysis report favorable to the plaintiff because the results of the report would have to suggest that the plaintiff and not the defendant was at fault in the case. Engineer A's services are terminated and his fee is paid in full. Thereafter, Attorney X, representing the defendant in the case, learns of the circumstances relating to Engineer A's unwillingness to provide a report in support of Attorney Z's case and seeks to retain Engineer A to provide an independent and separate engineering and safety analysis report. Engineer A agrees to provide the report.

Question from the NSPE:
Was it ethical for Engineer A to agree to provide a separate engineering and safety analysis report?

Going Beyond—Our Questions for a Deep Dive

1. In this case, does Engineer A potentially have "divided loyalties"? If so, what is the divide?
2. In certain cases where there is a potential conflict of interest, the conflict can be resolved if the engineer resigns from one role to take on another. Would having Engineer A resign from the role of "expert witness for Attorney Z" to take on the role of "expert witness for Attorney X" be enough to resolve the ethical dilemma in this case? If so why? If not, why not?

3. To what extent, if any, do engineers owe loyalties to former clients or employers? How should these loyalties be weighed against an engineer's loyalty to his or her current clients or employers?

4. One might argue that the answer to the previous question depends on the circumstance—for instance, it may depend on who the client or employer is, it may depend on what the job is, or it may depend on what else is at stake. If this argument is sound, then what circumstances do you think matter morally in such cases?

5. Could filling in more of the details of Case 85-4 make a moral difference in your judgments about the case?

Read the Board's Discussion and Conclusion

To read the discussion and conclusion of this case by members of the NSPE Board of Ethical Review, go to: www.nspe.org/resources/ethics/ethics-resources/board-ethical-review-cases/objectivity-engineer-retained-expert.

Case 06-8: Ethical Obligations as a Member of the U.S. Military

Ethical Obligations as a Member of the U.S. Military

Case 06-8
Year: 2006
Facts:

Engineer A is a professional engineer in private practice who is being mobilized as an Army Reserve engineer officer. Unlike previous roles as an Army officer (combat engineer, etc.), Engineer A is being mobilized as a design engineer and is expected to use his civilian skills and judgment as a professional engineer. Engineer A is advised that in the performance of his actions as a member of the military, Engineer A is subject to military law (Uniform Code of Military Justice, etc.), which would exempt Engineer A from civil liability associated with his work. However, Engineer A believes that he still has obligations as a professional engineer and that his professional and ethical obligations still apply.

Question from the NSPE:
Does Engineer A continue to have ethical obligations under the NSPE Code of Ethics as a member of the U.S. military?

Going Beyond—Our Questions for a Deep Dive

1. Does taking on a military role come with its own moral obligations? If so, do these obligations remain consistent both inside and outside of the context of war?
2. Is being exempted from civil liability the same thing as being exempted from moral liability? What, if anything, is the difference between these two types of liability?
3. To what extent, if any, do conflicting role responsibilities lead to divided loyalties in this case?
4. If conflicting roles are at issue in this case, then what is the nature of the divide? For instance, is the conflict between Engineer A's role as a military professional and his role as an engineering professional? Is the potential conflict between his role as a civilian and his role as a member of the military? Or is his conflict between his role as a member of the military and his role as a moral agent more generally?
5. Is there a hierarchy of role responsibilities in which one role responsibility could potentially trump another? If so, could this resolution be carried over to cases of divided loyalties?
6. Assume for a moment that Engineer A's military moral obligations trump his moral obligations as a civilian or a professional engineer to some extent. Is there any limit to when military obligations trump the moral obligations he has as a civilian or as a professional engineer?
7. Does Engineer A's professional role responsibilities change when he leaves his role as combat engineer and takes up a role as an Army Reserve officer?

Read the Board's Discussion and Conclusion

To read the discussion and conclusion of this case by members of the NSPE Board of Ethical Review, go to: www.nspe.org/resources/ethics/ethics-resources/board-ethical-review-cases/ethical-obligations-member-us-military.

Case 89-7: Duty to Report Safety Violations

Duty to Report Safety Violations

Case 89-7
Year: 1989
Facts:

Engineer A is retained to investigate the structural integrity of a 60-year old occupied apartment building which his client is planning to sell. Under the terms of the agreement with the client, the structural report written by Engineer A is to remain confidential. In addition, the client makes clear to Engineer A that the building is being sold "as is" and he is not planning to take any remedial action to repair or renovate any system within the building prior to its sale. Engineer A performs several structural tests on the building and determines that the building is structurally sound. However, during the course of providing services, the client confides in Engineer A and informs him that the building contains deficiencies in the electrical and mechanical systems which violate applicable codes and standards. While Engineer A is not an electrical nor mechanical engineer, he does realize those deficiencies could cause injury to the occupants of the building and so informs the client. In his report, Engineer A makes a brief mention of his conversation with the client concerning the deficiencies; however, in view of the terms of the agreement, Engineer A does not report the safety violations to any third party.

Question from the NSPE:
Was it ethical for Engineer A not to report the safety violations to the appropriate public authorities?

Going Beyond—Our Questions for a Deep Dive

1. Does Engineer A satisfy the conditions for a "strong prima facie obligation" to blow the whistle as suggested by Mike Martin?
2. Martin suggests that an engineer's obligation to blow the whistle depends, at least in part, on his or her other personal moral obligations. Do you agree with his position? If so, what sort of personal obligations might be relevant in this situation?
3. If Engineer A does have an obligation to blow the whistle, is the strength of this obligation dependent (as Martin suggests) on the level of legal protection in place for whistleblowers?
4. Does the fact that Engineer A is not an electrical engineer make any difference to his obligations in this case?
5. Could details about an engineer's specialty (for instance electrical engineering, mechanical engineering, etc.) ever make a difference to whether he or she is obligated to blow the whistle? What about an engineer's level of expertise—could that potentially make a difference to his or her moral obligations?

Read the Board's Discussion and Conclusion

To read the discussion and conclusion of this case by members of the NSPE Board of Ethical Review, go to: www.nspe.org/resources/ethics/ethics-resources/board-ethical-review-cases/duty-report-safety-violations.

Guided Further Reading

Further Reading 4.1: 'Organizational loyalty' by John Fielder

Find the Article

Fielder, J. (1992). Organizational loyalty. *Business and Professional Ethics Journal*, 11(1), 71–90. doi.org/10.5840/bpej199211122.

Read the article online by scanning the QR code or following the link below. Your college library will need to subscribe to the journal, and you may need to login via your library's website or use campus wifi to get access.

www.pdcnet.org/bpej/content/bpej_1992_0011_0001_0071_0090
Also available on JSTOR: www.jstor.org/stable/27800872

Preparing to Read

The notion of loyalty is conceptually linked to the notion of sacrifice—especially personal sacrifice. When we think of the obligations we have to be loyal to our dearest friends or family members, it seems natural to assume that fidelity demands that we be willing to sacrifice a great deal. However, arguably, the strength of these obligations is tied to our personal connections in these cases. What, if anything, underlies the putative obligation to be loyal to the organizations that we work for rather than to individuals we are personally connected to? What sorts of sacrifice might engineers be required to make for their employers, and how far should these obligations extend into their personal lives? In this reading, John Fielder takes a closer look at the concept of organizational loyalty in hopes of finding answers to these sorts of question.

Guided Reading Questions

1. Fielder claims that the NSPE's fourth canon highlights the same concerns as the agency model of organizational loyalty. After reading the fourth canon and the related provisions, do you agree with Fielder that the duties specified in the canon are to be interpreted as concerning agent loyalty? Or are there alternative ways of interpreting the ethical commitments alluded to in the fourth canon?

2. As Fielder puts it, "On the agency concept of loyalty the employee is seen as an extension of the principal who controls the agent." Is there any place for agent loyalty within engineering? Are there any circumstances under which an engineer might be subject to the duties of agent loyalty? For example, if an engineer is working for the government on a top-security project which is vital to national security, would the engineer owe the government agent loyalty?

3. Fielder argues that we need a better approach to organizational loyalty than agency loyalty. In particular he calls for an approach that better balances the interests of the employer and the other ethical obligations of employee. Do you agree? Or could the concept of organizational loyalty be amended somehow to make it more resistant to criticism?

4. Fielder surveys several potential approaches to organizational loyalty, including solutions by Ronald Duska, Richard De George, Marcia Baron, and Andrew Oldenquist. In your opinion, what are the benefits and drawbacks of each of these solutions? Do you agree with Fielder that Oldenquist's view is the "most useful"? Or do you think one of the other accounts presented is better with regard to "usefulness"?

5. Fielder agrees with Oldenquist that the additional obligations of loyalty stem from group membership. Fielder attempts to clarify

the notion of group membership as it relates to the concept of loyalty, and to answer several questions regarding the obligations of group loyalty. What do you think about Fielder's characterization of loyalty? Would it be better for us to interpret the NSPE's fourth Fundamental Canon as referring to obligations of group loyalty?

Further Reading 4.2: 'Whistle blowing and rational loyalty' by Wim Vandekerckhove and M. S. Ronald Commers

Find the Article

Vandekerckhove, W., & Commers, M. S. R. Whistle blowing and rational loyalty. *Journal of Business Ethics*, 53, 225–233 (2004). doi.org/10.1023/B:BUSI.0000039411.11986.6b.

Read the article online by scanning the QR code or following the link below. Your college library will need to subscribe to the journal, and you may need to login via your library's website or use campus wifi to get access.

https://link.springer.com/article/10.1023/B:BUSI.0000039411.11986.6b
Also available on JSTOR: www.jstor.org/stable/25123295

Preparing to Read

In the introduction to this chapter, we framed the "problem of whistleblowing" as a conflict between professional moral obligations that are sometimes incompatible in practice: loyalty and honesty or commitment to public wellbeing. However, Wim Vandekerckhove and M. S. Ronald Commers argue that these duties only seem to conflict. They claim that, by reframing the concept of loyalty, we can see that whistleblowing does not pose a moral dilemma for engineers.

Guided Reading Questions

1. Vandekerckhove and Commers point out that, as organizations become more complex and decentralized, a need for loyalty arises. What do you think—is there a connection between organizational structure and the need for loyalty?
2. Vandekerckhove and Commers reference Solomon's idea that loyalty is a "mutual obligation" in the sense that an employee's obligation to be loyal depends on what the company has done for the employee. Do you agree with the idea that loyalty is mutual in this sense? If so, what can an employee rightly expect from his or her company in exchange for loyalty?
3. Vandekerckhove and Commers introduce the concept of "rational loyalty" as a kind of loyalty not to the physical organization, but to the explicit statements of the organization's goals, values, and codes of conduct. Do a quick internet search of an organization you have worked for in the past, are currently working for, or would like to work for in the future to see if they have an explicit mission statement. Is their mission statement something that you would be willing to be loyal to?
4. Is loyalty a matter of actions, attitude, or both? Can you feel a sense of loyalty without acting loyal, or vice versa?
5. The concept of rational loyalty allows for an employee to blow the whistle in certain cases without being disloyal to the organization. Hence, Vandekerckhove and Commers argue, adopting the notion of rational loyalty dissolves apparent conflicts between an employee's duty to loyalty and his or her other duties—the duty to public safety for instance. Will employing the notion of rational loyalty ensure that engineers avoid every potential conflict between loyalty and their other duties?

Further Reading 4.3: 'Is whistle-blowing compatible with employee loyalty?' by Jukka Varelius

Find the Article

Varelius, J. (2009). Is whistle-blowing compatible with employee loyalty? *Journal of Business Ethics*, 85, 263–275. doi.org/10.1007/s10551-008-9769-1.

Read the article online by scanning the QR code or following the link below. Your college library will need to subscribe to the journal, and you may need to login via your library's website or use campus wifi to get access.

https://link.springer.com/article/10.1007/s10551-008-9769-1

Also available on JSTOR: www.jstor.org/stable/41315829

Preparing to Read

In the previous article, Vandekerckhove and Commers attempt to dissolve the problem of whistleblowing by arguing that it is not really a problem at all. In this article, Jukka Varelius criticizes this sort of strategy. She argues that whistleblowing is a genuine moral problem after all.

Guided Reading Questions

1. On what Varelius calls "the new conception of loyalty," whether an act is loyal depends on whether the employee aimed to promote the moral good of the organization. What do you think? Does loyalty to an organization demand that the employee aim for the moral good of that organization? Is there a difference between promoting the moral good of an organization and promoting the good of an organization?

2. Varelius offers several examples in which a person can be loyal to a morally bad entity—a Nazi organization or a mafia gang, for instance. These are examples of what she calls "the standard notion of loyalty." In the standard sense of loyalty, a person's loyalty depends on the fulfillment of his or her commitments to the object of loyalty regardless of whether the fulfillment of such duties is ultimately in the object's best interest or is otherwise morally acceptable. In your opinion, is loyalty in the "standard sense" of loyalty a virtue?

3. When it comes to engineering or business organizations, does the ordinary notion of loyalty apply? Does the duty to be "a faithful agent or trustee" of one's organization apply when the organization is morally corrupt in some way?

4. Varelius argues that it is not a central feature of loyalty that an individual must promote the good of the object of loyalty. She also argues that loyalty does not require that we adhere to the object's wishes or demands. What reasons does she give for these conclusions? Do you agree with these reasons?

5. Varelius contends that, in order to be justified in relying on the "new conception of loyalty" in codes of ethics, we must give a good reason for rejecting "the standard conception of loyalty." Do you agree? How should we decide how to interpret loyalty clauses in professional codes of ethics?

Bibliography

AppleInsider. (n.d.). NSA leaker Edward Snowden refuses to use Apple's iPhone over spying concerns—report. https://appleinsider.com/articles/15/01/21/nsa-leaker-edward-snowden-refuses-to-use-apples-iphone-over-spying-concerns---report.

Arendt, H. (1963, February 9). Eichmann in Jerusalem: I. *New Yorker*. www.newyorker.com/magazine/1963/02/16/eichmann-in-jerusalem-i.

Baron, M. (1984). *The Moral Status of Loyalty*. Kendall/Hunt. http://ethics.iit.edu/publication/Moral_status_loyalty_Baron.pdf.

BBC News (2014, January 17). Edward Snowden: Leaks that exposed US spy programme. www.bbc.com/news/world-us-canada-23123964.

Borchers, R. (2017, May 6). Ninth Circuit upholds convictions in economic espionage case. *Courthouse New Service*. www.courthousenews.com/ninth-circuit-upholds-convictions-economic-espionage-case.

Busch, P. L. (n.d). Time for another look at conflict of interest. *National Society of Professional Engineers (NSPE)*. www.nspe.org/resources/ethics/ethics-resources/other-resources/time-another-look-conflict-interest.

Carley, W. M., & Pasztor, A. (1999, July 7). Korean Air tries to fix a dismal safety record. *Wall Street Journal*. www.wsj.com/articles/SB931303249871932359.

Fielder, J. (1992). Organizational loyalty. *Business and Professional Ethics Journal*, 11(1), 71–90.

Gellman, B. (2013, December 23). Edward Snowden, after months of NSA revelations, says his mission's accomplished. *Washington Post*. www.washingtonpost.com/world/national-security/edward-snowden-after-months-of-nsa-revelations-says-his-missions-accomplished/2013/12/23/49fc36de-6c1c-11e3-a523-fe73f0ff6b8d_story.html.

Greenwald, G., & MacAskill, E. (2013, June 7). NSA Prism program taps in to user data of Apple, Google and others. *The Guardian*. www.theguardian.com/world/2013/jun/06/us-tech-giants-nsa-data.

Hotten, R. (2015, December 10). Volkswagen: The scandal explained. *BBC News*. www.bbc.com/news/business-34324772.

Jebb, R. C. (1900). *Sophocles: The Plays and Fragments. Part III. The Antigone* (3rd ed.). Cambridge University Press.

Kirk, D. (2002, March 26). New standards mean Korean air is coming off many 'shun' lists. *New York Times*. www.nytimes.com/2002/03/26/business/new-standards-mean-korean-air-is-coming-off-many-shun-lists.html.

Krall, J. R., & Peng, R. D. (2015, December 9). The difficulty of calculating deaths caused by the Volkswagen scandal. *The Guardian*. www.theguardian.com/news/datablog/2015/dec/09/the-difficulty-of-calculating-deaths-caused-by-the-volkswagen-scandal.

Leggett, T. (2018, May 5). How VW tried to cover up the emissions scandal. *BBC News*. www.bbc.com/news/business-44005844.

MacAskill, E., & Hern, A. (2018, June 4). Edward Snowden: 'The people are still powerless, but now they're aware.' *The Guardian*. www.theguardian.com/us-news/2018/jun/04/edward-snowden-people-still-powerless-but-aware.

Martin, M. W. (1992). Whistleblowing: Professionalism, personal life, and shared responsibility for safety in engineering. *Business and Professional Ethics Journal*, 11(2), 21–40.

Martin, M.W., & Schinzinger, R. (2005). *Ethics in Engineering* (4th ed.). McGraw-Hill.

McConnell, T. (2018). Moral dilemmas. In E. N. Zalta (Ed.), *The Stanford Encyclopedia of Philosophy* (Fall). https://plato.stanford.edu/archives/fall2018/entries/moral-dilemmas.

Muzzey, D. S. (1909). The Philosophy of Loyalty. By Prof. Josiah Royce [Review]. *International Journal of Ethics*, 19(4), 509–510. https://doi.org/10.1086/intejethi. 19.4.2377021.

New York Times. (2016, March 27–29). The Apple-F.B.I. case. www.nytimes.com/news-event/apple-fbi-case.

Rousseau, J.-J. (1984). *A Discourse on Inequality*. Penguin.

Royce, J. (1908). *The Philosophy of Loyalty*. The Macmillan Company.

Singer, P. (1972). *Famine, Affluence, and Morality*. Oxford University Press.

Stanley, B. (2006, January 9). Korean Air bucks tradition to fix problems. *Wall Street Journal*. www.wsj.com/articles/SB113676875085241209.

US Environmental Protection Agency (EPA). (2015, October 28). Learn about Volkswagen violations. www.epa.gov/vw/learn-about-volkswagen-violations.

US Environmental Protection Agency (EPA). (2015, September 18). Notice of violation [Letter]. www.epa.gov/sites/production/files/2015-10/documents/vw-nov-caa-09-18-15.pdf.

Valentine, J. P. (2015, September 18). EPA, California notify Volkswagen of Clean Air Act violations / carmaker allegedly used software that circumvents emissions testing for certain air pollutants. *US EPA*. https://19january2017snapshot.epa.gov/newsreleases/epa-california-notify-volkswagen-clean-air-act-violations-carmaker-allegedly-used_.html

Vandekerckhove, W., & Commers, M. S. R. (2004). Whistle blowing and rational loyalty. *Journal of Business Ethics*, 53, 225–233. doi.org/10.1023/B:BUSI. 0000039411.11986.6b.

Varelius, J. (2009). Is whistle-blowing compatible with employee loyalty? *Journal of Business Ethics*, 85, 263–275. doi.org/10.1007/s10551-008-9769-1.

Wilber, D. Q. (2016, February 4). The plot to steal the color white from DuPont. *Bloomberg*. www.bloomberg.com/features/2016-stealing-dupont-white.

Yu, R. (2009, August 23). Korean Air upgrades service, image. *USA TODAY*. https://usatoday30.usatoday.com/money/companies/management/profile/2009-08-23-travel-airlines-korea_N.htm.

Chapter 5

Honesty and Deception

"Avoid deceptive acts."

Of all of the NSPE canons, the one concerning deception appears to be the least deserving of further analysis. Nothing, it seems, is more straight-forward than honesty. It is just a matter of telling the truth. However, truth-fulness is not enough to secure honesty. Paul Grice offers an example that illustrates this point. Imagine you are applying for an internship. You ask your thermodynamics professor to write you a recommendation letter for the position. You are a bit worried about asking this particular professor for a letter because, as it happened, you did rather poorly in his class. However, to your surprise, the professor tells you that he would, quite truthfully, be able to write you a glowing recommendation. But it turned out, unbeknownst to the student, to read, "This student has excellent handwriting—the best I've ever seen" and nothing more. The professor did something wrong. But it isn't because he said something false. It's true that you have excellent hand-writing. It's also true that his report was quite positive—glowing in fact. The problem, as Grice points out, is that the literal meanings of our words often have little to do with what we actually communicate. Human communi-cation occurs in a sphere rich with contextual cues and assumptions. Yes, what your professor said was literally true. Nonetheless, given the context, the information about handwriting is hardly relevant. In fact, the absence of information about grades or your technical abilities speaks louder than the positive comments about your penmanship. That's because it's assumed that the writer would have included all of the relevant information. The fact that your professor had nothing more to say will lead the reviewers to conclude that the whole truth must be awfully unflattering.

Lying and Deception

Clearly, then, honesty is not just a matter of telling the literal truth. The information we omit is often more powerful than the information we include. Perhaps, then, honesty requires that we present *all* of the facts—the truth, the whole truth, and nothing but. However, there is a problem with this approach. Remember the last time you signed a contract online. Many internet agreements are tediously long and seemly incomprehensible. Even if you began in good faith to read the whole thing, you probably skipped at least some information simply to click "agree" at the bottom of the page. Hopefully, your trust in the company that prepared the contract was warranted, and you weren't harmed as a result of your agreement. However, you might not have been so lucky. In 2012, US medical billing service providers PaymentsMD and Metis Health released a service that would allow patients to access their full medical records though a patient portal. While registering for the service, many consumers unwittingly authorized PaymentsMD and Metis Health to collect sensitive medical information from third parties such as insurance companies, pharmacies, and laboratories.

What made this case controversial, at least until it was settled by the Federal Trade Association, is that PaymentsMD and Metis Health could correctly claim that the information regarding consent was available to consumers during the registration process. Unfortunately for users, the two companies made it almost impossible for their customers to find this information—concealing it in places where users had no reason to look. With one click of a button, patients signed away control of very private information. This case goes to show that truth can be as effective as falsehood as a means to deception. As PaymentsMD protested, the relevant information was there—all of it, in fact. But it was broken apart, displaced, and buried so far beneath piles of other "facts" that it might as well have been absent altogether. This case should make it plain that truth, even in its entirety, can sometimes be as good as a lie.

While PaymentsMD did not lie, it engaged in deception. The standard view is that lying is worse than mere deception. But cases like this have led some philosophers to deny that there is a difference between lying and mere deception. Consider an example by Jennifer Saul (2012): Frieda is allergic to peanuts. George, who wants to kill Frieda, invites her over for dinner and prepares the meal with a deadly amount of peanut oil. Frieda asks whether there are any peanuts in the meal. George tells her that there are not. He never says that the meal is safe for her to eat. He never says that it does not contain peanut oil. He just says that there are no peanuts in the meal. In this example, George does not lie to Frieda. He merely deceives her. But, Saul argues, George's deception was just as wrong as it would have been if he had lied. Is Saul right about this?

Perhaps one thing the defender of the traditional view could say is this: whether George lied or merely deceived, he is on his way to performing a terrible act—an act of murder. Let's assume for a moment that lying is indeed at least a bit worse than mere deception. Still, it feels cold and inappropriate to try to measure out and quantify that difference when these comparatively minor acts are embedded in the much worse act of killing. Killing is so bad that the difference between lying and merely deceiving seems to vanish. In cases like this, we think to ourselves, why worry about whether George's act is at least a bit less wrong than it would have otherwise been if he had lied. After all, either way what he did amounts to murder. We might say something very similar about the PaymentsMD example. It would be cold comfort to tell the victims of PaymentsMD that, although they were deceived in such a way that their private information was compromised, at least they weren't lied to. So one of the issues on which the debate between Saul's view and the traditional view hinges is whether the peanut oil example and whether the PaymentsMD example can be explained away in this manner. The issue is this: is the intuition that the acts in the relevant examples are not at all different due to the fact that they really aren't different; or is it instead due to the fact that, although the acts are different, they are each part of an act that is much worse? And, whatever difference there is between lying and mere deception, it is small in comparison to the larger acts of murder or violation and of privacy in which those acts are embedded.

Another issue on which the debate between Saul and the traditional view hinges concerns whether the proponent of the traditional view can give a plausible explanation of why lying might be worse than mere deception. Some philosophers suggest that lying is worse because in cases of deception the victim is more responsible for the falsehood that they believe. But Saul points out that this explanation is implausible. If I am mugged because I knowingly walked in an unsafe area, I would bear some responsibility for what happened. But the mugger's act would be just as wrong as it would have been if I had walked in a safe area. There are other explanations philosophers give for thinking that lying is worse than mere deception. But Saul argues that all such explanations fail.

The Value of Honesty

Honesty is not as straightforward as it seems. What does honesty require if not merely telling the truth? To answer this question, it will be useful to think about some reasons for avoiding deception—not practical reasons, but moral ones. What is the **moral value** of honesty? Both Mill and Kant had answers to this question. They each stressed the moral significance of honesty. But they gave very different reasons for doing so.

Honesty and Happiness

We can begin with John Stuart Mill. At first, it is a bit surprising to hear that an arch consequentialist like Mill championed honesty. Cases where lying appears to maximize utility are readily at hand. In fact, often the very reason people are inclined towards deception is because it allows them to escape some harm or obtain some benefit. We might imagine, then, that when faced with the choice between a painful truth and a pleasant lie, the steadfast Utilitarian would almost always choose the lie.

It's true that, according to Utilitarianism, honesty is not always the best policy. Mill was clear that there are cases in which we are morally obligated to lie. For instance, we may need to lie to save an innocent person from harm. However, Mill was keenly sensitive to the role that honesty can play in human happiness. Recall that, according to Mill's Utilitarianism, happiness is the fundamental unit of moral value—it is the thing that grounds all moral obligations and prohibitions. Relationships are undoubtedly among the greatest contributors to human happiness. Trust is essential to human relationships, and honesty is key to trust. There are few things that wound us more deeply than to discover that someone we love and rely on has been dishonest with us. And Mill argued that even seemingly innocent "white lies"—those told to avoid awkwardness or hurt feelings—could be corrosive to close personal relationships. Small lies often grow into larger ones over time; lies that have the potential to break the relational bonds forged by trust. Of course, close personal relationships are the not only kinds that matter to human happiness. Others matter too. And, as essentially social creatures, few of us can hack it on our own. We need one another not only to survive, but also to thrive.

Honesty and Power

Like the relationships between individual human beings, the relationships between business and customers, governments and the populous, civil servants and the public all depend to some extent on trust. Granted we don't (and shouldn't) trust a government or a company in the same way we might trust a parent or a spouse. This is because these relationships are different in kind. A company, for instance, doesn't have the same level, or even the same sort, of responsibility to its consumers as a husband does to his wife or a mother to her child. However, trust is still essential to any kind of working relationship. Professional relationships exist because one party, in essence, passes control of some area over to the other. For such a venture to succeed, it is necessary that each entity can be trusted to do right by the other. Some **care ethicists** argue that there is an essential **asymmetry** involved in many relationships (professional relationships included). They claim that, as a result, one party is sometimes more vulnerable to being taken advantage of than the other. In such cases the person (or persons) in a **position of power** has a responsibility to protect the weaker party and to take care not to take advantage of them. Dishonesty, of course, is an excellent tool for manipulation. In most cases, we have good reason to believe that those who seek to manipulate us do not have our best interests in mind. Professional relationships that involve manipulation, such as the one between PaymentsMD and its clients, are untenable if not downright destructive.

Honesty and Autonomy

Immanuel Kant gave another reason for valuing honesty apart from the instrumental role it plays in sustaining human happiness. One reason for emphasizing honesty was linked to its role in supporting human autonomy. In order to truly exercise our autonomy, we have to understand and properly weigh the choices available to us. Information is key to freedom. For instance, imagine that you are having a conversation with your doctor about treatment options for disease X. Your doctor describes an experimental treatment with a 20 percent rate of success. You agree to the treatment only to find out later that there was another option with a 95 percent success rate. Did you freely choose to undergo the experimental treatment? The intuitive answer is "no." Granted, no one forced you to give your consent to the more dangerous option; but it seems clear that you could not have freely chosen it without complete knowledge of all of available options along with the risks and benefits involved with each. "Knowledge," as the saying goes, "is power."

Sometimes, however, information interferes with autonomy. Imagine again that you are in the doctor's office and that the doctor describes every possible treatment in excruciating detail using a mountain of technical information one would need an MD to understand. Would this kind of exhaustive description of your options help or hinder your choice? Or imagine that the doctor offers you an enticing but risky treatment option when she has good reason to believe that you do not have sufficient medical experience to properly understand the risks of the particular procedure. Can you freely choose an option when you can't properly conceive of the risks? Clearly, in some cases, the "whole truth" can be unhelpful and even harmful. We might say then that, like "uncritical loyalty" (a subject we discussed in Chapter 4), **uncritical honesty** can be a dangerous thing.

The Problem of Full Disclosure

This tension between offering too little or too much information is as present in engineering as it is in medicine. The **Problem of Full Disclosure**, as we will call it, is especially acute for engineers. Engineering decisions involve a large measure of specialized technical information—information that we would not necessarily expect the public to comprehend. Being provided with a flood of information, especially information that one does not have the expertise to fully understand, can be as disorienting and debilitating as having no information at all. Gene sequencing and biological engineering provide examples in which information is key to autonomy, as well as examples of the opposite scenario in which too much technical information hinders autonomy. For instance, a genetic test that gives specific and actionable information, such as the BRCA gene test for breast cancer susceptibility genes, enhances autonomy by giving individuals specific information on breast cancer risk, thereby allowing individuals to decide whether preventive surgery is warranted. On the other hand, a genetic sequencing test that gives an individual her entire genetic code (an estimated 3×10^9 characters in length), while technically providing more information, hinders autonomy because the information is highly technical, too confusing, and not actionable.

Furthermore, even if all of the relevant technical information is made available to the public, they may not be motivated to comb through it. This is because individual members of the public may feel less invested in trying to understand this technical information regarding public engineering projects than they would technical information relating to personal health. In that case, simply "putting the information out there" is not enough. "The Ethics of Truth-Telling and the Problem of Risk" by Paul B. Thompson helps us better understand the problem of full disclosure as it applies to situations involving the communication of risk. Thompson offers some suggestions for how experts can communicate vital information, such as information regarding risk, to non-experts. His view, in brief, is that the public uses the term "risk" in a different way than experts do. And the public finds salient and begins to fear risks in ways that are different from experts. For these reasons, in communicating information regarding risk, engineers and other scientists should adopt a number of policies. Two of the most salient for our purposes are: first, don't use "risk" and "probability" interchangeably. For example, never say "There is no zero risk." The public will hear that differently than an engineer or a scientist. And, second, if possible, present information in such a way that the non-expert will use his own values, rather than your values, to make a decision. Whether an option is a risk may be something the expert is able to determine, but not the lay person. However, given that something is a risk, the values of the lay person may be significantly different from those of the expert. And the expert in that case should do her best to empower the lay person to make a decision based on his own values.

Honesty: Some Unanswered Questions

At this point it should be clear that looking to Kant, Mill, and others does not answer the moral question about honesty once and for all. Instead, it raises further ethical questions about the limits of an engineer's professional obligations. For instance, with regard to the duty to protect autonomy, we might ask: "To what extent is it an engineer's job to facilitate public understanding of technical decisions?" After all, we may not think engineers always have the time or inclination to be public educators. And, why think that the burden of education falls solely on the shoulders of engineers? To what extent does the public have an obligation to educate themselves about such decisions? Surely, making engineers solely responsible for public knowledge undermines the public's independence in some sense.

There is simply no escaping these kinds of question. However, for the philosophically minded there is no need to escape. Moral problems are among the most pressing problems there are. As with any worthwhile pursuit, we should expect the project of moral problem solving to be interestingly long and to demand a tremendous amount of our intellectual resources. Each new question uncovers a new layer of complexity in the moral life, and it is worth pursuing each dimension slowly and carefully. As our investigation progresses, we may use the insights we have gathered along the way as tools for future work. Most importantly, the more we practice asking and answering such questions, the better we get at it.

Understanding Trust

As our discussion of Mill earlier in the chapter showed, trust is relevant to morality. Mill's concern was that for society to work people need to trust one another. And, in particular, he thought that we need to be honest in order to trust each other. But there are other cases in which trust is important. Think about the examples considered so far in this chapter. There is the PaymentsMD scandal. There is the story about Frieda's peanut allergy. There is the example about the doctor offering you a treatment with a 20 percent rate of success when he could have offered you a treatment with a 95 percent rate of success instead. There is the example contrasting the BRCA test for breast cancer with a test that provides the patient with their entire genetic code. All these examples involve trust. Consumers trusted PaymentsMD not to deceive them. Frieda trusted George not to deceive her when she asked whether there were peanuts in the meal he prepared. You trust doctors to give you all the relevant information about possible treatments. You trust those who administer screening tests to omit irrelevant information. Trust is clearly an important concept in moral philosophy. But what is trust? When is trust morally acceptable? When does morality demand distrust?

Trust and Reliance

To answer these questions, we must first distinguish between trust and mere reliance. Suppose you relax on your porch in the early afternoon and go inside to watch your favorite show only when your neighbor, who always walks at 3:30pm, leaves his house. In this case you rely on your neighbor to keep the time. But you do not exactly trust him. It would be misplaced to feel betrayed by your neighbor if, on a certain day, he decided not to go for a walk and as a result you missed your favorite show. Contrast this with a case in which your friend promises to drive you to the airport. You pack your bags. You wait outside your house. And your friend never shows. It turns out that he decided to get drunk and play videogames instead. In this case you rely on your friend to take you to the airport. But you also trust him. Different reactions are appropriate and different reactions are likely when trust, as opposed to mere reliance, is broken or misplaced. It would be appropriate and natural to feel anger toward your friend and to demand an apology from him for failing to take you to the airport. But it would be inappropriate and unnatural to react in the same way to your neighbor who failed to leave his house. Furthermore, trust always has a moral dimension to it. Your neighbor has done nothing wrong in deciding to go for a walk at a different time—but has done something wrong by getting drunk instead of taking you to the airport.

Trust and Vulnerability

Different reactions are appropriate to the violation of trust than to mere reliance. But why is this? What exactly is trust? Annette Baier has defended one particularly influential theory of trust. On her view, trust involves exposing oneself to harm. When we trust someone, we trust them with the care of something. Her view is that A trusts B with the care of something if and only if A accepts vulnerability to B's possible but not expected ill-will or incompetence regarding the care of that thing. To distrust someone is to not accept such vulnerability.

This can be made clear with some examples. Go back to the example in which your friend fails to take you to the airport and gets drunk instead. In this case you have trusted your friend with the care of your travel plans and transportation. You have accepted vulnerability to your friend in such a way that if he wants to interrupt your travel plans, if he is too eager to prioritize something else, or if he is simply too incompetent, your plans will be ruined or made more difficult to accomplish. For another example, suppose you enter the library late at night. You look around and see a few people hanging out. You judge that these people are not a threat and you continue to enter the library. In this case you have trusted the other people in the library with the care of a number of things. You trust them with your autonomy and freedom. You trust them not to interrupt you or nag you or attack you. Baier suggests that there are a number of goods that would not be possible without trust. We need to trust others in order for certain things to be created or sustained. We cannot create or sustain goods such as health, our children, conversation, writing, governments, markets, and so on without trust.

Think about how Baier's theory applies to real-world cases. Members of the public trust engineers—they *must* because most members of the public don't have the relevant technical knowledge to know whether a given engineering product is a risk. Recall the VW case discussed in Chapter 4. The public purchased and allowed the sale of VW cars because they trusted the engineers to design products that complied with regulations regarding fossil fuel emissions. In doing so, the public exposed itself to harm. Those who purchased VW products, and those who allowed VW products to be sold, made themselves vulnerable to clever engineers who were able to design cars that passed emissions tests while exceeding emissions limits when on the road. The PaymentsMD example is another such case. The public trusted that their private information would be secure, and that the forms they were asked to sign would honestly communicate all relevant information. The public accepted vulnerability to PaymentsMD on these matters. And their trust was violated.

Self-Deception

So far in this chapter, we have focused on an engineer's obligation to be honest with the public. However, engineers also have an obligation to be honest with themselves. In our more vulnerable moments, all of us are tempted to use loopholes to justify our moral shortcomings. "I didn't *lie*," we might say. And while strictly speaking it might be true, we now know that the strict truth isn't really what is important about honesty. The sort of reasoning we use to rationalize our poor behavior is a form of **self-deception**—perhaps the most dangerous form of deception, morally speaking. When the pressure is on, it's not difficult for us to convince ourselves that our duty to honesty is easily discharged. The very phrasing of the canon "avoid deceptive acts," though it centers on deception rather than truth, can leave us vulnerable to self-deception if we take it literally. It might seem as if all that is required of us is to steer clear of wanton acts of manipulation. Since few of us strive to be overtly deceptive, it's natural to think that we can satisfy this canon without much difficulty. However, we now understand that there is much more to it than that. There are times when protecting autonomy and trust will require more than merely *avoiding* deception. Instead it will take a tremendous amount of deliberateness, effort, and courage. And, more than anything, it will take being honest with ourselves—to admit, not just when we succeed in holding ourselves to these high standards, but also when we fail.

Understanding Self-Deception

What is self-deception? A natural thought is that self-deception should be modeled after the sort of regular, interpersonal, deception we have already discussed. In interpersonal deception, one person tries to get another person to consciously believe something that they themselves consciously believe to be false. So self-deception would occur when a person consciously tries to get themself to believe something they consciously believe is false. But how could one trick themself into believing something they know is false? It is easy to see how deception could occur between people. I know that what I'm trying to get the person to believe is false. But he doesn't. And he doesn't know that I'm tricking him. But when I deceive myself, I know the relevant belief is false. And I know I'm playing a trick on myself. So how can *self*-deception occur?

Self-deception, though a bit trickier than interpersonal deception, can occur in at least two ways. First, people have conscious and unconscious parts. If I'm stealing money from the register at work, and I recognize that it's wrong but feel bad about it, my subconsciousness might trick me into believing that I'm not doing anything wrong by making some rationalization seem plausible. So while I might go from consciously believing what I'm doing is wrong to consciously believing it's permissible, I never consciously believe both at the same time. I only consciously believe it's permissible while, at most, retaining some unconscious awareness that it's wrong. Second, it might be that self-deception doesn't happen at just one time, but that it is a process extended over time. Imagine again that I'm stealing from the register at work. I want the money but I don't want to retain the belief that I'm a thief. So I steal the money, cover up all the evidence, create evidence that I didn't do it, and then, a few years later, I forget what I've done. In that case I've deceived myself because I forgot that I tricked myself. Furthermore, it is possible to arrive at true beliefs accidentally or by an unreliable process. If I flip a coin and decide to believe the number of stars in the universe is even on the basis of that flip, it might very well be a true belief. So, imagine that I convince myself that stealing is permissible by taking a pill that induces the belief that stealing is permissible. In that case, I'm aware of the trick I played on myself. But I might simply think that I've come to a true belief by an unreliable means.

Questions Regarding Self-Deception

So far, we have been considering questions about what self-deception is and how it can occur. But there are also important questions concerning the morality of self-deception. First, to what extent is someone who is self-deceived responsible for their self-deception? Some think that self-deception that occurs due to the conscious decisions of a person makes that person morally responsible for their predicament. On the other hand, if one thinks that self-deception is caused primarily by one's unconsciousness, then one might think that a self-deceived person is off the hook. We have many unconscious biases. While some of them are unfortunate, many people do not think we are morally responsible for the relevant biases or for their consequences. If self-deception is caused by just another one of these unconscious biases, then one might think the self-deceived are not morally responsible for their situation. On the other hand, to the extent that we are all somewhat aware of these biases, and to the extent that we can do things to mitigate them, such as exposing ourselves to ideas and people that challenge our deeply held beliefs, perhaps even if self-deception is unconscious, we could still be at least partly morally responsible for it. Others suggest that even if self-deception is caused entirely by the unconscious, we are still blameworthy for it to at least some extent. After all, our unconsciousness is a part of us. And so there is a part of us that is deceptive.

So one issue is whether one is responsible in cases of self-deception. Another issue is whether self-deception is good or bad. And, if it is bad, why? One of the primary ways in which self-deception might be bad in the context of engineering concerns the consequences of self-deception. It is plausible that self-deception played a role in many of the problematic engineering cases we have discussed. In the case of the VW scandal, for instance, it would have been easy for an engineer to rationalize rigging an engine to pass emissions tests. Perhaps the engineers working on this project thought that they were just following orders and so they were off the hook. Perhaps they told themselves that other companies were doing it too. Perhaps they told themselves that worries about climate change are overblown. Any of these is a plausible mechanism for eliminating guilt and going through with the problematic engineering project. For another example, self-deception might be part of the explanation for cases of plagiarism. In 2006 the mechanical engineering department at Ohio University became embroiled in a plagiarism scandal. It turned out that at least 36 masters' theses were plagiarized. The fault wasn't just with the students. Faculty members were fired and reprimanded for what happened. Perhaps the faculty members told themselves that, in accommodating plagiarism or looking the other way, they were simply helping out their students. Perhaps, in a desire to get their students jobs, they subtly encouraged them to plagiarize without being fully conscious of what they were doing.

Plagiarism and Deception

Another form of deception relevant to the work of an engineer is plagiarism. This can be deceptive in the interpersonal sense. For example, you might well know that an idea is not yours. But you do your best to convince others at your engineering firm that it is yours. But plagiarism need not take this explicit and interpersonal form. It can have a more subtle, self-deceptive shape. One could deceive oneself into thinking that an idea is one's own when it really belongs to another. Certainly that seems wrong. But why? And what makes it wrong?

One answer is that plagiarism involves stealing intellectual property (IP). And stealing is wrong. So plagiarism is wrong too. This is the **stealing explanation** of the wrongness of plagiarism. Understanding this explanation of the wrongness of plagiarism requires thinking a bit more about what it takes to own something and what it takes for something to become one's property.

One influential theory of ownership is due to John Locke. Locke holds that one owns something if one mixes one's labor with that thing and if it is previously unowned. Imagine you are walking through the woods and find an unowned mushroom. You pick up the mushroom, take it home, and cook it in a stir-fry. In this case you have taken something previously unowned, the mushroom, and have mixed your labor with it by cooking it into your stir-fry. On Locke's theory, you own the mushroom. And that seems right.

The core idea of Locke's theory is attractive and influential. But there are some complications. One is that the theory seems to make it too easy to own property: Suppose you are the first person to travel to Mars. You clear out a plot of land, plant a flag, and send a radio signal back to Earth in which you say "Sorry losers, Mars belongs to me!" You mixed your labor with Mars. It was previously unowned. But it seems a bit much to think that you can now claim all of Mars for yourself.

One could try to fix this problem by pointing out that when you clear out a plot of land you only mix your labor with a small part of Mars. What matters isn't that you mix your labor with *any* part of what is unowned at all, however small. What matters is instead that your labor *permeates* what was unowned. In the Mars example, your labor permeates the small plot of land. So you own that. But it doesn't permeate the entirety of Mars. So you don't own the planet as a whole. But this fix won't work. Imagine you create a machine that will go through all of Mars and scratch the entire surface. Or imagine you pour a can of radioactive tomato juice into the ocean and a molecule of the juice finds its way to every part of the ocean, turning the whole thing red. In these cases your labor permeates Mars and your labor permeates the ocean. But you do not own either.

What to say about examples like this? One suggestion is to add to the theory the idea that in claiming property you have to leave as much or better for others. So, if you just take a plot of land on Mars, others can come after you and take as much or better. But if you take the entirety of Mars, then all the other people coming to Mars are out of luck. But this strategy will make it too difficult to own property. Imagine Mars has a lot of potentially valuable land. You are the first to Mars and take the very best plot of land but leave plenty of other very good land for others. It seems like you can now claim ownership of that plot of land. Or imagine you are in an unowned cave and happen to see a lone diamond stuck together with other rocks. You break the diamond out of the rock and take it. One might think the diamond is now yours even if there is nothing as good waiting for other discoverers.

So perhaps we can say this about Locke's theory: the core idea is attractive. Perhaps something like Locke's theory might be true. But the proponent of the theory will have to do some work to avoid problematic examples like the ones discussed above.

Another potential difficulty in applying Locke's theory to intellectual property concerns whether intellectual property even exists. Is it really possible to own something as abstract and intangible as a song or an idea or a paper? Some skeptics of intellectual property doubt that such things can be owned. They accept the **physical possession theory of ownership**, according to which the ownership of something requires the physical possession of that thing. And since you can't physically possess an idea, that idea can't be your property. It is impossible to own an idea. Defenders of intellectual property address this problem by denying that ownership requires the physical possession of something. They accept the **power theory of ownership**, according to which ownership is the right to a power. In particular: to own something is to have the right to the power to keep others from activities involving that thing. To own a song isn't to own some abstract entity. It is instead to have the right to the power to keep others from using that song, or using that song without paying you. You can't own an abstract idea. But you can own and have the right to control the physical manifestation of an idea.

So, how does all of this apply to engineering? Recall the Ohio University academic plagiarism scandal. In that case masters' theses plagiarized previously published work and passed it off as the work of the engineering students. Professors were fired as a result. In that case students, with the aid of faculty, are alleged to have taken ideas that others previously and claimed that those ideas were their own. So, although those involved in the scandal might have genuinely mixed their labor with the relevant ideas, those ideas were not unowned. And so they were stolen.

Go back to the discussion of honesty and deception. One of the lessons of the Grice and PaymentsMD examples was that one can be dishonest and one can deceive without explicitly saying anything false. In the present case, consider an engineering thesis containing formulas, claims about materials,

186 Honesty and Deception

claims about regulations, etc. It is possible that a plagiarized thesis could contain only true information. But, nevertheless, it can be dishonest and fail to live up to the admonition to avoid deceptive acts.

Chapter 5 Key Terms and Concepts

Moral Value
Care Ethicists
Asymmetry
Position of Power
Uncritical Honesty
Problem of Full Disclosure

Self-Deception
The Stealing Explanation
The Physical Possession Theory of
    Ownership
The Power Theory of Ownership

Chapter 5: End of Chapter Reading and NSPE Board of Ethical Review Cases

Guided Core Reading   188

> *Core Reading 5.1:* 'The ethics of truth-telling and the problem of risk' by Paul B. Thompson (excerpts)
> *Core Reading 5.2:* 'Trust and antitrust' by Annette Baier (excerpts)

NSPE Board of Ethical Review Cases   195

> *Case 99-7:* Disclosure—Advising Client to Exercise Judgment When Disclosing Information to Engineer (1999)
> *Case 97-11:* Duty to Disclose Disciplinary Complaint to Client (1997)
> *Case 79-5:* Academic Qualifications (1979)

Guided Further Reading   200

> *Further Reading 5.1:* 'Just go ahead and lie' by Jennifer Saul
> *Further Reading 5.2:* 'Commentary: Informed consent in engineering and medicine' by Roland Schinzinger and Mike W. Martin
> *Further Reading 5.3:* 'Plagiarism: Words and ideas' by Mathieu Bouville

Tip: If you can't use the QR codes, use the hyperlinks found on the book's webpage instead: www.routledge.com/9781138183865.

Guided Core Reading

Core Reading 5.1: 'The ethics of truth-telling and the problem of risk' by Paul B. Thompson (excerpts)

Preparing to Read

What is risk? How should experts, such as engineers, communicate the risks associated with various alternatives to the public? Thompson considers and rejects various proposals. He argues that the literature on risk communication fails to take into account a distinction between risk as event prediction and risk as problem classifying. He then gives a new account of the problems facing risk communication and four dictums for ethical risk communication.

Excerpted from: Thompson, P. B. (1999). The ethics of truth-telling and the problem of risk. *Science and Engineering Ethics*, 5, 489–510. doi.org/10.1007/s11948-999-0050-5. © Springer Nature 1999, reprinted with permission. Internal references omitted.

[A]ttempts at risk communication … fall into paradox …. [T]he … public overreacts, except when they under-react …. [T]hey tend to view risks as either more or less serious than … evidence would warrant….

Models of risk communication … presuppose that the information being supplied is intended for use in calculative weighing of options ….Yet … risk figures in non-deliberative practice, too …. [W]hen a particular activity or course of action is classified as 'risky' it is moved into the deliberative realm and singled out for scrutiny….

The dilemma arises because there … are … contexts in which it is … important to make people aware of the probability that harm may accompany unexceptional and ordinary activities. However, one would not wish … to lead … people to make substantial revisions in the cognitive filters that help them focus on so-called risky activities….

On the one hand, risk communicators *should* provide all relevant information on relative probabilities because doing so is … their responsibility …. On the other hand, risk communicators *should not* promote messages that might lead to an inappropriate revision of our cognitive filters because doing so is misleading and will lead to false judgments about risk….

Reliability of Information and Evaluation of Risk

The … public … is likely to reflect uncertainty in its estimation of … risks…. For example, people may regard the risk of buying a used car as significant, not only because there is an objective probability of repair costs and financial losses associated with the car itself, but because they regard their potential sources of information about used cars as highly unreliable....

[F]actors involved in assessing the reliability of information contribute to the divergence between expert and lay estimates of risk. After all, the experts are the public's source of information about nuclear power, biotechnology, or whatever. Although experts may have concerns about uncertainty or incompleteness of information, they would not suspect themselves of duplicity or culpable ignorance. The lay person clearly might, however, and this suspicion could reasonably lead them to regard risks associated with the technology in question as greater than that reported. It is also possible that a feeling of confidence in the authorities responsible for a given activity will make people think of that activity as less risky....

What should risk communicators do ...? Any used car dealer certainly knows that certain communication techniques will increase a potential customer's estimate of the dealer's honesty and reliability: look your customers in the eye; speak in a calm tone of voice; don't use pressure; acknowledge and validate the customer's concerns. As a matter of fact, many of the used car dealer's techniques are disconcertingly similar to the kinds of advice being given to risk communicators today. There is an interesting irony here. The more these techniques are deployed as a way of limiting the distorting affects [sic] of information reliability, the more we tend to think of them as ethically questionable....

Furthermore, when the techniques are detected, they increase the audience's tendency to believe that the source is unreliable ....We discount the message of the salesman who masters the techniques of obtaining trust precisely because we think that people who would do this are untrustworthy....

The Case of Food Safety

... There is no intra-scientific disagreement about the relative probabilities that microbial contamination and pesticide residues will cause injury to food consumers....Although there is disagreement about the effects of long-term exposure to pesticide, there is little doubt that, overall, the probability of death or injury from microbial contamination vastly exceeds that of death or injury from consuming pesticide residues, perhaps by several orders of magnitude....

However ... the public is far more concerned about pesticide residue than microbial contamination....

When people believe that there is "no risk" associated with ordinary consumption of food, they do not believe that there is zero probability of harm. What they believe is that under normal circumstances there is no reason to be particularly mindful of vague possibilities that lurk in the background.

Instead, we devote time and presence of mind to things that are newly apparent within our environment. Pesticide residues are relatively recently discovered; microbial food poisoning has always been with us....

Truth-Telling and Communicative Discourse

These observations lend support to four dicta for risk communicators.

1st Dictum of Ethical Risk Communication: Never say 'risk' when you mean 'probability'. While many scientists and engineers may use these terms interchangeably, members of the general public do not. Why fight it? One can tell the truth about the probability of a given harm by specifying the harm and stating its rough likelihood, or one may talk about the 'chance' of a given event or outcome. It is not necessary to say more than this by saying that this probability of harm is "the risk".

2nd Dictum of Ethical Risk Communication: Never say, There is 'No zero risk' .... It is true that there are no circumstances in which the future holds zero probability of harm. It does not follow that everything involves risk. In some contexts, the whole point of calling something a risk is to distinguish it from a broad category of "not risks" to which we will pay no further attention....

3rd Dictum of Ethical Risk Communication: Empower when possible. The two problems discussed in this paper become especially troubling from an ethics perspective when people have no choice but to rely on expert opinion .... [A] lay person may rely on [their] own values in deciding whether or not to base action on an expert's prediction....

4th Dictum of Ethical Risk Communication: Everyone is responsible for public trust. The best way to earn confidence is to always be right. Since that seems unlikely, and since not every risk problem can be resolved with informed consent, scientists, engineers and their professional organizations should actively explore better ways to strengthen the communicative context for discussing technological risks. This is admittedly an open-ended dictum that goes well beyond what has been shown in this paper. It points toward an underdeveloped area in science and engineering ethics....

Guided Reading Questions

1. Thompson thinks a paradox arises in risk communication. Do you agree?
2. Thompson argues that there are two ways that we think about risk. One is deliberative. The other is non-deliberative. Suppose Thompson is right about this. In that case, do you think both ways of thinking about risk are valuable? In your opinion, what are the relative strengths and weaknesses of each approach?

3. Explain the food safety example Thompson discusses. Do you think the public is right to interpret the risks in the relevant way? Or do you think they are mistaken and should worry much more about microbial food poisoning than pesticide residues?
4. What are Thompson's four dictums of ethical risk communication? How do the dictums help with the problems that concern him? Do you agree that his dictums are helpful? Or do you see any problems with them?

Read the Full Article

You can read the full article online by scanning the QR code or following the link below. Your college library will need to subscribe to the journal, and you may need to login via your library's website or use campus wifi to get access.

https://link.springer.com/article/10.1007/s11948-999-0050-5

Core Reading 5.2: 'Trust and antitrust' by Annette Baier (excerpts)

Preparing to Read

In this paper Baier develops an account of the morality of trust. She specifies when a trust relationship has become corrupted. Baier begins by identifying the need for an account of the morality of trust and its absence in previous moral philosophy. She then discusses different varieties of trust. Baier argues that a trust relationship is morally decent just in case its continuation need not rely on threats or coverups of breaches of trust.

Excerpted from: Baier, A. (1986). Trust and antitrust. *Ethics*, 96(2), 231–260. doi.org/10.1086/292745. © 1986 University of Chicago, reprinted with permission. Internal references omitted.

TRUST AND ITS VARIETIES

… Trust … is shown by us … not only with intimates but with strangers…. We often trust total strangers, such as those from whom we ask directions in foreign cities, to direct rather than misdirect….We trust those we encounter in lonely library stacks to be searching for books, not victims….

Trust … is accepted vulnerability to another's possible but not expected ill will….

The … thing to attend to is why we typically … leave things … we value close enough to others for them to harm them. The answer … is that we need their help in creating, and … looking after the things we most value…. Accepting such an analysis, taking trust to be a three-place predicate (A trusts B with valued thing C) will involve some distortion and regimentation of some cases, where we may have to strain to discern any definite candidate for C, but I think it will prove more of a help than a hindrance.

One way in which trusted persons can fail to act as they were trusted to is by taking on the care of more than they were entrusted with—the babysitter who decides that the nursery would be improved if painted purple and sets to work to transform it, will have acted, as a babysitter, in an untrustworthy way, however great his good will….

Admittedly there are many cases of trust where "caring for C" seems much more than A expects of B even when there is no problem in finding a fairly restricted value for C. Suppose I look quickly around me before proceeding into the dark street or library stacks …, judge the few people I discern there to be nondangerous, and so go ahead. We can say that my bodily safety, and … pocketbook, are the goods I am allowing these people to be in a position to threaten. I trust them, it seems, merely to leave me alone. But this is not quite right, for should a piece of falling masonry or toppling books threaten to fall on my head, and one of these persons leap into action and shove me out of this danger, I would regard that I had trusted these strangers to do a case for gratitude, not for an assault charge …. So what do I trust strangers in such circumstances to do? Certainly not anything whatever as long as it is done with good will, nor even anything whatever for my bodily safety and security of property as long as it is done with good will. Suppose someone I have judged nondangerous as I proceed into the stacks should seize me from behind, frightening but not harming me, and claim with apparent sincerity that she did it for my own good, so that I would learn a lesson and be more cautious in the future. I would not respond with gratitude but demand what business my long-term security of life was of hers, that she felt free to subject me to such unpleasant educational measures....

It is fairly easy, once we look, to see how this special vulnerability is involved in many ordinary forms of trust. We trust the mailman to deliver and not tamper with the mail, and to some extent we trust his discretion in interpreting what "tampering" covers.... What do we trust our mailmen to do or not to do? To use their discretion in getting our mail to us, to take enough interest in us and in the nature of our mail, (compatibly with their total responsibility) to make intelligent decisions about what to do with it when such decisions have to be made....

[N]ot all the variables involved in trust are yet in view. One which the entrusting model obscures rather than highlights is the degree of explicitness.... [T]rust relationships need not be so express, and some important forms of them cannot be verbally acknowledged.... Trust between infant and parent is such a case....

A MORAL TEST FOR TRUST

I now turn to the question of when a given form of trust is morally decent, so properly preserved by trustfulness and trustworthiness, and when it fails in moral decency....

I ... propose a test for the moral decency of a trust relationship, namely, that its continuation need not rely on successful threats held over the trusted, or on her successful cover-up of breaches of trust. We could develop and generalize this test into a version of an expressibility test, if we note that knowledge of what the other party is relying on for the continuance of the trust relationship would, in the above cases of concealment and of threat advantage, itself destabilize the relation. Knowledge of the other's reliance on concealment does so fairly automatically, and knowledge of the other's partial reliance on one's fear of his revenge would tend, in a person of normal pride and self-assertiveness, to prompt her to look for ways of exploiting her discretionary powers so as to minimize her vulnerability to that threat.... Should the wife come to realize that the husband relies on her fear of his revenge ... to keep her more or less trustworthy, that knowledge should be enough to begin to cure these weaknesses and to motivate untrustworthiness. Similarly, should the truster come to realize that the trusted relies on her skill at covering up or on her ability to charm him into forgiveness for breaches of trust ..., that realization will help cure that blindness and gullibility. A trust relationship is morally bad to the extent that either party relies on qualities in the other which would be weakened by the knowledge that the other relies on them. Where each relies on the other's love, or concern for some common good, or professional pride in competent discharge of responsibility, knowledge of what the other is relying on in one need not undermine but will more likely strengthen those relied-on features. They survive exposure ... in a way that some forms of stupidity, fear, blindness, ignorance, and gullibility normally do not....

Guided Reading Questions

1. Baier thinks we trust strangers. Why does she think this? Do you agree?
2. How are the varieties of trust connected to the varieties of vulnerabilities? Do you agree with Baier that trust essentially involves vulnerability?
3. What is infant trust? What non-verbal aspects of trust does it illustrate? Do you agree with Baier that an infant trusts its parents? In the context of engineering, does the public ever exhibit this sort of trust? Or is public trust in engineers necessarily more explicit?
4. What is Baier's expressibility test for the morality of trust? She thinks trust can be bad. Do you agree? If so, what are some examples of bad trust that you have encountered. If not, why not?

Read the Full Article

You can read the full article online by scanning the QR code or following the link below. Your college library will need to subscribe to the journal, and you may need to login via your library's website or use campus wifi to get access.

www.journals.uchicago.edu/doi/pdfplus/10.1086/292745
Also available on JSTOR: www.jstor.org/stable/2381376

NSPE Board of Ethical Review Cases

Case 99-7: Disclosure—Advising Client to Exercise Judgment When Disclosing Information to Engineer

Disclosure—Advising Client to Exercise Judgment When Disclosing Information to Engineer

Case 99-7
Year: 1999
Facts:

Engineer A is a consulting engineer and provides civil and environmental engineering services for public and private clients. Among the standard practices that Engineer A has incorporated when initially meeting with clients is to explain to the client that in an effort to fulfill his obligation as a faithful agent and trustee to the client, the client should be advised that should Engineer A discover a danger to the public health and safety, he (Engineer A) has an ethical obligation to report such violations of the law to the appropriate public authorities and, therefore, the client "should exercise judgment and discretion when providing information to him or making him aware of facts and circumstances that could involve a violation of the law."

Question from the NSPE:
Was it ethical for Engineer A to advise the client in the manner described?

Going Beyond—Our Questions for a Deep Dive

1. What information might be implicitly, though not explicitly, communicated to clients by Engineer A's statements?
2. Engineer A stated something true when he said he had a duty to act as a faithful agent or trustee to his clients. But is it also true that, in order to fulfill that duty, Engineer A had an obligation to alert clients of his duty to report dangers to public health and safety?
3. In your opinion, is Engineer A simply fulfilling his professional obligation to act as a faithful agent or trustee? Or is Engineer A betraying his professional obligation to hold paramount the safety and wellbeing of the public?
4. Is Engineer A's warning consistent with his duty to hold paramount the safety and welfare of the public, or does it compromise that obligation to any extent? Does "holding paramount" public safety and welfare mean that this obligation must be weighed more heavily than other obligations?
5. Suppose a client was involved in unlawful activity that would seriously compromise public health and safety. And suppose further that the client would have disclosed this information to Engineer A, but that the client purposely hid this information from Engineer A as a result of Engineer A's warning. In your opinion, would Engineer A be responsible with regard to any harm that came to the public as a result of the client's decision to withhold the information.
6. We do not know Engineer A's motives for warning his client of his duty to report dangers to public health and safety. However, we can hypothesize about his motives. What could some possible motives for Engineer A's actions be? For instance, is Engineer attempting to protect his client? Is he attempting to avoid a potential ethical dilemma? Do intentions matter in this case, or only the actions themselves?

Read the Board's Discussion and Conclusion

To read the discussion and conclusion of this case by members of the NSPE Board of Ethical Review, go to: www.nspe.org/resources/ethics/ethics-resources/board-ethical-review-cases/disclosure-advising-client-exercise.

Case 97-11: Duty to Disclose Disciplinary Complaint to Client

Duty to Disclose Disciplinary Complaint to Client

Case 97-11
Year: 1997
Facts:

Engineer A is retained by Client B to perform design services and provide a Critical Path Method (CPM) schedule for a manufacturing facility. Engineer A prepares the plans and specifications and the CPM schedule.

During the rendering of services to Client B on this project, the state board of professional engineers contacts Engineer A regarding an ethics complaint filed against Engineer A by Client C relating to services provided on a project for Client C that are similar to the services being performed for Client B. Client C alleges that Engineer A lacked the competence to perform the services in question. Engineer A does not believe it is necessary to notify Client B of the pending complaint. Later, through another party, Client B learns of the ethics complaint filed against Engineer A and tells Engineer A that he is upset by the allegations and that Engineer A should have brought the matter to Client B's attention.

Question from the NSPE:
Was it unethical for Engineer A to not report to Client B the ethics complaint filed against Engineer A by Client C?

Going Beyond—Our Questions for a Deep Dive

1. What reasons might Engineer A have for thinking that reporting the complaint to Client C was unnecessary? When might it be necessary to report this kind of information to a client?
2. In order to make an autonomous decision, an individual has to have access to the relevant information regarding that decision. Was the information regarding the complaint relevant to Client C's decision to retain Engineer A or was it superfluous to it?
3. In general, what sort of information might be relevant to a client's decision to retain the services of an engineer? What sort of information is not relevant?
4. Does it make a difference, morally, that the complaint in this case was pending and not yet verified. If the complaint against Engineer A had

been verified rather than alleged, would Engineer A have had a duty to report the information regarding the complaint to Client C?

5.   Arguably, the fact that Client B did not hear about the complaint from Engineer A led to a loss of trust of Client B in Engineer A. If Engineer A had disclosed the information about the complaint, would it have saved Client B's trust in Engineer A? Could disclosing the information have any negative effects on trust?

6.   Does the state board of professional engineers have any obligation to make Engineer A's current clients aware of the pending complaint against Engineer A? What if the complaint had been verified?

Read the Board's Discussion and Conclusion

To read the discussion and conclusion of this case by members of the NSPE Board of Ethical Review, go to: www.nspe.org/resources/ethics/ethics-resources/board-ethical-review-cases/duty-disclose-disciplinary-complaint.

Case 79-5: Academic Qualifications

Academic Qualifications

Case 79-5
Year: 1979
Facts:

Engineer A received a Bachelor of Science degree in 1940 from a recognized engineering curriculum, and subsequently was registered as a professional engineer in two states. Later, he was awarded an earned "Professional Degree" from the same institution. In 1960 he received a Ph.D. degree from an organization which awards degrees on the basis of correspondence without requiring any form of personal attendance or study at the institution, and is regarded by state authorities as a "diploma mill." Engineer A has since listed his Ph.D. degree among his academic qualifications in brochures, correspondence, and otherwise, without indicating its nature.

Question from the NSPE:
Was Engineer A ethical in citing his Ph.D. degree as an academic qualification under these circumstances?

Going Beyond—Our Questions for a Deep Dive

1. Presumably, Engineer A did not provide any additional information about the nature of his bachelor or professional degree. Instead, he left the reader to fill in that information on their own. Do you think he was wrong not to include such information? Why or why not?
2. Imagine that Engineer A had independently completed PhD-level work commensurate with the kind he would have completed at an accredited university PhD program (perhaps through self-study). However, assume he has not received a degree from any institution—accredited or otherwise. Would it be unethical for him to list a PhD as an academic qualification?
3. If a client found out that Engineer A had received a PhD from a "diploma mill," how might this affect the client's trust in the profession? If engineers regularly received degrees in this way, how might it affect the public's perception of engineering as a profession?

Read the Board's Discussion and Conclusion

To read the discussion and conclusion of this case by members of the NSPE Board of Ethical Review, go to: www.nspe.org/sites/default/files/resources/pdfs/Ethics/EthicsResources/EthicsCaseSearch/1979/BER%2079-5.pdf.

Guided Further Reading

Further Reading 5.1: 'Just go ahead and lie' by Jennifer Saul

Find the Article

Saul, J. (2012). Just go ahead and lie. *Analysis*, 72(1), 3–9. doi.org/10.1093/analys/anr133.

Read the article online by scanning the QR code or following the link below. Your college library will need to subscribe to the journal, and you may need to login via your library's website or use campus wifi to get access.

https://academic.oup.com/analysis/article-abstract/72/1/3/269290

Also available on JSTOR: www.jstor.org/stable/41340787

Preparing to Read

In this article, Jennifer Saul argues that in many cases lying is no worse than merely deceiving someone. She begins by providing a counterexample to the claim that lying is always worse than misleading. Saul then considers and rejects various attempts to explain why lying might be worse, and offers an explanation of why we are tempted to think lying is worse. In the end, although there are some cases in which lying is worse than mere deception, in general one should just lie when faced with a need to deceive.

Guided Reading Questions

1. Saul thinks that, in the case of Frieda and George, lying is no different than mere deception. Why does she think this? Do you agree?
2. One explanation for the badness of lying is this: In cases of mere misleading, the audience is partly responsible for the deception. In cases of lying, the audience is not. So that is why lying is worse. Why does Saul think the story about the two muggers is a problem for this explanation? Is Saul right? Or do you disagree?
3. How is the idea that we sometimes need to deceive supposed to explain why lying is worse than misleading? How is the story about the different brands of gun a problem for this explanation?
4. What is Saul's explanation for why we tend to think lying is worse than mere deception? Do you agree with Saul's explanation?
5. What, according to Saul, are the contexts in which lying is much worse than mere deception? How might Saul's insight be applied to engineering contexts?

Further Reading 5.2: 'Commentary: Informed consent in engineering and medicine' by Roland Schinzinger and Mike W. Martin

Find the Article

Schinzinger, R., & Martin, M.W. (1983). Commentary: Informed consent in engineering and medicine. *Business and Professional Ethics Journal*, 3(1), 67–77. doi.org/10.5840/bpej19833143.

Read the article online by scanning the QR code or following the link below. Your college library will need to subscribe to the journal, and you may need to login via your library's website or use campus wifi to get access.

www.pdcnet.org/bpej/content/bpej_1983_0003_0001_0067_0077

Also available on JSTOR: www.jstor.org/stable/27799821

Preparing to Read

Our discussion of the "Problem of Full Disclosure" makes it apparent that it isn't always clear how engineers can fulfill their duty to be honest while satisfying their obligation to safeguard public well-being. This brings us back to an issue that we first discussed in Chapter 1: informed consent. In this article, Roland Schinzinger and Mike W. Martin emphasize the relevance of this topic to engineering ethics.

Guided Reading Questions

1. In what respects is medicine similar to engineering? In what respects do the obligations of engineers compare to those of doctors? In what respects do they differ? Compare and contrast the American Medical Association's Code of Ethics to the NSPE's Code of Ethics (see www.ama-assn.org/topics/ama-code-medical-ethics).

What are some notable similarities and some notable differences with regard to the types of obligations referred to in each code?

2. Schinzinger and Martin argue that, in a sense, engineering involves "social experimentation." This is because (1) engineering involves a great deal of risk, and (2) engineers are usually in a privileged position compared to the public when it comes to understanding these risks. What do you think about the characterization of engineering as a "social experiment"?

3. Schinzinger and Martin claim that if engineering involves social experimentation members of the public have the right to informed voluntary consent when subject to the risks of a technological experiment. Do you agree with this argument? If so, whose duty is it to inform the public of the risks from engineering projects—engineers, policy makers, ethicists, someone else?

4. Long claims that informed consent is not relevant in engineering in the way that it is in medicine. This is because, he argues, engineering and medicine are importantly dissimilar. He offers three arguments for his position—what Schinzinger and Martin label the Consenter Identification Problem, the Proxy Problem, and the Dissident Minority Problem. What do you think of Long's arguments? Are they successful?

5. Schinzinger and Martin offer detailed responses to each of Long's arguments. What do you think about their responses? Can you think of any potential criticisms of their responses? How do you think Schinzinger and Martin might defend their views against the criticisms you raise?

Further Reading 5.3: 'Plagiarism: Words and ideas' by Mathieu Bouville

Find the Article

Bouville, M. (2008). Plagiarism: Words and Ideas. *Science and Engineering Ethics*, 14, 311–322. doi.org/10.1007/s11948-008-9057-6.

Read the article online by scanning the QR code or following the link below. Your college library will need to subscribe to the journal, and you may need to login via your library's website or use campus wifi to get access.

https://link.springer.com/article/10.1007/s11948-008-9057-6

Preparing to Read

In this chapter, we've emphasized that a major component of an engineer's obligation to be honest and avoid deception is academic integrity. One aspect of academic integrity is, of course, plagiarism. Most people will agree with the statement "Plagiarism is wrong"; but few can claim to fully understand what plagiarism is or why it is wrong. This is at least in part because the concept of plagiarism itself is notoriously murky. In this article, Mathieu Bouville attempts to clear up some of the murkiness, and offer us greater insight into the nature of plagiarism and our obligations towards academic integrity.

Guided Reading Questions

1. Bouville describes various complexities surrounding the word "plagiarism"—including vagueness in its definition and inconstancy in its use. Think back to your introduction to the concept of plagiarism in college or primary school. Do Bouville's remarks resonate with your experience? What reasons were you given for thinking plagiarism was wrong? Do those reasons hold up upon further scrutiny?

2. Bouville argues that, in science, ideas matter more than words when it comes to the morality of plagiarism. That is because, he claims, science aims at producing scientific knowledge, which is about facts, theories, and concepts, not words. He suggests that words are not essential to science in the way that they are essential to a discipline such as poetry. Do you agree with Bouville on these points?

3. If Bouville is right that ideas are more important than words in science, does it follow that it is permissible for a Person A to copy Person B's words in order for A to better express her original ideas?

4. Bouville examines several arguments against plagiarism with the goal of determining whether these arguments apply to words or original intellectual contributions. What do you think about each of these arguments? What do you think about Bouville's response to each argument?

5. Bouville claims that one reason we focus on words rather than ideas when it comes to plagiarism is because plagiarism software makes it relatively easy to detect strings of copied words. He points out several potential problems with using strings of words or software detection to define plagiarism. What do you think about the issues Bouville raises? Do they give us reason to stop using plagiarism detection software?

Bibliography

Baier, A. (1986). Trust and antitrust. *Ethics*, 96(2), 231–260.

Bouville, M. (2008). Plagiarism: Words and ideas. *Science and Engineering Ethics*, 14, 311–322. doi.org/10.1007/s11948-008-9057-6.

Carson, T. L. (2006). The definition of lying. *Noûs*, 40(2), 284–306.

Deweese-Boyd, I. (2017). Self-deception. In E. N. Zalta (Ed.), *The Stanford Encyclopedia of Philosophy* (Fall). https://plato.stanford.edu/archives/fall2017/entries/self-deception.

Gladwell, M. (2015, April 27). How do we build a safer car? *New Yorker*. www.newyorker.com/magazine/2015/05/04/the-engineers-lament.

Grice, P. 1989. *Studies in the Way of Words*. Harvard University Press.

Guenin, L. M. (2005). Intellectual honesty. *Synthese*, 145(2), 177–232.

Hawley, K. J. (2014). Trust, distrust and commitment. *Noûs*, 48(1), 1–20.

Kant, I. (1797). On a supposed right to lie because of philanthropic concerns.

Levy, N. (2004). Self-deception and moral responsibility. *Ratio*, 17(3), 294–311.

Lynch, K. (2016). Willful ignorance and self-deception. *Philosophical Studies*, 173(2), 505–523.

Mahon, J. E. (2016). The definition of lying and deception. In E. N. Zalta (Ed.), *The Stanford Encyclopedia of Philosophy* (Winter). https://plato.stanford.edu/archives/win2016/entries/lying-definition.

Mill, J. S. (2004). *Utilitarianism* (The Project Gutenberg EBook of Utilitarianism). www.gutenberg.org/files/11224/11224-h/11224-h.htm.

Miller, C. (2017). Honesty. In W. Sinnott-Armstrong & C. Miller (Eds.), *Moral Psychology, Volume V: Virtue and Character* (pp. 237–273). MIT Press.

Nozick, R. (2013). *Anarchy, State, and Utopia*. Basic Books.

Saul, J. (2012). Just go ahead and lie. *Analysis*, 72(1), 3–9.

Schinzinger, R., & Martin, M. (1983). Commentary: Informed Consent in Engineering and Medicine. *Business and Professional Ethics Journal*, 3(1), 67–77.

Shapin, S. (1995). Trust, honesty, and the authority of science. In R. E. Bulger, E. M. Bobby, & H.V. Fineberg (Eds.), *Society's Choices: Social and Ethical Decision Making in Biomedicine* (pp. 388–408). National Academy Press.

Tallant, J. (2017). Commitment in cases of trust and distrust. *Thought: Fordham University Quarterly*, (4), 261–267.

Thompson, P. B. (1999). The ethics of truth-telling and the problem of risk. *Science and Engineering Ethics*, 5(4), 489–510.

Van Leeuwen, N. (2013). Self-deception. In H. LaFollette (Ed.), *International Encyclopedia of Ethics*. Wiley-Blackwell.

Von Hippel, W., & Trivers, R. (2011). The evolution and psychology of self-deception. *Behavioral and Brain Sciences*, 34(1), 1–16.

Chapter 6

Professional Honor

"Conduct themselves honorably, responsibly, ethically, and lawfully so as to enhance the honor, reputation, and usefulness of the profession."

The final NSPE canon is perhaps the broadest and most far-reaching. It calls upon engineers to not only safeguard the **honor**, reputation, and usefulness of the profession but also to improve upon them. This is a tall order considering that engineering is already one of the most respected and trusted professions. As long as the laws concerning engineering practice are clear, the idea of behaving lawfully is more or less straightforward. However, what does it mean to behave honorably, responsibly, and ethically if not to just act within the bounds of the law? It would be easy to dismiss these additions as mere platitudes—buzzwords used to set the tone of the canon but that do not point to any additional requirements for engineers. However, this is not the case. As we have already seen in Chapter 1, ethical norms and legal norms are distinct. In that case behaving ethically cannot be reduced to being law-abiding. Because of the fast pace of technological advancement, our laws will not always be able to keep pace with the ethical issues raised by emerging technologies. And, because of the moral fallibility of humankind, laws created by human beings may not always align properly with morality—for instance, some may be unjust, inhumane, irresponsible, etc. For engineers the, moral responsibility is more fundamental than legal responsibility. Furthermore, in the context of engineering as a profession, the notion of honor has a special role to play in connection to moral responsibility.

In Chapter 5, we learned about the epistemic and moral dangers that can result when the public loses trust in the honesty and objectivity of scientists and engineers. But, in addition to safeguarding against the erosion of public trust, engineers also have a responsibility to encourage public trust by "promoting the honor, reputation and usefulness of the profession." But what does this mean, and how should it be accomplished?

We will begin this chapter by exploring the notion of professional responsibility and by confronting some common excuses for evading responsibility. Next, we will step back and begin "rethinking" the notion of responsibly—focusing on developing positive moral **character** traits rather than simply avoiding wrongdoing. Here we will think about the difference between doing what's required and going "above and beyond" the call of duty. Finally, we will ask what it takes to be a morally exceptional engineer—one who continually seeks to "go beyond."

Problems for Professional Responsibility

On January 28, 1986 the US Presidential State of the Union Address was postponed for the first time in history. In place of his scheduled address, then President Ronald Reagan delivered a poignant 650-word speech on the loss of the Space Shuttle *Challenger* and the death of its seven crew members. Millions watched the ***Challenger* disaster** unfold live on CNN. The viewers included hosts of school children to whom the National Aeronautics and Space Administration (NASA) had provided access to the broadcast. Though the public had witnessed shuttle launches in the past, this flight held special interest. This was in part because the mission included the first civilian crew member: Christa McAuliffe, a 37-year-old high school teacher from New Hampshire. In his speech Reagan extolled the *Challenger* crew for their bravery in accepting the dangerous mission. He also praised the government's transparency in allowing the public to bear witness to the event:

> I've always had great faith in and respect for our space program, and what happened today does nothing to diminish it. We don't hide our space program. We don't keep secrets and cover things up. We do it all up front and in public. That's the way freedom is, and we wouldn't change it for a minute.
>
> (Reagan, 1986)

Although the tragedy may have transpired "up front and in public" it would take the formation of a special investigative commission, led by former Secretary of State Roger Williams, to uncover the cause of the disaster. The investigators discovered details which are now infamous. The O-ring seal on the shuttle's solid rocket booster lost its elasticity on the cold winter morning of the launch and broke apart. The disintegration of the O-rings sent flames from the booster that reached the external engine and caused the space craft to tear apart.

Perhaps the most heartbreaking detail of the case was that the crash itself could have been avoided had the O-rings been tested at sufficiently low temperatures.

Furthermore, the Rogers Commission discovered that both NASA and the company that designed the solid rocket boosters, Morton Thiokol, were aware of the potential problem with the O-rings. Six months before the crash Roger Boisjoly, a Morton Thiokol engineer, had discovered worrisome data regarding the O-rings when reviewing the rocket boosters. Boisjoly first voiced his concern on July 19, 1985. According to Boisjoly, his concerns were largely ignored. Boisjoly persisted, and eventually a "Seal Task Team" was formed to investigate the issue. In a memo sent to his superiors at Morton Thiokol on July 31, 1985 (primarily Robert Lund, Vice President of Engineering), Boisjoly warned that if the problem with the O-rings was not addressed, "The result could be a catastrophe of the highest order, loss of human life."

At a teleconference between Morton Thiokol and NASA, Boisjoly and members of the Seal Task Team, which included Arnie Thompson and Bob Ebeling, made a case for delaying the launch of the *Challenger* shuttle until testing could be done to confirm the rockets were safe. When NASA asked the Vice President of the Space Booster Project, Joe Kilminster, for his recommendation he replied that he did not recommend the launch. NASA officials stated their displeasure at the recommendations, and even questioned the accuracy of the data. At this point, Kilminster called for a five-minute private conference with the other Morton Thiokol managers to re-evaluate the data presented by Boisjoly and Thompson. Here is Boisjoly's description of what happened next:

> [A]s soon as the mute button was pushed our general manager, Jerry Mason, said in a soft voice, "We have to make a management decision." I became furious when I heard this because I knew that an attempt would be made by management to reverse our recommendation not to launch.

Some discussion had started between the managers when Arnie Thompson moved from his position down the table to a position in front of the managers and once again tried to explain our position by sketching the joint and discussing the problem with the seals at low temperature. Arnie stopped when he saw the unfriendly look in Mason's eyes and also realized that no one was listening to him. I then grabbed the photographic evidence showing the hot gas blow-by and placed it on the table and, somewhat angered, admonished them to look and not ignore what the photos were telling us, namely, that low temperature indeed caused more hot gas blow-by in the joints. I too received the same cold stares as Arnie with looks as if to say, "Go away and don't bother us with the facts." At that moment I felt totally helpless and felt that further argument was fruitless, so I, too, stopped pressing my case.

What followed made me both sad and angry. The managers who were struggling to make a pro-launch list of supporting data actually supported a decision not to launch. During the closed managers' discussion, Jerry Mason asked in a low voice if he was the only one who wanted to fly. The discussion continued; then Mason turned to engineering VP Bob Lund and told him to take off his engineering hat and put on his management hat. The decision to launch resulted from the yes vote of only the four senior executives since the rest of us were excluded from both the final decision and the vote poll. The telecon resumed, and Joe Kilminster read the launch support rationale from a handwritten list and recommended that the launch proceed. NASA promptly accepted the recommendation to launch without any probing discussion and asked Joe to send a signed copy of the chart. The change in decision so upset me that I do not remember Stanley Reinhartz of NASA asking if anyone had anything else to say over the telecon. The telecon was then disconnected so I immediately left the room feeling badly defeated.

(Boisjoly, 1987)

In acknowledgement of his efforts to stop the launch, Boisjoly was awarded the Prize for Scientific Freedom and Responsibility by the American Association for the Advancement of Science (AAAS). Boisjoly's efforts were unquestionably praiseworthy. However, given the power of the Seal Task Team's information, we can't help but ask: Could he or should they have done more? Should Boisjoly and Thompson, for instance, have pushed past the "cold stares" of the managers and protest the launch until the very end? Should the Seal Task Team have tried to rally additional support from Boisjoly's colleagues in hopes of convincing his superiors of the legitimacy of his concerns? Should they have alerted the astronauts directly so they could make an informed decision about the risk? Should they have gone to the press to warn of the potential catastrophe in hopes that the public would put pressure on NASA to stop the launch?

Such measures may seem "above and beyond" the call of duty, but keep in mind that this was literally a life or death situation. And, because of the expertise of members of the Seal Task Team and their familiarity with the technical details of the project, there was perhaps no one in a better position to push for acknowledgment of the truth. In this case, despite his efforts, as engineers, aren't Boisjoly and the Seal Task Team at least partially responsible for the disaster?

The members of the Seal Task Team seem to have been conflicted on this point. When speaking about his role in the *Challenger* case Boisjoly said:

I must emphasize, I had my say, and I never [would] take [away] any management right to take the input of an engineer and then make a decision based upon that input ... I have worked at a lot of companies ... and I truly believe that ... there was no point in me doing anything further [other] than [what] I had already attempted to do.

(Goldberg 1987, p. 156)

Bob Ebeling seems to have felt differently. Thirty years after the incident, an interview with NPR shows that he was still plagued by regret:

Ebeling retired soon after Challenger. He suffered deep depression and has never been able to lift the burden of guilt. In 1986, as he watched that haunting image again on a television screen, he said, "I could have done more. I should have done more."

He says the same thing today, sitting in a big easy chair in the same living room, his eyes watery and his face grave. The data he and his fellow engineers presented, and their persistent and sometimes angry arguments, weren't enough to sway Thiokol managers and NASA officials. Ebeling concludes he was inadequate. He didn't argue the data well enough.

(Berkes, 2016)

Was Ebeling's guilt justified? Or was Boisjoly right that they fully discharged their obligations as engineers? For many reasons, it seems unfair to hold Boisjoly and the members of the Seal Task Team responsible for the disaster. After all, weren't they all just cogs in a much larger machine—a machine that they lacked the power to control? For instance, as a staff engineer, Boisjoly was embedded in various levels of management at Morton Thiokol—including a Manager of Applied Mechanics, a Director of Engineering Design, the Vice President of the Space Booster Program, the General Manager of Morton, and the Vice President of Engineering, to name a few. And Morton Thiokol was only a sub-contractor, one of many hired by NASA to work on the enormously complex project of constructing a space shuttle. NASA itself is not an independent body, but a part of the United States Federal Government. With so many entities involved, how is it possible to attribute responsibility to a single person—especially a person working under so many layers of bureaucracy? Furthermore, how much power did Boisjoly and the other engineers like Ebeling and Thompson really have in the situation? If the managers and directors of the project had the authority to make the final call, should they alone be held responsible for the consequences of their decision? And if Boisjoly and his colleagues hadn't stopped protesting, would their managers simply have replaced them with other less scrupulous engineers? In that case, what choice did these men really have?

Although few engineers will find themselves in a position to prevent a disaster on the scale of the *Challenger* crash, many can relate to Boisjoly's feelings of frustration and helplessness. Engineering projects rarely involve a single engineer working in isolation. Rather, such projects involve teams of professionals working as members of larger companies—companies which might themselves be embedded in larger organizations. Engineers who are not managers may have the authority to report a problem, but may not have the power to effect a solution. Like Boisjoly, they may find even their strongest recommendations overruled. Furthermore, engineers may have good reason not to question a decision made by management. Often the engineers working "on the ground" with the most technical components of a project are not privy to the "big picture" aspects of a complex project. Something that appears to be a problem at the micro level may dissolve when viewed at the macro level. It seems that when it comes to questions about moral responsibility in engineering, the answer is always "It's complicated."

However, as Michael Davis argues, the fact that moral responsibility in engineering is a complicated notion should not lead us to conclude that it doesn't exist. And it should not tempt us into thinking that engineers can never be held responsible for their actions. In the excerpt of his article included in this text, Davis examines several arguments designed to show that, for reasons such as the one just considered, it is impossible to assign responsibility to engineers. Davis concludes that, though responsibility in engineering is a complex matter, none of these arguments succeed in showing that engineers are immune from claiming responsibility in their practice. As a complement to this conclusion, Davis attempts to shed light on the kinds of responsibilities engineers have as members of organizations. Finally, he offers a reason why it is in an engineer's best interest to take responsibility for their actions, even when others may find reason to avoid it.

Rethinking Responsibility

Before reading this chapter, you may already have been familiar with the *Challenger* disaster. If you are, it is hardly surprising. Engineering catastrophes such as this loom large because of their tragic and sensational nature. For many members of the public, news about engineering disasters is the only sort of information about engineering they receive. This is understandable to some extent. Safety is a chief concern of engineers. So, in most cases, if a job goes well no one hears about it. In that case, when we see an engineer appear in the news, it is more likely that he or she is a subject of scrutiny as opposed to praise. When something goes wrong, we want to know who is to blame. It seems natural then that so much of the literature on engineering ethics is devoted to making sure engineers, as professionals, are not blame-worthy in their conduct.

However, some engineers and ethicists have begun to worry that the focus on the "negative aspects of engineers" such disasters, is actually counterproductive to encouraging ethical conduct. It's only natural for us to want to avoid blame and the guilt that may be associated with it. This can lead us to try to avoid responsibility altogether. And though guilt and the avoidance of it can be one motivating factor for ethical behavior, it is arguably not the most effective one. Moral problems are like technical problems in their complexity and sensitivity to context. In that case, perhaps we ought to think more about what sorts of strategies work best for problem solving. If we are thinking of moral issues in terms of ethical problem solving, it doubtful that guilt and blame will be at the top of our strategy list.

In his article "Responsible Engineering: The Importance of Character and Imagination" Michael S. Pritchard argues that the literature on engineering ethics has focused too much on wrongdoing in engineering and how to avoid or prevent it. Instead, Pritchard says, we ought to focus on the positive in engineering practice, including the things that go right. In particular, we should look to engineers who have demonstrated superlative moral behavior, and try to figure out what it is about them that caused them to act the way they did. Here notice that, although Pritchard is calling attention to particular praiseworthy actions of engineers, his focus is on character. He is assuming that certain character dispositions are what matters for right action. His suggestion is that we ought to look to positive moral exemplars, and to cultivate the kinds of character traits that allow them (engineers) to excel with regard to moral situations. In this respect, Pritchard's suggestion should remind us of Aristotle's brand of virtue ethics, discussed in Chapter 2. Like Aristotle, Pritchard believes that character is key to morality. And he believes that having "settled dispositions" or "virtues" matters just as much as performing right actions. Pritchard's views have much in common with the views of Jon Alan Schmidt, also discussed in Chapter 2. In Schmidt's view, blind adherence to rules, though morally instructive, is the mark of a moral novice rather than an expert. He suggests that professional excellence in engineering is inseparable from moral excellence, and that both are best achieved by focusing on the character of the acting professional. Schmidt even went so far as to suggest that a revival in a virtue-based approach to engineering ethics would lead to renewed motivation for engineers to actively engage in professional responsibility.

Pritchard explains that one reason character is especially important in the field of engineering is connected to an issue we discussed in Chapter 5: public trust. No one action or even collection of actions can establish trust. We trust a person or an organization when we believe that they are the sort of person or organization that will continually strive to do the right thing. We trust people when they have developed the sort of dispositions that regularly result in virtuous behavior. We trust organizations that are structured around virtuous ideals and that, because they are led by and employ virtuous people, manage to regularly live up to those ideals. When we trust a person or organization, we are more tolerant of the occasional misstep. Accidents may perhaps weaken our trust, but they will not destroy it. And our trust in a person or organization may be strengthened by such trials if the person or organization handles them ethically.

Members of the public rarely have contact with the individual engineers on whom they rely. Rather, they are familiar with engineers in the abstract, as members of a profession. And it isn't at all clear that the public has an accurate perception of engineering as a profession, technically or ethically. Indeed, the US National Academy of Engineering (NAE) has recognized an "image problem for engineering" in the twenty-first century. An NAE committee investigated public opinion of scientists versus engineers, and the results were troubling. The general public perceives that engineers, more than scientists, create economic growth, strengthen national security, and make strong leaders. However, the public also believes that, compared with scientists, engineers do little to save lives, are less sensitive to societal concerns, and do not care as much about their communities. The NAE committee went a step further and focused on the views of parents of teenagers. The study revealed that parents perceive engineers as smart problem solvers, and believe engineering is a solid career. Yet parents also perceive engineers as narrowly focused on technical details, rather than engaged with social or human dimensions of technology. When well-prepared first-year college students are asked why they do not choose to study engineering, the general response is that they prefer to enter a profession that will enable them to help others and make the world a better place to live.

At this point we can see how public trust and the honor of the engineering profession are inseparable from one another. In order for the public to trust engineers, they have to believe that, as professionals, they are the sort of people who will strive to live up to the **ideals of the profession**—ideals like the ones articulated in the NSPE Code of Ethics.

Pritchard argues that not only is it beneficial for engineers to develop character traits like **creativity** and imagination, it is essential. For instance, consider the NSPE's Code of Ethics. As we have seen, understanding the code's provisions and applying them to actual engineering practice is no simple matter. Pritchard points out that many important provisions of the code are open to interpretation in the sense that it isn't clear exactly what it takes to satisfy them. He also draws attention to the fact that the NSPE provides little guidance as to how such provisions ought to be interpreted. If we are thinking of a code of ethics as a rulebook for behavior, then any **vagueness** or ambiguity in the code can be frustrating. Anyone who has ever played a board game knows how maddening it can be when the rules are unclear about what players exactly ought to do in any given situation.

Here is it important to realize that the code of ethics provided by the NSPE is not meant to serve as a rulebook. Rather, it is intended to serve as general guidelines for ethical behavior. If, for instance, we were to try to use the Fundamental Canons to solve ethical dilemmas as one would use a rulebook to play a game, we would find the canons to be pretty unhelpful— they simply do not contain enough information about how they ought to be applied in real-life situations. It is also worth pointing out that the NSPE does provide an extensive list of resources designed to help engineering professionals interpret the code. But, more significantly, it is important to understand that the vagueness in the Fundamental Canons is by design. The Fundamental Canons of the NSPE are what van de Poel and Royakkers call **aspirational codes**. In their words, an aspirational code "expresses the moral values of a profession or company. The objective of such a code is to express to the outside world the kind of values the profession or company is committed to" (2011, pp. 1132–1134).

There is good reason for aspirational codes to be vague. First, in general, we aspire to general principles, not particular concrete guidelines. When an organization has aspirational codes that align with moral values, this helps lay the foundation of public trust. This is because these codes make up part of the "brand" of the organization—the values that the public associates with that organization. Because so many professional organizations in engineering prioritize ethical ideals, the **engineering brand** has become closely associated with moral values such as integrity, courage, honesty, objectivity, and the like. This hard-won reputation is well worth safeguarding. The second reason that aspirational codes are designed to be vague is that they must be able to be applied to every possible situation. As we have seen, in real life, moral dilemmas are incredibly complex and the answers often hinge on subtle contextual details. Take for instance the issue of paternalism, discussed in Chapter 1, in relation to public safety. It would be impossible to articulate a code that dictated particular actions in every situation. And, even if we could come up with such a code, it would be so long and complex that sifting through it would be completely overwhelming.

However, taken another way, Pritchard's point about the vagueness of the codes stands. Because of their vagueness, codes of ethics are not enough to ensure ethical behavior. Rather, they help illuminate the boundaries of impermissible behavior and guide us toward exceptional behavior. Pritchard's point echoes that of Schmidt's article (see Guided Core Reading 2.2). So, if the code requires interpretation to be applicable to real-world situations, how do we become faithful interpreters of the code?

Pritchard points out that responsibility comes on a spectrum, one that ranges from doing the bare minimum to going above and beyond—what ethicists call the **morally supererogatory**. He notes that, in our ordinary lives, most of us spend the majority of our time hovering between the two extremes. How you choose to fulfill your obligations is a matter of how committed you are to them. Having a minimal or even a moderate commitment to ethical behavior will not help engineers live up to ideals as high minded as the **dedication** to public safety. Dedication is not the sort of thing that admits of minimal involvement.

How does an engineer become the kind of person that strives for more than the minimum fulfillment of his or her duty? How does one become committed to the ideals of the profession? How does one become invested in developing the sort of character that Pritchard suggests? Mike Martin's view of **personal meaning** may help us answer these questions.

Personal Meaning

In his article "Personal Meaning and Ethics in Engineering," Mike W. Martin argues that, when it comes to engineering, ethicists have ignored the role that personal meaning and personal commitments play in the fulfillment of professional obligations.

By personal meaning, Martin is referring to the collection of things that make life worth living. A **meaningful** life may include aesthetic concerns, religious concerns, professional concerns, relationship concerns, moral concerns, etc. Personal meaning has both subjective and objective meaning. **Subjective meaning** involves those things that make life worth living from the perspective of the person who is living it. Subjective meaning can vary from individual to individual, depending on what they value. **Objective meaning** is the sort of meaning that is independent of what any individual values. For instance, we might say of a person that they lived a worthwhile life because of the good that person did for humanity. In this sense, a person's life could be objectively valuable even if they themselves did not find meaning in it. There has been a great deal of debate in philosophy about whether objective meaning really exists and, if so, what it consists in. However, we can set that question aside for now and focus on subjective personal meaning.

Personal commitments are commitments we undertake to achieve those things that make life worth living. For instance, if relationships are part of what makes life worth living for you, then perhaps a commitment to your family or friends will be among your personal commitments. Personal commitments generate obligations, but, because not all of us will have the same personal commitments, not all of us will have the same obligations. Personal commitments are manifested in a web of "desires, concerns, and projects." According to Martin, this web helps constitute one's character. Personal meaning and personal commitments are obviously closely intertwined. He explains that: "Meaning connects directly with motivation and commitment, with what people care about deeply in ways that evoke interest and energy, and create pride or shame in work" (Martin, 2002 p. 547).

Martin identifies different kinds of meaning based on different sources of motivations or commitments. These are: **craft motives, compensatory motives**, and **motives of moral concern**. Craft motives include things such as technical expertise, technological enthusiasm, creative expression, etc. Compensatory motives include items such as money, fame, power, prestige, and the like. Motives of moral concern include integrity, respect, concern for others, etc. Are some motives more essential for ethical engineering? Obviously, being motivated by moral concerns can be advantageous in fulfilling one's moral obligations. But what about craft motives and compensatory motives: aren't they antithetical to moral concerns in engineering?

Martin argues that personal commitments are often ignored in professional life because it is assumed that pursuing personal interests is at odds with the fulfillment of one's professional obligations. This is especially true of craft motives and compensatory motives. Professionalism is associated with putting aside your personal interests and focusing on the shared standards of the profession. This sort of thinking might carry over into expectations about professional ethics as well. The idea is that pursuing personal interests can lead one to ignore one's ethical obligations as a professional. For instance, Wernher von Braun, designer of the V2 Rocket, became a controversial figure in part because he prioritized personal commitments such as ambition and technological enthusiasm over concern for public wellbeing. According to satirist Tom Lehrer in his 1965 song "Wernher von Braun":

"Once the rockets go up, who cares where they come down?
That's not my department!" says Wernher von Braun.

The idea that personal commitments can hinder professional ethics has some merit to it. As we have seen in Chapter 5, personal bias—something that can stem from personal interests—can lead to a lack of objectivity. However, on the whole it is a mistake to think that personal commitments are necessarily the enemy of moral commitments. Rather, if properly connected, such commitments can enhance one another.

The engineering profession offers a distinctive opportunity to connect these personal and moral commitments. This is because ethical ideals including humanitarian concerns are an essential part of the job. In that case, engineers have good reason to allow the ethical commitments of the profession to become personal commitments—ones that are reflected in the web of desires, concerns, and projects that help make up a person's character.

For many engineers and scientists, creativity is an important part of who they are. Expression of creativity, then, is a major motivation for entering the fields of engineering and science. In his article "Moral Creativity in Science and Engineering Ethics" Martin discusses the lives and careers of several exceptionally creative individuals, including Gertrude B. Elion. Martin argues that individuals like Elion provided great benefit to humanity precisely because they combined scientific creativity with moral creativity. Elion, a Nobel laureate biochemist, channeled her creativity, curiosity, and determination into cancer research. Although her work provided a major contribution to humanity, her motive for pursuing cancer research was a personal one: the death of her grandfather from stomach cancer.

What happens when our values and commitments align? One answer is that it brings **satisfaction**. This is because personal commitments and values are part of who we are. For this reason, we are more invested in the projects that reflect our authentic selves.

Arguably, Elion lived a meaningful life in both the subjective and the objective sense because she was deeply and personally invested in projects that reflected her personal and moral commitments. Her personal investment in her work drove her to gladly go beyond the minimum, professionally and morally.

Engineers can take pride in going above and beyond the call of duty. They can find personal and professional satisfaction in seeing their personal interests and individual abilities matched to their moral commitments—commitments such as honesty, loyalty, objectivity, competence, and public wellbeing.

Chapter 6 Key Terms and Concepts

Professional Honor
Character
Challenger Disaster
Ideals of the Profession
Creativity
Vagueness
Aspirational Codes
The Engineering "Brand"
Morally Supererogatory
Dedication
Personal Meaning

Meaningful (Life/Work)
Subjective Meaning
Objective Meaning
Personal Commitments
Craft Motives
Compensatory Motives
Motives of Moral Concern
Personal and Professional
    Satisfaction

Chapter 6: End of Chapter Reading and NSPE Board of Ethical Review Cases

Guided Core Reading — 220

Core Reading 6.1: 'Ain't no one here but us social forces' by Michael Davis (excerpts)

Core Reading 6.2: 'Moral creativity in science and engineering' by Mike W. Martin (excerpts)

NSPE Board of Ethical Review Cases — 227

Case 08-10: Public Welfare—Design of Medical Equipment (2008)

Case 13-3: Engineering Judgment Overruled—Faulty Workmanship (2013)

Case 12-1: Academic Integrity—Obligation of Engineering Faculty Who Becomes Aware of Cheating (2012)

Guided Further Reading — 232

Further Reading 6.1: 'Engineering codes of ethics and the duty to set a moral precedent' by Eugene Schlossberger

Further Reading 6.2: 'Responsible engineering: The importance of character and imagination' by Michael S. Pritchard

Further Reading 6.3: 'Engineering ethics beyond engineers' ethics' by Joseph M. Basart and Montse Serra

If you can't use the QR codes, use the hyperlinks found on the book's webpage instead: www.routledge.com/9781138183865.

Guided Core Reading

Core Reading 6.1: "'Ain't no one here but us social forces": Constructing the professional responsibility of engineers' by Michael Davis (excerpts)

Preparing to Read

Davis's primary concern in this article is to address the concern that engineers, for various reasons, cannot be held responsible for the failures of the technology they help create. He begins his article by clarifying the concepts of responsibility—articulating and discussing nine senses of the word "responsibility." He continues by canvassing seven arguments that seek to show that, in many situations, engineers are not responsible for their actions (or lack of action) with regard to engineering practice. We have included one here: "The Argument from Institutional Constraints." Davis offers reasons for this argument. He ends by offering a rational justification for why it is in engineers' best interest to take responsibility for their actions and for the technology they develop.

Excerpted from: Davis, M. (2012). 'Ain't no one here but us social forces': Constructing the professional responsibility of engineers. *Science and Engineering Ethics*, 18, 13–34. doi.org/10.1007/s11948-010-9225-3. © Springer Nature 2010, reprinted with permission. Internal references and notes generally omitted.

Institutional Constraint

[The Argument from Institutional Constraint] seeks to undercut the claim that engineers have a choice. Lynch and Kline state it nicely:

> Most engineers operate in an environment where their capacity to make decisions is constrained by the corporate or organizational culture in which they work. Engineers are rarely free to design technologies apart from cost and schedule pressures imposed by a corporate hierarchy, a government agency concerned with its image, or market pressures. (Lynch and Kline 2000, 210)

Lynch and Kline are certainly right that most engineers do (and always have) worked in large organizations. Except for those engineers high in the organization, working in such an organization means working within a framework that others have constructed, one that necessarily drastically limits what an individual engineer can do. Of course, the other side of working within a large organization is that one's choices, while limited by cost, market, organizational politics, and the like, can have much larger effects than the same sort of choice outside the organization. To design a small plane in one's own little company is unlikely to affect many people. To design just the riveting for the wing of the Boeing 737 is likely to have a much larger effect.

...

Can an engineer have responsibility for what her employer does—or just for what she does within the narrow bounds where she is free? I see no reason why the engineer cannot take responsibility for what her employer does, however large the employer. She has voluntarily accepted employment with that employer, and can break off that association at any time just by giving notice. ... At a minimum, an engineer should be willing to give an account of an employer's conduct and to accept some blame for what it does when what it does deserves blame (just as she might accept credit if the employer does something creditable). An engineer who declines to accept that minimum responsibility but continues to benefit from the employment will seem much like that great but greatly flawed engineer in Tom Lehrer's song:

"Once the rockets are up, who cares where they come down? That's not my department," says Wernher von Braun.

While engineers work in departments, they work for an organization. If the organization's name is on the rocket, they may have something to answer for when it comes down—even if their department has nothing to do with rockets.

That, however, is not the end of the argument from institutional constraint. The main point of the argument is to free engineers from responsibility for what is "their department", that is, for what they in fact help to bring about. The engineers are causal factors but (the argument runs) the organization so hems them in that they are not free enough to be faulty causes. The engineer who prepares a plan for a project is not responsible for it because she could have prepared no other. She had "no choice.

This version of the argument from institutional constraint has at least three flaws (beside the one already discussed). Each flaw is serious in itself. One is logical. The engineer always has at least one other choice, that is, not to prepare the plan. That other option may be suicidal, but—as a matter of logic—it always exists. Morally, there is an important difference between "no choice" and "no attractive choice".

The second flaw is conceptual. Engineers are hired to exercise engineering judgment on behalf of their employer. Where judgment is necessary, there must be at least two options, aside from preparing no plan. If there is only one option, a technician can prepare the plan. Even if engineers do not make the final decision, they must make the initial decisions on almost any project they undertake. That decision-making power, that freedom to choose, is what, as a conceptual matter, distinguishes an engineer from a mere technician. The argument from institutional constraint is not a reason why engineers cannot be responsible for how they exercise that decision-making power—in the faulty-cause, accountability, or liability sense of responsibility. They have the necessary freedom to choose.

The third flaw is empirical. Those of us who have watched engineers at work have noticed that many of the decisions engineers make are in fact final. Superiors review them but, unless something is clearly wrong, the superior will not enquire deeply into the decision. Going along with engineering decisions is generally more efficient than getting a second opinion or overruling the engineer "on principle". As a matter of fact, most engineers in large organizations have considerable decision-making power. Whenever that is true, the argument from institutional constraint simply does not apply....

The Rationality of Taking Responsibility

... Though people are generally thought to shy away from responsibility-as-liability or as-accountability, engineers do not seem to. Instead, they seem to claim certain responsibilities most of us, even technically trained managers and other technologists, try to avoid.... Some might well wonder whether I have described a mass pathology rather than explained why engineers can have such moral responsibilities. Why take on responsibilities others do not want?

...

What engineers gain by taking on responsibilities others avoid are several tasks or offices which, as a matter of fact, have become a relatively lucrative occupation. Creating a lucrative occupation is rational enough to justify accepting the moral responsibility (both accountability and liability) making it possible (provided the tasks accepted are also morally permissible—as they seem to be). The very barriers to moral responsibility that technology and organization throw up are opportunities for a profession willing to make overcoming them their responsibility.

Reference

Lynch, T., & Kline, Ronald. (2000). Engineering practice and engineering ethics. *Science, Technology, & Human Values*, 25, 195–225.

Guided Reading Questions

1. What is the Problem of Institutional Constraint? What is the "main point" of the Argument from Institutional Constraint?
2. Davis points to several flaws with the Argument from Institutional Constraint. Do you find these arguments convincing—why or why not?
3. Can you think of any counterarguments to Davis's criticisms? How do you think Davis might respond to these counterarguments?
4. What reason does Davis give for thinking that it is in an engineer's best interest to "take on" responsibility for what they do (or do not do)?
5. Can you think of ways in which it would be in your best interest to "take on" responsibility for what you do as an engineer?

Read the Full Article (optional)

You can read the full article online by scanning the QR code or following the link below. Your college library will need to subscribe to the journal, and you may need to login via your library's website or use campus wifi to get access.

https://link.springer.com/article/10.1007%2Fs11948-010-9225-3

Core Reading 6.2: 'Moral creativity in science and engineering' by Mike W. Martin (excerpts)

Preparing to Read

In this article, Martin explains how, by exercising the non-moral trait of creativity, scientists and engineers can have a profound moral impact both on society and on themselves. Additionally, he emphasizes the connection between personal commitments and personal meaning. He argues that personal meaning and personal commitments can play a role in moral motivation and contribute to a meaningful life.

Excerpted from: Martin, M. W. (2006). Moral creativity in science and engineering. *Science and Engineering Ethics*, 12, 421–433. doi.org/10.1007/ s11948-006-0043-6. © Springer Nature 1969, reprinted with permission. Internal references and notes omitted.

Is Creativity a Virtue?

When, if ever, is creativity in science and engineering a virtue? The word "virtue" has two meanings. In a wide (and somewhat archaic) sense, virtues include admirable traits and excellences of all kinds, whether moral or non-moral. Non-moral excellences include athletic ability, musical talent, intelligence, and physical vitality. In a narrow sense, virtues are specifically moral excellences, such as honesty, courage, fairness, and beneficence. Creativity is a virtue in the wide sense, for it is a much-admired excellence in almost all domains of human activity. But does scientific and technological creativity ever amount to moral creativity?

The standard view seems to be that creativity in science and engineering is not a moral virtue because it is defined in terms of non-moral scientific and engineering criteria rather than moral criteria.... Yet, consider Gertrude B. Elion, a Nobel Laureate biochemist.... Elion deliberately focused her career on cancer research, beginning with her choice of chemistry as a college major, in direct response to the death of her beloved grandfather from stomach cancer. Like other women during the 1930s and 1940s, she faced enormous obstacles, including being denied entrance to doctoral programs, despite graduating from college with highest honors. She sought jobs with an eye to finding any opportunity to do research. When she finally managed to find a job at a drug research company, owing to the shortage of male workers during World War II, she became a passionate and tireless investigator. The drugs she discovered saved countless children with leukemia who advanced from invariably fatal to an 80% survival rate. She also developed new research techniques for comparing nucleic acid metabolism in normal and abnormal cells. Throughout her writings she expresses joy in being able to help—a joy that helped sustain her passion for science. One of her colleagues claimed that during her fifty years as a researcher she did more good for the human race than Mother Teresa....

As a second illustration, consider Jonas Salk. Prior to his discovery of the first polio vaccine, tens of thousands of children were maimed or killed each year. Parents lived in terror of the disease, and at the height of the epidemic each year they would drastically restrict their children's activities in order to protect them from the plague. In addition to his spectacular success in finding a vaccine for polio, Salk pioneered the possibility of vaccinations that have more long-lasting effects than traditional immunizations.... Salk's lifetime of research was infused with a strong sense of responsibility to help humanity by reducing suffering....

Elion and Salk manifested several moral virtues in exemplary degrees: benevolence, beneficence, generosity, self-discipline, perseverance, self-respect (in believing in themselves) and courage (in taking risks and struggling against formidable obstacles). Their creativity is interwoven with these virtues. Because of this interweaving, I suggest their scientific creativity is also moral creativity. Indeed, as a disposition manifested over a lifetime, it is a moral virtue enmeshed in a configuration of good motives, good intentions, morally-committed activity, and morally desirable consequences.

...

Meaningful Lives of Creative Persons

Virtues are Janus-faced; they tend to contribute to the flourishing of both other people and the individuals manifesting them.... Thus far I have emphasized good consequences for society, but creativity also contributes to the meaning and self-fulfillment of scientists and engineers—topics that are themselves neglected in professional ethics....

Meaningful lives have a core of commitments—to activities, individuals, groups, perspectives, or ideals—that provide coherence and a sense of worthwhileness. Similarly, character is a "nexus of projects" through which we form an identity and pursue worthwhile ends.... Character is not an abstract pattern of virtues of vices in an individual, but rather value-structured commitments and projects; they are excellences which enable us to pursue valuable endeavors. These core commitments include specifically moral concerns. Thus, a sense of felt responsibility and concern for others was an important part of Elion and Salk's self-identity. Yet, meaningful lives have additional moral significance, beyond the specific moral commitments they embody, for they pertain to the morally-resonant ideas of self-fulfillment and authenticity.

The commitments and deep caring that we make central to our identities reflect our talents, opportunities, and interests. Insofar as we cherish creativity, it is especially important that individuals identify, affirm, and nurture their talents.... But individuals often have multiple talents, and there is no general moral requirement to pursue a talent they have no interest in developing. Authenticity is the dominant value guiding choices in pursuing self-fulfillment, or at least it has been since the middle of the nineteenth century. Authenticity is the idea, in Charles Taylor's words, that "each of us has an original way of being human" and that it is important to be true to oneself.... Each of us must discover what this "true self" is, and that discovery can itself involve person-, group-, or history-relative creativity. Hence, authenticity is connected with the idea, voiced by Matthew Arnold, that "the exercise of a creative power, that a free creative activity, is the true function of man."...

...

The creativity of scientists and engineers contributes to the meaning of their lives while advancing their disciplines. The two are connected: the meaning individuals derive from their work comes in part through the advancement of their discipline in tune with the values defining their professions. Standards define what it means to make creative advances. To be sure, rebellion might play a key role in overthrowing dogmas. Nevertheless, standards and creativity go together. Individuals are creative by submitting to standards of excellence, where those standards include creative advancement of understanding and technological innovation. In more personal terms, personal authenticity unfolds (in part) through disciplined inquiry and devotion to one's profession.

Guided Reading Questions

1. What makes your life worth living, for you? What kinds of personal commitments are tied to your conception of personal meaning? In what ways could your personal commitments be connected to your moral commitments through your work?
2. Elsewhere, Martin says that "moral values are embedded in engineering." What does he mean by this? What are some particular examples of this embedding? How might engineering differ from other professions on this point?

3. How do the lives and careers of Elion and Salk illustrate Martin's point that creativity can contribute to a meaningful life?

4. Martin argues that creativity is not given adequate attention in engineering ethics. Why is this? What sorts of connections to morality might creativity have?

5. In what ways does creativity manifest itself in your work? How might expressing this creativity be of benefit both to others and to yourself?

Read the Full Article

You can read the full article online by scanning the QR code or following the link below. Your college library will need to subscribe to the journal, and you may need to login via your library's website or use campus wifi to get access.

https://link.springer.com/article/10.1007/s11948-006-0043-6

NSPE Board of Ethical Review Cases

Case 08-10: Public Welfare—Design of Medical Equipment

Public Welfare—Design of Medical Equipment

Case 08-10
Year: 2008
Facts:

Engineer A, an experienced professional engineer, is employed by MedTech, a company that manufacturers [*sic*] medical equipment. A key company product is respirators that are used in hospitals. Engineer B, a company colleague of Engineer A, asks Engineer A to evaluate a respirator designed by MedTech for infant use. Following his review, although not an expert on respirators, Engineer A determines that a relief valve intended to protect against overpressure being applied to the infant's lungs may have been incorrectly placed so that under certain circumstances, an infant could potentially experience dangerously high pressure levels—although no incidents have been reported. Correcting the error would involve stopping the manufacturing process for part of a week to correct [the] problem. Engineer A brings the issue and his proposed solution to the attention of the appropriate manager, who is not an engineer, and Engineer A assumes that the matter will be taken care of immediately. However, a month later Engineer A learns from Engineer B that nothing has been done to correct the issue. Hundreds of new respirators are now on the market, and Engineer A is concerned about the increasing likelihood of a tragic event. Engineer A again urges the manager to take immediate action. When the manager indicates that the matter is still being looked into by a design team, Engineer A indicates that if prompt measures are not taken to correct the problem, he will be compelled to report the matter to an appropriate federal regulatory agency.

Question from the NSPE:
Was it ethical for Engineer A to indicate that if prompt measures are not taken to correct the problem, he will be compelled to report the matter to an appropriate federal regulatory agency?

Going Beyond—Our Questions for a Deep Dive

1. Were there any other solutions Engineer A might have pursued before threatening to report the matter to the appropriate regulatory agency?
2. Did Engineer A fulfill his duty in reporting his proposed solution to the appropriate manager? Or is he obligated to follow up on the situation to make sure the problem is corrected?

3. If Engineer A does decide to pursue the issue until it is corrected, to what extent is he "heroic" and to what extent is he "just doing his job"?
4. Where is the line, if any, between basic professional obligation and going "above and beyond"? In your opinion, can these two things be separated in engineering practice?

Read the Board's Discussion and Conclusion

To read the discussion and conclusion of this case by members of the NSPE Board of Ethical Review, go to: www.nspe.org/resources/ethics/ethics-resources/board-ethical-review-cases/public-welfare-design-medical-equipment.

Case 13-3: Engineering Judgment Overruled—Faulty Workmanship

Engineering Judgment Overruled—Faulty Workmanship

Case 13-3
Year: 2013
Facts:

Engineer A works for the State X Department of Transportation and is the in-house project manager on a construction project being performed by Contractor Q for State X. Contractor Q submits a change order for Engineer A's approval on work already performed by Contractor Q. The normal practice is for a contractor to first seek review and approval of a change order by the project manager (in this case, Engineer A) before commencing the work. Engineer A believes, in his engineering judgment, the change order is actually the result of Contractor Q's faulty workmanship and not the result of any changes directed or required by State X. Following a lengthy conversation between the Engineer A and Contractor Q during which Engineer

A informs Contractor Q that he will not sign off on the change order, Contractor Q contacts Supervisor B who supervises Engineer A. The next day, Supervisor B, who is not a professional engineer, directs Engineer A to sign off on the change order.

Question from the NSPE:
Would it be ethical for Engineer A to sign off on the change order?

Going Beyond—Our Questions for a Deep Dive

1. In what respects, if any, is Engineer A's situation in this case similar to Roger Boisjoly's situation in the Space Shuttle *Challenger* case?
2. Could Engineer A use "the Argument from Institutional Constraint" (discussed in the excerpt from Michael Davis) to justify signing off on the change order? How might Davis respond to such an argument from Engineer A?
3. Are there any creative solutions available to Engineer A to avoid signing the order if he thinks doing so would be unethical?
4. In your opinion, should individuals such as Supervisor B be allowed to have the final say regarding decisions in which engineering expertise is required?
5. Looking beyond this particular case, what do you imagine having a job working under a supervisor such as Supervisor B would be like? Is it the sort of job that would be conducive to a "meaningful" career in Martin's sense of the term?

Read the Board's Discussion and Conclusion

To read the discussion and conclusion of this case by members of the NSPE Board of Ethical Review, go to: www.nspe.org/resources/ethics/ethics-resources/board-ethical-review-cases/engineering-judgment-overruled-faulty.

Case: 12-1: Academic Integrity—Obligation of Engineering Faculty Who Becomes Aware of Cheating

Academic Integrity—Obligation of Engineering Faculty Who Becomes Aware of Cheating

Case 12-1
Year: 2012
Facts:

Engineer A, a licensed professional engineer, is a full-time engineering faculty member at a large university. Engineer A is currently involved in a series of accreditation visits being conducted by an academic accreditation group and not readily available to students and faculty. However, following an accreditation meeting, Engineer A is told by one of Engineer A's students, Student X, that during a recent written engineering examination in a class taught by faculty member Engineer B, Student X observed Student Y using a phone to photograph a test question with the apparent purpose of sending the photograph to a second student— seeking the second student's assistance on the test question. Student X advised Engineer A that after she immediately reported the incident to Engineer B, Engineer B spoke to Student Y, but there did not appear to be any further consequences resulting from Student Y's actions.

Question from the NSPE:
What are Engineer A's ethical obligations under the circumstances?

Going Beyond—Our Questions for a Deep Dive

1. Does Engineer A have a larger professional obligation to do something about the alleged academic integrity violation? Or are Engineer A's obligations restricted to matters relating to accreditation?
2. Does Engineer A have the moral authority to pursue further action regarding Student Y's actions once she has notified Engineer B of the incident?
3. Under what conditions, if any, are engineers permitted or obligated to monitor and/or correct the moral decisions of their peers?
4. Is an engineer even "off the clock" with regard to his or her professional moral obligations? For instance, imagine that Engineer A was on vacation and happened to witness a violation of academic integrity while visiting a colleague at a university. Would Engineer A be justified in ignoring the incident?

5. How do matters concerning academic integrity relate to the honor, reputation, and usefulness of the profession?
6. What is the relationship between academic integrity and personal integrity? What might Mike Martin say about the relationship between academic integrity and a meaningful life or career?

Read the Board's Discussion and Conclusion

To read the discussion and conclusion of this case by members of the NSPE Board of Ethical Review, go to: www.nspe.org/resources/ethics/ethics-resources/board-ethical-review-cases/academic-integrity-obligation.

Guided Further Reading

Further Reading 6.1: 'Engineering codes of ethics and the duty to set a moral precedent' by Eugene Schlossberger

Find the Article

Schlossberger, E. (2016). Engineering codes of ethics and the duty to set a moral precedent. *Science and Engineering Ethics*, 22, 1333–1344. doi.org/10.1007/s11948-015-9708-3.

Read the article online by scanning the QR code or following the link below. Your college library will need to subscribe to the journal, and you may need to login via your library's website or use campus wifi to get access.

https://link.springer.com/article/10.1007%2Fs11948-015-9708-3

Preparing to Read

Arguably, one specific way in which engineers can promote the reputation of the profession is by participating in morally praiseworthy behavior such as performing pro bono services or taking a stand on major moral issues. Another is for engineering to avoid morally blameworthy behavior such as associating with disreputable individuals or organizations. In this article, Eugene Schlossberger examines what he claims is at the heart of these "public service-related" obligations—"the proclamative principle." In exploring this principle, Schlossberger sheds light on an engineer's responsibility to act as a moral exemplar.

Guided Reading Questions

1. Schlossberger asks why engineers should be obligated to perform public outreach services such as educating the public or pro bono work when many other professions are not. Do you agree that engineers have this kind of obligation? Why or why not? Do you agree that individuals from other professions—anthropologists, philosophers, economists, for example—do not?

2. Schlossberger suggests that one reason for thinking that engineers have a special obligation to educating the public is that doing so helps engineers avoid acting paternalistically because informing the public helps foster public autonomy. Can you think of any other reasons why engineers might have the obligation to perform public outreach?

3.   Schlossberger argues that one reason why engineers have a duty to perform public outreach services is that engineers enjoy certain benefits that society provides, called "opportunity capital." According to him, opportunity capital includes things such as "licensure, education, roads, a currency system, and more." Do you agree with Schlossberger's argument here? If so, does this argument apply only to engineering or could it be applied to other professions as well?

4.   The duty of association refers to an engineer's obligation to refrain from associating with bad actors. Schlossberger offers two potential reasons for why engineers might be subject to the duty of association. Do you agree with either of these reasons? Is the duty of association clause redundant in a code of ethics given other codes that refer to an engineer's duty to protect public welfare?

5.   Do engineers have a special obligation to serve as a moral example or set a moral precedent for others? Do engineers have a special obligation to "live their principles"? Schlossberger has his own answers to these questions. What do you think about his answers?

Further Reading 6.2: 'Responsible engineering: The importance of character and imagination' by Michael S. Pritchard

Find the Article

Pritchard, M. S. (2001). Responsible engineering: The importance of character and imagination. *Science and Engineering Ethics*, 7, 391–402. doi.org/10.1007/s11948-001-0061-3.

Read the article online by scanning the QR code or following the link below. Your college library will need to subscribe to the journal, and you may need to login via your library's website or use campus wifi to get access.

https://link.springer.com/article/10.1007/s11948-001-0061-3

Preparing to Read

In this article, Michael Pritchard argues that we ought to shift our focus in engineering ethics away from the negative aspects of engineering, such as wrongdoing and blame. Instead, he calls on us to focus on the positive aspects of engineering, such as situations in which engineers display exemplary behavior. Our goal in examining such cases is to find moral exemplars—individuals that display virtuous character dispositions. Pritchard argues that, in particular, the disposition to be imaginative is of great importance to engineering ethics. In support of this point, he offers an example taken from engineering practice: the story of William LeMessurier and his involvement with the then Citicorp Center in downtown Manhattan. Pritchard argues that cases like LeMessurier's show that character and imagination can do more to help engineers fulfill their professional responsibility than any list of prescribed actions ever could.

Guided Reading Questions

1. Pritchard claims that focusing on the negative aspects of engineering, such as disaster cases, can be a hindrance to exemplary behavior. Do you agree? If so, should we stop talking about disaster cases in engineering ethics? Do discussions of disaster cases still have a role in engineering ethics education, even if they are problematic in certain respects?
2. Pritchard says that one of the tests of character is what a person does when no one is watching. Is this the case? Why or why not? Can you think of examples from your own life where you demonstrated exemplary behavior even when no one else was watching? If so, what motivated you to do this? If not, what do you think kept you from "doing the right thing"?
3. What is Pritchard's reason for thinking that "character and imagination can assist the end of protecting the public in ways that no list of required course of actions can specify"? Do you agree with his reasoning?
4. Do you think that LeMessurier behaved heroically or was he "just doing his job"? Is there really a difference between these two things in engineering?
5. What does Pritchard mean when he says LeMessurier was "prepared to be lucky"? What are some concrete ways in which engineers could "prepare themselves to be lucky" in Pritchard's sense?

Further Reading 6.3: 'Engineering ethics beyond engineers' ethics' by Joseph M. Basart and Montse Serra

Find the Article

Basart, J. M., & Serra, M. (2013). Engineering ethics beyond engineers' ethics. *Science and Engineering, Ethics* 19, 179–187. doi.org/10.1007/s11948-011-9293-z.

Read the article online by scanning the QR code or following the link below. Your college library will need to subscribe to the journal, and you may need to login via your library's website or use campus wifi to get access.

https://link.springer.com/article/10.1007/s11948-011-9293-z

Preparing to Read

So far in this chapter and in this book, we have assumed that engineers have weighty responsibilities that go beyond the sorts of obligations associated with many other professions. However, how far do these responsibilities extend into an engineer's personal life? How much "heroism" is required of engineers as part of the job? In this article, Joseph M. Basart and Montse Serra explore the boundaries of engineers' professional obligations in a world that is increasingly dependent on the technologies they help develop.

Guided Reading Questions

1. Basart and Serra introduce the persona of the "heroic engineer," which they characterize as "a self-reliant engineer both ready and willing to confront many challenges and perils for the sake of others." Do you see this persona reflected in any of the NSPE's

codes of ethics? Have you seen this persona reflected in any of the articles that you have read in this text?

2. In your opinion, is the concept of the heroic engineer useful in engineering ethics? Is it inspiring or is it unrealistic? Does it help or hinder the pursuit of ethics in engineering?

3. Basart and Serra argue that the concept of the heroic engineer reinforces the perception of ethical engineers as solitary actors who are willing to make great personal sacrifices for the sake of their ethical commitments. They give reasons for thinking that the heroic engineer should not be the default model for the ethical engineer. Do you agree with the reasons they offer?

4. Basart and Serra suggest that we should abandon the picture of engineering ethics in which engineers "discover in their conscience or wisdom both: (a) the correct answer to a moral dilemma they are confronted with, and (b) the courage to carry it out unhesitatingly." What might be the benefits of abandoning this picture? What might be the drawbacks of abandoning it?

5. Basart and Serra voice concerns about the effectiveness of engineering ethics courses and case studies in ethical development for engineering. Do you agree with the reasons they offer for these concerns? What do you think about the alternative route to engineering ethics that Basart and Serra suggest?

Bibliography

Basart, J. M., & Serra, M. (2013). Engineering ethics beyond engineers' ethics. *Science and Engineering Ethics*, 19(1), 179–187.

Berkes, H. (2016, January 28). 30 years after explosion, Challenger engineer still blames himself. *The Two Way* [NPR blog]. www.npr.org/sections/thetwo-way/2016/01/28/464744781/30-years-after-disaster-challenger-engineer-still-blames-himself.

Boisjoly. R. M. (1985, July 31). SRM O-ring erosion/potential failure criticality. [Memo to R. K. Lund]. https://catalog.archives.gov/id/596263/1/public?contributionType=transcription.

Boisjoly, R. M. (1987). Ethical decisions: Morton Thiokol and the space shuttle *Challenger* disaster [Conference presentation]. American Society of Mechanical Engineers Annual Meetings. http://onlineethics.org/cms/7123.aspx.

Davis, M. (2001a). 'Doing the minimum': What is 'the minimum' for engineers. *Science and Engineering Ethics*, 7(2), 283–283.

Davis, M. (2001b). Ordinary reasonable care is not the minimum for engineers. *Science and Engineering Ethics*, 7(2), 286–290.

Davis, M. (2012). 'Ain't no one here but us social forces': Constructing the professional responsibility of engineers. *Science and Engineering Ethics*, 18(1), 13–34.

Doorn, N. (2012). Responsibility ascriptions in technology development and engineering: Three perspectives. *Science and Engineering Ethics*, 18(1), 69–90.

Goldberg, S. (1987). The space shuttle tragedy and the ethics of engineering. *Jurimetrics*, 27(2), 155–159.

Martin, M. W. (2002). Personal meaning and ethics in engineering. *Science and Engineering Ethics*, 8(4), 545–560. doi.org/10.1007/s11948-002-0008-3.

Martin, M. W. (2006). Moral creativity in science and engineering. *Science and Engineering Ethics*, 12(3), 421–433.

Online Ethics Center (OEC). (2016). Roger Boisjoly: The Challenger disaster. www.onlineethics.org/Topics/ProfPractice/Exemplars/BehavingWell/RB-intro.aspx.

Pritchard, M. S. (2001a). Responsible engineering: The importance of character and imagination. *Science and Engineering Ethics*, 7(3), 391–402.

Pritchard, M. S. (2001b). Response to 'ordinary reasonable care is not the minimum for engineers' (M. Davis). *Science and Engineering Ethics*, 7(2), 291–297.

Reagan, R. (1986, January 28). Explosion of the Space Shuttle *Challenger* Address to the Nation. *NASA*. https://history.nasa.gov/reagan12886.html.

Schlossberger, E. (2016). Engineering codes of ethics and the duty to set a moral precedent. *Science and Engineering Ethics* 22, 1333–1344. doi.org/10.1007/s11948-015-9708-3.

Schmidt, J. A. (2014). Changing the paradigm for engineering ethics. *Science and Engineering Ethics*, 20(4), 985–1010.

Van de Poel, I., & Royakkers, L. *Ethics, Technology, and Engineering: An Introduction.* Wiley-Blackwell. Kindle Edition.

Van de Poel, I., Fahlquist, J., Doorn, N., Zwart, S., & Royakkers, L. (2012). The problem of many hands: Climate change as an example. *Science and Engineering Ethics*, 18(1), 49–67.

Vest, C. M. (2011). The image problem for engineering: An overview. *The Bridge*, 41(2), 5–12. https://nae.edu/Publications/Bridge/51063/51071.aspx.

Werhane, P. (2001). The myth of minimums: Response to 'Ordinary reasonable care is not the minimum for engineers.' *Science and Engineering Ethics*, 7(2), 298–302.

Index

academic pressure 115–116
accountability 52, 116, 222
advisors 79, 91
American Conference of Governmental
   Industrial Hygienists (ACGIH) 120
analytical thinking xxii
antitrust law xiii
Apple 143, 149
applied ethics xxii, 6–7, 8, 20; value
   conflicts in 8–11
apprenticeship model of engineering 77
approximate truth 18
Arendt, Hannah xxviii, 143, 145
argument from absent
   disagreement 15–16
argument from explanation 12–14, 15, 16
argument from widespread moral
   disagreement 16
Aristotle xxvi, 75, 76–77, 77–78, 79–80,
   83–84, 85, 86, 213
Arnold, M. 226
aspirational codes 215
asymmetry in relationships 176
attitude loyalty xxviii, 145
attunement 76
authenticity 226
automation 82–83
autonomous vehicles 7, 9–11, 27–33,
   82–83
autonomy 9, 25–26, 42–43, 44, 52, 158;
   and honesty 177, 179; moral 46; and
   Problem of Full Disclosure 178

Baier, A. 180–181, 191–194
banality of evil xxviii, 145
Beauchamp, T. L. 24
beliefs, justified 109

beneficence, principle of 9, 25,
   146
Berkes, H. 211
biomedical engineering 113, 148
biomedical research 125–126
biotechnology 148
Boeing 144
Boisjoly, R. 209–210, 210–211, 212
BP Deepwater Horizon oil rig 78
Braun, W. von 217, 221
Bridgman, P. 127
Brindell, S. xxvii, 116
Buchanan, A. 91

Canterbury Television (CTV) building,
   Christchurch, New Zealand 73–74
care ethicists xxix, 176
Cech, E. A. xxvi, 46, 49, 56–60
Celebrex 126, 127
Challenger disaster 208–212
Chapman, M. W. 80
character, personal xxx, 157–158, 208,
   213–214, 225
Charette, R. N. 83
Childress, J. F. 24
clinical experiments 26
codes of ethics 94; vagueness in 215;
   see also National Society of Professional
   Engineers (NSPE) Code of Ethics
cogito 111
collective consent 25
collegiality 158
Collingridge, D. 22, 25
Columbia "Prayer Study" 127
combustion 16–18, 19
commitments, personal 216–218
compensatory motives 217

competence xxvi, 73–74, 82;
    complications for determining 74–75;
    ethical xxvi, 75–76, 78, 86; public 77;
    social 79; technical xxvi, 75, 86
conflicting loyalties 142, 152–153
conflicts of interest xiii
consensus fallacy 122
consent: collective 25; informed 23,
    25, 52, 53
consequentialism xxix, 3–4, 8, 175–176
control dilemma 22
converse sheer size fallacy 119–120
Copernicus, N. 110
Cowan, R. S. 77
craft motives 217
creativity xxvi, 214, 218, 224–227
culture of ethics 78
Cummings, M. L. xxvi, 47, 52–54
cybersecurity 148

Davis, M. xxix, 212, 220–223
De Winter, J. 115
deception xxviii–xxix, 185–186; lying and
    xxix, 173–175; and plagiarism xxix,
    183–186; self-deception xxix, 181–183
dedication 216
Deepwater Horizon oil rig 78
degenerate loyalty xxvii, 143
delay fallacy 121
deontology xxix, 4–6, 8
depoliticization of engineering 56–58
Descartes, R. xxvii, 109–111
descriptivist relativism 18–19
discrimination 59; avoidance of xiv, 28–29
distributive justice xxv, 41, 47–49
diversity xiv
Doctrine of Double Effect (DDE) 5–6
Doctrine of the Mean 85
doubt, method of 100–111
driverless cars see autonomous vehicles
DuPont titanium oxide espionage
    case 141

Ebeling, B. 209, 211
Edison, T. 59
Eichmann, A. 145
Elion, G. B. 218, 224–225
ends and means 5–6
energia 79–80, 84
engineering brand 215
Environmental Protection Agency
    (EPA) 144

episteme 93, 94
epistemic questions 46
epistemology 109
equality 47; see also inequality
error theory 12, 15, 16
ethical competence xxvi, 75–76, 78, 86
ethical engagement 79–80
ethical judgment 75–76, 157, 158
eudaimonia 95–96
European Expert Group on Science and
    Governance 23
evidence-sharing 114, 125
excellence xxix, 84–85, 86–87, 213
exemplars, moral xxvi, 77–78, 213
experimental technology 22–27
expertise: moral xxvi, 85, 86–87;
    technical 86
explaining well 116–117
explanation, argument from 12–14, 15, 16
expressibility test 193
external goods of engineering 96
external validity 113

Facebook 112, 143
fallacies of risk xxvii, 111–112, 117,
    119–124
fallibility 109
Federal Bureau of Investigation (FBI) 149
Federal Trade Commission xiii
Felt, U. 23
fiduciary obligations 141
Florman, Samuel 83
Food and Drug Administration (FDA)
    114, 126
food safety 189–190
Ford, H. 48
fracking 48
full disclosure, problem of xxix, 177–178
funding 112, 127

Galileo Galilei 110
gas industry 148
General Relativity 8
genuine loyalty 147–149
Goldberg, S. 211
Google 143, 144
Gould, G. 84–85
Grice, P. xxviii, 173, 185

Haack, S. xxvii, 113, 114, 115, 124–129
Hansson, S. O. xxvii, 112, 119–124
happiness, and honesty 175–176

harm: avoidance of 157; prevention of 156–157; *see also* non-maleficence
Hauser, M. 115–116
health and safety 41, 42
hedonic act utilitarianism (HAU) 3–4, 5
hedonic utility 3–4
helmet laws 44–45
heuristics 95
Holocaust 145
honesty xxviii–xxix, 173–174, 178–179, 185–186; and autonomy 177, 179; and happiness 175–176; and power 176–177; uncritical 177; value of 175–177
honor, professional xxix, 207, 214
Hrachovec, Jennifer 126
Hwang Woo Suk 127

ideals of the profession 214
incrementalism 24, 25
indemnification xii, xiii
inequality 47, 48–49, 58–59; structural 48
information reliability 188–189
informed consent 23, 25, 52, 53
Infuse TM 113
Institute of Electrical and Electronics Engineers (IEEE) 28, 82
institutional constraint 220–222
integrity 157, 158; *see also* scientific integrity
intellectual property (IP) 184, 185
intending and foreseeing 5–6
internal goods of engineering 95–96
internal validity 113

Jobs, S. 59
judgment: ethical 75–76, 157, 158; practical (*phronesis*) 76–77, 80, 93, 94, 95
justice 9, 25–26, 49; distributive xxv, 41, 47–49; social xxvi, 49, 56–60, 77
Justice Department xiii
justice virtues 158
justified beliefs 109

Kant, I. 175, 177
Kelly-Detwiler, P. 78
Kilminster, J. 209, 210
Kline, R. 220
know-how, moral 85–86
knowledge 93–94, 109; propositional 78; theoretical 94

Korean Air 144–145
Kosolosky, L. 115
Kramer, A. D. I. 112
Krulwich, R. 84–85
Kuhn, T. S. 93

Large Man 2–3, 4, 6
law(s) 11, 207; paternalistic 44–45
learning, trial-and-error 25
Lehrer, T. 217, 221
liability insurance xii–xiii
Liew, W. 141
Lin, P. 27–33
Locke, J. 184, 185
loyalty xxvii–xxviii, 141–149, 151–154, 158; attitude xxviii, 145; conflict of 142, 152–153; degenerate xxvii, 143; divided 141–143, 149; genuine 147–149; predatory 143–144; *see also* whistleblowing
Lund, R. 209, 210
lying xxix, 173–175, 176
Lynch, T. 220

Maegerle, R. 141
Marcuse, H. xxvi, 80–82, 83
Martin, M. W. xxviii, xxx, 23, 83, 145, 155–159, 216–218, 224–227
Mason, J. 209, 210
maximising 4
meaning: objective 216; personal xxx, 216–218; subjective 216
meaningful life/work 216, 225–226
medical journals 125–126
Mencken, H. L. 127
mentors/mentorship xxvi, 77, 78–79, 89–92
Merck 114, 126
meritocracy, ideology of 58–60
metaethics 11–16, 20
Method of Doubt 110–111
Metis Health 174
Mill, J. S. 175–176, 179
Model T Ford 48
moral autonomy 46
moral exemplars xxvi, 77–78, 213
moral expertise xxvi, 85, 86–87
moral know-how 85–86
moral objectivism 16
moral statements 11–12, 16
moral value of honesty 175–177
morally supererogatory 216

Morton Thiokol 209, 211
motives: compensatory 217; craft 217;
    of moral concern 217
Musk, E. 83

National Academy of Engineering
    (NAE) 214
National Aeronautics and Space
    Administration (NASA) 209, 210, 211
National Security Agency (NSA) xxvii,
    148; PRISM program 142, 143
National Society of Professional
    Engineers (NSPE) Board of Ethical
    Review (BER) xii, xxiii; opinions of
    xiv–xvi
National Society of Professional
    Engineers (NSPE) Code of Ethics
    xi–xii, xiii, xxiii; Fundamental Canons
    xvii, xxiii
naturalness, fallacy of 120
New England Journal of Medicine (NEJM)
    114, 126
New York Times 126
non-maleficence, principle of 9, 10,
    24–25, 26, 146
normative ethics 1–3, 6, 7, 8

Obama, B. 48
objective meaning 216
objectivity xxvi–xxvii, 109–110, 111,
    112–113; scientific 18–20, 109, 113
observations 17–18, 20
Ohio University plagiarism scandal
    183, 185
oil industry 148
Organ Harvest 2, 3, 4, 7
ostrich's fallacy 120
ownership 184–185; physical possession
    theory of 185; power theory of 185
oxidation theory 17, 18, 19

paradigms: in ethics 94; in
    philosophy 93–94
paternalism xxv, 41, 43–45, 46, 215
paternalistic action 43, 44
PaymentsMD 174, 175, 179, 181, 185
Payne, C. 45
Peirce, C. S. 127
personal character xxx, 157–158, 208,
    213–214, 225
personal commitments 216–218
personal meaning xxx, 216–218

pessimistic induction 18, 19, 20
pharmaceutical companies 114–115,
    125–126, 148
philosophy of science 16–20
phlogiston theory 17, 18, 19
phronesis 76–77, 80, 93, 94, 95
physical possession theory of
    ownership 185
physics 8
plagiarism xxix, 183–186; stealing
    explanation of the wrongness of 184
Plato 77
Popper, K. 23, 24–25
power: and honesty 176–177; position of
    176–177
power theory of ownership 185
practical judgment (*phronesis*) 76–77, 80,
    93, 94, 95
praxis 95
predatory loyalty 143
PRISM program 142, 143
Pritchard, M. S. xxix–xxx, 213–215
privacy 52, 53, 54, 142–143
probability 178, 190
Problem of Full Disclosure xxix, 177–178
professional honor xxix, 207, 214
professional responsibility xxix–xxx, 41,
    208–216, 220–223
professionalism xxx, 217
proof-seeking fallacy 121
proportionally grave reason 5–6
propositional knowledge 78
public competence 77
public good 77, 142, 146, 147–148, 158
public recognition 77
public trust 112–113, 127, 190, 207,
    213–214, 215
public welfare 41–43
public wellbeing xxv, 41–49, 146–147
public-spirited virtues 158
publication pressure 115, 125

Quantum Mechanics 8
Quine, W. V. O. xxvii

RAND Center for Catastrophic Risk
    Management 78
rationality 123; of taking responsibility
    222; technological (technical) xxvi,
    80–83, 94
Raytheon 144
Reagan, R. 208

reason 84
relevant explanations 116
reliability of information 188–189
reliance, and trust 179–180
responsibility 73, 158; professional
    xxix–xxx, 41, 208–216, 220–223;
    rationality of taking 222
risk 117; assessment 95; communication
    95, 178, 188, 189, 190; deliberative and
    non-deliberative thinking about 188;
    fallacies of xxvii, 111–112, 117,
    199–124; management 95; reliability of
information and evaluation of 188–189
role models 77, 78, 79, 89
Roman Catholic Church 109–110
Royakkers, L. 215
Royce, J. xxvii, 143–144, 148, 149,
    151–154
Rust (videogame) 9

Salk, J. 225
satisfaction, personal and professional 218
Saul, J. xxviii–xxix, 174, 175
Schinzinger, R. 23, 145
Schmidt, J. A. xxvi, 85–86, 93–96,
    213, 215
science, objectivity of 18–20, 109, 113
scientific integrity xxvii, 113–114,
    124–128; erosion of 125–126, 127–128;
    lack of 114–116
seatbelt laws 44, 45
self-deception xxix, 181–183
self-direction, virtues of 157
self-driving vehicles *see* autonomous
    vehicles
semiconductor industry 148
sensitivity 76
sheer size fallacy 119
Snowden, E. xxvii, 142–143, 148
social competency 79
social engineering xxvii, 112–113
social experiments, new technologies as
    23, 24–25
social justice xxvi, 49, 56–60, 77
Socratic method 77
Spectrum magazine 82–83
Spitler, T. 141
stakeholders, direct and indirect 52
standards 226
Stealing Explanation 184
STEM disciplines 80
structural inequality 48

subjective meaning 216
subjectivism 14–16
Sudbø, J. 127
sustainable development xiv
Swazey, J. 89, 90

Taylor, C. 226
team-work virtues 158
techne 93, 94
technical competence xxvi, 75, 86
technical expertise 86
technocratic fallacy 121–122
technological mediation xxv, 41, 45–47
technological (technical) rationality xxvi,
    80–83, 94
telos 84
theoretical knowledge 94
Thompson, A. 209
Thompson, P. B. xxix, 178, 188–191
Toyota safety crisis (2009—10) 111–112
trial-and-error learning 25
Trolley 1–2, 3, 4, 5–6
Trolley Problem 3, 4, 6, 7
trust 52, 176, 179–181, 189, 191–194;
    expressibility test for morality of 193;
    public 112–113, 127, 190, 207,
    213–214, 215; and reliance 179–180;
    and vulnerability 180–181, 193
truth xxix, 174; approximate 18

unconscious bias 183
uncritical honesty 177
underdetermination problem 17–18,
    19, 20
unobservable entities 18
usability 52, 53–54
utilitarianism 156, 176; *see also* hedonic
    act utilitarianism (HAU)

vaccinations 7, 47, 225
vagueness in codes of ethics 215
validity, internal and external 113
value 46
value conflicts in applied ethics 8–11
value laden nature of technology 45–46
value neutrality 45
value-sensitive design (VSD) xxvi,
    47, 52–55
Van de Poel, I. 22–27, 215
Verbeek, P.-P. 45
Vertu cell phone 48
Vioxx 114, 126, 127

virtue of all virtues 76
virtue ethics 76–78, 94, 213
virtue(s) xxix, xxx, 84, 157–158, 224
virtuous engineering 95–96
vulnerability, and trust 180–181, 193
VW Emissions scandal 144, 181, 183

Wallace, D. F. xxiii
Weil, V. xxvi, 78–79, 89–92
wellbeing, public xxv, 41–49, 146–147
whistleblowing xxviii, 11, 146–148,
    155–159; avoid-harm argument 157;
and character and virtue 157–158;
personal considerations xxviii,
156–157; prevent-harm argument
156–157; prima facie obligation
to whistleblow xxviii, 156; problem
of 146; professional-status
argument 157
Wildavsky, A. 25
Williams, R. 208
Winterkorn, M. 144

Zachary, G. P. 77